COOK'S
ILLUSTRATED

~ 2017 ~

Published by
America's Test Kitchen
21 Drydock Avenue, Suite 210E
Boston, MA 02210

ISBN: 978-1-945256-36-3
ISSN: 1933-639X

To get home delivery of *Cook's Illustrated* magazine, call 800-526-8442 inside the U.S., or 515-237-3663 if calling from outside the U.S., or subscribe online at www.CooksIllustrated.com/Subscribe.

In addition to *Cook's Illustrated* Annual Hardbound Editions available from each year of publication (1993–2017), America's Test Kitchen offers the following cookbooks:

The Complete Slow Cooker
The Complete Make-Ahead Cookbook
The Complete Mediterranean Cookbook
The Complete Vegetarian Cookbook
The Complete Cooking for Two Cookbook
The Complete Cooking for Two Cookbook Gift Edition
Cooking at Home with Bridget and Julia
What Good Cooks Know
Cook's Science
The Science of Good Cooking
The Perfect Cookie
Bread Illustrated
Master of the Grill
Kitchen Smarts: Questions and Answers to Boost Your Cooking I.Q.
Kitchen Hacks: How Clever Cooks Get Things Done
100 Recipes: The Absolute Best Way to Make the True Essentials
The New Family Cookbook
The America's Test Kitchen Cooking School Cookbook
The Cook's Illustrated Meat Book
The Cook's Illustrated Baking Book
The Cook's Illustrated Cookbook
The America's Test Kitchen Family Baking Book
The Best of America's Test Kitchen (2007–2018 Editions)
The Complete America's Test Kitchen TV Show Cookbook (2001–2018)
Food Processor Perfection
Pressure Cooker Perfection

Vegan for Everybody
Naturally Sweet
Foolproof Preserving
Paleo Perfected
The How Can It Be Gluten-Free Cookbook: Volume 2
The How Can It Be Gluten-Free Cookbook
The Best Mexican Recipes
Slow Cooker Revolution 2: The Easy Prep Edition
Slow Cooker Revolution
The Six-Ingredient Solution
The America's Test Kitchen Do-It-Yourself Cookbook
1993–2017 Cook's Illustrated Master Index
Cook's Country Annual Hardbound Editions from each year of publication (2005–2017)

THE COOK'S ILLUSTRATED ALL-TIME BEST SERIES
All-Time Best Sunday Suppers
All-Time Best Holiday Entertaining
All-Time Best Appetizers
All-Time Best Soups

COOK'S COUNTRY TITLES
One-Pan Wonders
Cook It in Cast Iron
Cook's Country Eats Local
The Complete Cook's Country TV Show Cookbook, 10th Anniversary Edition

Visit our online bookstore at www.CooksIllustrated.com to order any of our cookbooks listed above. You can also order subscriptions, gift subscriptions, and any of our cookbooks by calling 800-611-0759 inside the U.S., or at 515-237-3663 if calling from outside the U.S.

BC = Back Cover

NUMBER 144

JANUARY & FEBRUARY 2017

COOK'S
ILLUSTRATED

Seared Pork Chops
Hotter Pan, Juicier Chops

Weeknight Bolognese
Deep Flavor in Less Time

Rating Slow Cookers
We Looked Under the Hood
and Guess What We Found

Cauliflower Gratin
Creamy Without Cream

Easier Gumbo
It's All About the Flour

Cast-Iron Skillets
How to Choose, Season, and
Cook in This All-Purpose Pan

French Butter Cake

Basque Scrambled Eggs
Warm Winter Salads
Tasting Crushed Tomatoes

CooksIllustrated.com
$6.95 U.S. / $7.95 CANADA

0 2>
7 25274 62805 6

COOK'S
ILLUSTRATED

JANUARY & FEBRUARY 2017

PAGE 8

BACK COVER ILLUSTRATED BY JOHN BURGOYNE

Sushi

SUSHI

Japan has hundreds of types of sushi, including CHIRASHI (meaning "scattered"), a bowl of rice topped with fish and other ingredients such as nori (seaweed), roe, and vegetables. INARI features sushi rice stuffed into a fried bean curd, cabbage, or thin omelet wrapper. To make OSHI, rice and other ingredients are layered and pressed into a box called an *oshibako* and cut into rectangles. There are various types of rolled, or *maki*, sushi: HOSOMAKI consists of rice spread with a single thin filling and then rolled up in nori and cut into pieces; FUTOMAKI has multiple colorful fillings. URAMAKI, or inside-out rolls, have the rice on the outside and the nori and fillings in the center. TEMAKI, or "hand" rolls, are made by wrapping a cone of seaweed around rice and fillings. To make NIGIRI, fish, egg, or vegetable slices are dabbed with wasabi and placed on top of mounds of rice. GUNKAN, or "battleship," sushi are small cups of seaweed and rice that hold toppings in place. MUSUBI is made by forming rice into a ball or triangle shape around a filling.

AMERICA'S
TEST KITCHEN
RECIPES THAT WORK

America's Test Kitchen is a real 2,500-square-foot kitchen located just outside Boston. It is the home of more than 60 test cooks, editors, and cookware specialists. Our mission is to test recipes until we understand exactly how and why they work and eventually arrive at the very best version. We also test kitchen equipment and supermarket ingredients in search of products that offer the best value and performance. You can watch us work by tuning in to *America's Test Kitchen* (AmericasTestKitchen.com) and *Cook's Country from America's Test Kitchen* (CooksCountry.com) on public television and listen to us on our weekly radio program on PRX. You can also follow us on Facebook, Twitter, Pinterest, and Instagram.

EDITORIAL STAFF

Chief Executive Officer David Nussbaum
Chief Creative Officer Jack Bishop
Editorial Director John Willoughby
Executive Editor Amanda Agee
Deputy Editor Rebecca Hays
Executive Managing Editor Todd Meier
Executive Food Editor Keith Dresser
Senior Editors Andrea Geary, Andrew Janjigian, Lan Lam,
    Chris O'Connor
Senior Editors, Features Elizabeth Bomze, Louise Emerick
Associate Editor Annie Petito
Test Cooks Daniel Cellucci, Steve Dunn
Assistant Test Cook Mady Nichas
Senior Copy Editor Krista Magnuson
Copy Editor Jillian Campbell
Executive Editor, Cook's Science Dan Souza
Science Editor Guy Crosby, PhD, CFS
Director, Creative Operations Alice Carpenter

Executive Editor, Tastings & Testings Lisa McManus
Managing Editor Scott Kathan
Deputy Editor Hannah Crowley
Associate Editors Lauren Savoie, Kate Shannon
Assistant Editor Miye Bromberg
Editorial Assistant Carolyn Grillo

Test Kitchen Director Erin McMurrer
Assistant Test Kitchen Director Leah Rovner
Test Kitchen Manager Alexxa Benson
Lead Senior Kitchen Assistant Meridith Lippard
Senior Kitchen Assistant Taylor Pond
Lead Kitchen Assistant Ena Gudiel
Kitchen Assistants Erick Aroche-Paz, Gladis Campos,
    Blanca Castanza

Design Director Greg Galvan
Photography Director Julie Cote
Art Director Susan Levin
Designer Maggie Edgar
Art Director, Marketing Melanie Gryboski
Deputy Art Director, Marketing Janet Taylor
Associate Art Director, Marketing Stephanie Cook
Senior Staff Photographer Daniel J. van Ackere
Staff Photographer Steve Klise
Assistant Photography Producer Mary Ball
Styling Catrine Kelty, Marie Piraino

Senior Director, Digital Design John Torres
Executive Editor, Web Christine Liu
Managing Editor, Web Mari Levine
Senior Editor, Web Roger Metcalf
Associate Editors, Web Terrence Doyle, Briana Palma
Senior Video Editor Nick Dakoulas
Test Kitchen Photojournalist Kevin White

BUSINESS STAFF

Chief Financial Officer Jackie McCauley Ford
Production Director Guy Rochford
Imaging Manager Lauren Robbins
Production & Imaging Specialists Heather Dube,
    Sean MacDonald, Dennis Noble, Jessica Voas
Senior Controller Theresa Peterson
Director, Business Partnerships Meghan Conciatori

Chief Digital Officer Fran Middleton
VP, Analytics & Media Strategy Deborah Fagone
**Director, Sponsorship Marketing & Client
    Services** Christine Anagnostis
National Sponsorship Sales Director Timothy Coburn
Client Services Manager Kate Zebrowski
Partnership Marketing Manager Pamela Putprush
Director, Customer Support Amy Bootier
Senior Customer Loyalty & Support Specialists
    Rebecca Kowalski, Andrew Straaberg Finfrock
Customer Loyalty & Support Specialist Caroline Augliere

**Senior VP, Human Resources & Organizational
    Development** Colleen Zelina
Human Resources Director Adele Shapiro
Director, Retail Book Program Beth Ineson
Retail Sales Manager Derek Meehan
Associate Director, Publicity Susan Hershberg

Circulation Services ProCirc

Cover Illustration: Robert Papp

PRINTED IN THE USA

WHO KNEW?

Here at *Cook's Illustrated*, we're not about celebrity chefs or luxury travel or lifestyle anything. We're about one thing: getting into the kitchen and cooking. That might seem like a narrow focus but, in fact, cooking is an inexhaustible subject. Just when you think you know everything about some dish or ingredient, you find out there's more to it.

Sometimes you discover something about an ingredient that affects how you should cook it. The particular nature of the fiber in cauliflower, for example, led us to a technique that creates a creamy sauce for our Modern Cauliflower Gratin (page 11) without any actual cream. And what we learned about how the skin of ordinary beans interacts with acid led to the perfect compromise between saving time and imbuing flavor in our recipe for New England Baked Beans (page 15).

Sometimes, on the other hand, you discover the importance of the manner in which an ingredient is made. That's what happened to Annie Petito when working on Weeknight Tagliatelle with Bolognese Sauce (page 9). She thought she finally had both the flavor and the texture of her sauce just right. But when she added the sauce to the pasta, the tagliatelle sucked up all the sauce and the dish ended up dry rather than luscious. It was frustrating and puzzling, but it eventually led to a discovery: Pasta extruded through brass dies, as good-quality Italian pastas are, has a rough surface that soaks up a lot of liquid. Less-expensive pasta is often extruded through Teflon dies, which gives it a smooth surface that absorbs very little. If you want your pasta to be properly coated, the sauce needs to be calibrated to take this difference into account. Who knew? But now we do, and so do you.

And sometimes what you discover is that something you already knew applies to the cooking situation you're in right now. Read our story "The Easiest Carrot Side Dish" (page 19), and you'll discover why Andrea Geary found herself recalling her French culinary instructor striding through the kitchen bellowing, "Salty like the SEA!" Turns out he knew what he was bellowing about.

–The Editors

FOR INQUIRIES, ORDERS, OR MORE INFORMATION

COOK'S ILLUSTRATED MAGAZINE

Cook's Illustrated magazine (ISSN 1068-2821), number 144, is published bimonthly by America's Test Kitchen Limited Partnership, 17 Station St., Brookline, MA 02445. Copyright 2016 America's Test Kitchen Limited Partnership. Periodicals postage paid at Boston, MA, and additional mailing offices, USPS #012487. Publications Mail Agreement No. 40020778. Return undeliverable Canadian addresses to P.O. Box 875, Station A, Windsor, ON N9A 6P2. POSTMASTER: Send address changes to *Cook's Illustrated*, P.O. Box 6018, Harlan, IA 51593-1518. For subscription and gift subscription orders, subscription inquiries, or change of address notices, visit AmericasTestKitchen.com/support, call 800-526-8442 in the U.S. or 515-248-7684 from outside the U.S., or write to us at *Cook's Illustrated*, P.O. Box 6018, Harlan, IA 51593-1518.

CooksIllustrated.com

At the all-new CooksIllustrated.com, you can order books and subscriptions, sign up for our free e-newsletter, or renew your magazine subscription. Join the website and gain access to 23 years of *Cook's Illustrated* recipes, equipment tests, and ingredient tastings, as well as companion videos for every recipe in this issue.

COOKBOOKS

We sell more than 50 cookbooks by the editors of *Cook's Illustrated*, including *The Cook's Illustrated Cookbook* and *Paleo Perfected*. To order, visit our bookstore at CooksIllustrated.com/bookstore.

EDITORIAL OFFICE 17 Station St., Brookline, MA 02445; 617-232-1000; fax: 617-232-1572. For subscription inquiries, visit AmericasTestKitchen.com/support or call 800-526-8442.

QUICK TIPS

⊰ COMPILED BY ANNIE PETITO ⊱

Safely Storing a Corkscrew

Shaun Breidbart of Pelham, N.Y., has found that if he keeps a cork on the end of his corkscrew, he won't stab his hand when reaching into the drawer to grab it. Plus, he always has an extra cork if he needs one for an open wine bottle.

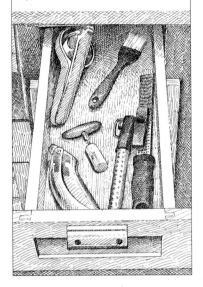

Homemade Rolling Pin Guide for Pie Dough

Marcia Thomas of Evanston, Ill., doesn't own a rolling pin guide for pie dough, so she made her own with two rulers, which are roughly the same thickness as rolled-out pastry should be. As she starts to approach the desired dough thickness, she places the rulers on either side of the dough round so that the pin rolls on top of them, which ensures that she ends up with uniformly rolled dough.

Remembering to Remove the Bay

Jennifer Meisenkothen of Mount Airy, Md., came up with a way to remind herself to remove bay leaves from soups before she purees them. She cuts two slits in a plastic coffee can lid and writes "remove the bay" on it. Then she slides the lid onto the plug of her blender so that when she goes to puree the soup, she has to remove the reminder before she can plug the blender in.

Salt-and-Pepper Grinder

Michael Marrone of Pittsburgh, Pa., keeps a pepper grinder filled with equal amounts of black peppercorns and coarse salt. The seasonings' relatively similar size keeps them well blended in the grinder and makes for an even sprinkling of both in a single twist. (Using a zipper-lock bag as a funnel makes it easy to load the seasonings into the grinder.)

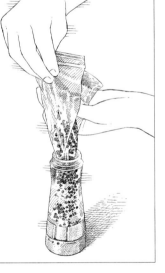

Portioning Frosting with Ease

Sarah Quigley of San Francisco, Calif., likes to use a 2-tablespoon portion scoop to dollop frosting onto cupcakes. It ensures that all the cupcakes are equally frosted and that the dollops of frosting are even and easy to spread.

Makeshift Flame Tamer

When Fran Bindon of Fairfax, Va., needs to cook foods, such as polenta, over very low heat, she stacks two burner grates from her gas stove over the flame. This way, the pot or pan is farther from the heat source and the food cooks as gently as possible.

Cardboard Box Cubby

Sharon Sayers of Rochester, N.Y., likes to save the cardboard inserts from boxes of wine to use as cubby-like slots for keeping long boxes of aluminum foil, plastic wrap, and other kitchen wraps neatly organized.

SEND US YOUR TIPS We will provide a complimentary one-year subscription for each tip we print. Send your tip, name, address, and daytime telephone number to Quick Tips, *Cook's Illustrated*, P.O. Box 470589, Brookline, MA 02447 or to QuickTips@AmericasTestKitchen.com.

ILLUSTRATION: JOHN BURGOYNE

Space-Saving Storage for Glassware

In her small city apartment, Phyllis Erikson of Nassau, N.Y., stores drinking glasses, wine glasses, and coffee mugs by arranging them rim up and rim down to fit more in a small cabinet or on a shelf.

Stovetop-Steamed Tortillas

To soften and warm tortillas without using a microwave, Jeff Fair of Seattle, Wash., places a tortilla on a wire rack set over a pot of simmering water. He leaves the tortilla over the heat only briefly to ensure that it doesn't get overly moist, flipping it once or twice so that it warms through evenly. (You can also stack up to four tortillas at a time.)

Parchment Paper Origami

To tame the curl of a freshly cut sheet of parchment paper, Michael LaFosse of Haverhill, Mass., folds evenly spaced, parallel creases in both the short and long directions. When unfolded, the creased grid helps to keep the paper from rolling back into a cylinder, and it also works as a guide for evenly spacing cookie dough. (The number of pleats may be adjusted for more or fewer spots depending on what is being baked.)

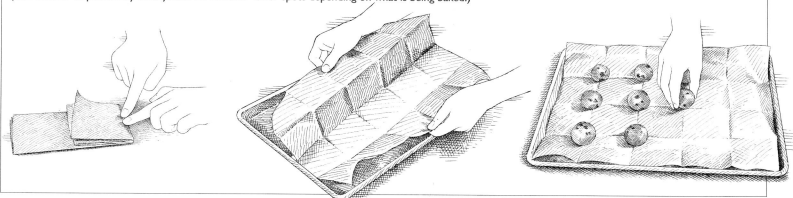

Makeshift Splatter Guard

When mixing dough or batter with a handheld or stand mixer, Betty Meyer of Greenville, S.C., keeps dry ingredients contained by making a splatter guard from a paper plate. She cuts a line from the edge to the center of a paper plate, cuts a 2-inch circle out of the middle of the plate, and positions the cut-out plate over the bowl.

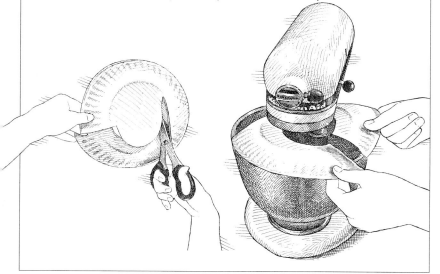

Hot Handle Reminder

When roasting foods in a skillet in the oven, Henny Wright of Dallas, Texas, hangs a potholder on the oven door so it's at the ready to cover his hand before transferring the hot skillet to the stovetop. He then leaves the potholder over the pan's handle to help him remember (and signal to others) that the handle is still hot.

Pan-Seared Thick-Cut Pork Chops

We always knew that the key to chops with a deep sear is a screaming-hot pan.
What we didn't know is that it's also the trick to producing a juicy, tender interior.

> BY ANDREW JANJIGIAN <

For the best thick-cut pork chops, cut them yourself and (mostly) leave them be in a cast-iron skillet.

P ork chops seem like a good candidate for a weeknight meal: They're quick to cook and, when given a nice crusty sear, are flavorful. But since most pork is pretty lean, chops are easy to overcook, resulting in leathery, dried-out meat. Thicker chops—which require more time to cook through—give you a wider window of time to build up a solid sear before the interiors are overdone. But after looking for thick-cut (1½ inches or thicker) chops at a number of supermarkets and coming up short, I realized that if I wanted a juicy interior and a substantial crust, I was going to have to butcher a pork roast into chops myself.

Chop Chop

Although rib bones insulate meat from heat, helping prevent overcooking, I decided right off the bat that I'd cut boneless chops for two reasons. First, the rib bones can be a challenge to slice through. Second, you don't get to decide how thick to make the chops, since that is dictated by the spacing between the ribs (usually about an inch). Starting with a boneless roast would make it possible to fashion chops of any thickness.

As for the type of roast, I considered both blade-end and center-cut loin roasts. Blade-end roasts come from near the shoulder of the animal and contain more fat, which made for slightly juicier chops. But that wasn't enough to overcome the cut's drawbacks: For one thing, the fattier parts are found only at the very end of the roast, meaning that you can't cut four identical chops. This roast also tends to widen toward the blade end, making it impossible to cut chops of equal thickness and weight. On the other hand, a center-cut roast, which comes from the pig's back, is compact, cylindrical, and lean from end to end, making it ideal for home-cut chops. What's more, it's readily available in most supermarkets.

See the Sear
A step-by-step video is available at CooksIllustrated.com/feb17

I cut my center-cut pork loin roast crosswise into four even pieces. The thickness of the chops varied slightly depending on the diameter of the loin, but I found that starting with a 2½-pound roast guaranteed chops at least 1½ inches thick.

Flip Answer

We typically brine or salt pork to season it and enhance or maintain the meat's juiciness. But since the moisture added by brining would impede browning, I dismissed it—I didn't want to wait 45 minutes for the surface to dry out. As it turned out, salting the meat also interfered with developing a rich crust since it brought some of the meat's moisture to the surface. I decided to simply season the meat just prior to cooking. But here was the crux of the problem: To get the rich mahogany crust and juicy interior I was after, I needed to cook the meat both at high heat and more gently at the same time, a seeming contradiction.

Spotlight on Sauce

Our easy no-cook sauces add richness to the lean chops, but a little bit goes a long way: Too much sauce will make the crust on the pork soggy.

Until now, I'd been using a basic approach to searing, cooking the chops in a stainless-steel skillet with a couple of teaspoons of oil over high heat and flipping them once. But the skillet never got hot enough to produce a great crust. I switched to a cast-iron skillet, which gets—and stays—exceptionally hot, even when four thick chops (which absorb a lot of heat from the metal) are added. The trick with cast iron is to preheat it thoroughly, so I put it in a cold oven set to 500 degrees and waited for the oven to come to temperature, by which time the pan would be well saturated with heat—the method we used in our Cast Iron Steaks with Herb Butter recipe (November/December 2016). I also added more oil (2 tablespoons total) to the pan, which ensured that the chops, which tended to pull away from the pan here and there as they cooked, made full contact with the heat and seared evenly.

Now that the exterior was gorgeously brown, I focused on the interior. The chops needed to hit 140 degrees for serving, but that didn't mean I had to keep them in the pan to get them there, since they'd continue to cook off heat—the phenomenon referred to as carryover cooking. Usually, we remove meat from direct heat about 5 to 10 degrees shy of the serving temperature to avoid overcooking, but I wondered if the extreme heat I was getting on the chops' exteriors would allow me to take the meat off the heat sooner. In other words, could I use the high heat to my advantage?

It sounded counterintuitive, but it actually worked brilliantly. By the time the chops were seared on both sides, the meat registered 125 degrees, and there was more than enough residual heat on their surfaces to push them to 140 as they rested under foil. The only flaw was the gray band of overcooked meat that developed just below the surface as each side spent several minutes sitting over the heat to sear. The fix was to flip the chops every couple of minutes as they cooked, which slowed down cooking and just about eliminated the overcooked layer of meat.

The chops ultimately spend the same amount of time in contact with the pan as they would with

Hotter Pan, Juicier Chops

Searing pork chops in a blazing-hot cast-iron skillet was an obvious way to brown them deeply. But as we discovered, it was also a great way to keep a relatively lean cut juicy. That's because the internal temperature of the chops continues to rise off the heat—the phenomenon referred to as carryover cooking—and the hotter the exteriors of the chops got, the more heat there was to transfer to the centers. As a result, we were able to take the chops off the heat 15 degrees shy of the serving temperature and rely on much gentler residual heat to finish cooking them as they rested.

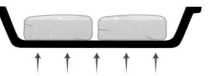

START COOKING IN THE PAN

A superhot skillet builds up heat
on the chops' exteriors.

FINISH COOKING ON THE PLATE

As the chops rest, residual heat brings
their interiors to a safe temperature.

TECHNIQUE | DIY THICK-CUT PORK CHOPS

Most supermarkets don't carry superthick (at least 1½ inches) boneless chops. Fortunately, it's a cinch to cut them yourself from a center-cut loin roast.

If necessary, trim to square off ends. Divide roast in half crosswise. Divide each half again crosswise to form 4 equal-size chops.

---

uninterrupted searing on each side, but with every flip, some of the heat that accumulates in the chop dissipates, preventing overcooking on the interior.

No brining. No salting. No fancy techniques. These were by far the easiest pork chops I'd ever made, and they looked and tasted great. But to give the recipe plenty of utility—even for company, since thick-cut chops are nice for entertaining—I decided to develop a few sauces to dress up the chops. I made them intensely flavored and relatively rich to give the meat plenty of character, but they're still quick enough to whip up any night of the week. In a nod to the vinegar-pepper topping commonly found in Italian pork chop recipes, I created a roasted red pepper–vinegar sauce. I also pulled together a couple of pesto-like concoctions: a French mint persillade (a parsley-based sauce with garlic and oil) and a Sicilian-inspired walnut and raisin pesto.

PAN-SEARED THICK-CUT BONELESS PORK CHOPS
SERVES 4

Look for a pork loin that is 7 to 8 inches long and 3 to 3½ inches in diameter. We strongly prefer using natural pork here. Using pork that is enhanced (injected with a salt solution) will inhibit browning. This recipe works best in a cast-iron skillet, but a 12-inch stainless-steel skillet will work. Serve the chops with one of our sauces (recipes follow), if desired. Our recipe for Walnut-Raisin Pesto is available for free for four months at CooksIllustrated.com/feb17.

I (2½- to 3-pound) boneless center-cut pork
  loin roast, trimmed
  Kosher salt and pepper
2 tablespoons vegetable oil

1. Adjust oven rack to middle position, place 12-inch cast-iron skillet on rack, and heat oven to 500 degrees. Meanwhile, cut roast crosswise into 4 chops of equal thickness.

2. When oven reaches 500 degrees, pat chops dry with paper towels and season with salt and pepper. Using potholders, remove skillet from oven and place over high heat. Being careful of hot skillet handle, add oil and heat until just smoking. Add chops and cook, without moving them, until lightly browned on first side, about 2 minutes. Flip chops and cook until lightly browned on second side, about 2 minutes.

3. Flip chops and continue to cook, flipping every 2 minutes and adjusting heat as necessary if chops brown too quickly or slowly, until exteriors are well browned and meat registers 125 to 130 degrees, 10 to 12 minutes longer. Transfer chops to platter, tent with aluminum foil, and let rest for 15 minutes (temperature will climb to 140 degrees). Serve.

ROASTED RED PEPPER–VINEGAR SAUCE
MAKES ABOUT I CUP

Red wine vinegar or sherry vinegar can be substituted for the white wine vinegar, if desired.

¾ cup jarred roasted red peppers, rinsed and
  patted dry
2 jarred hot cherry peppers, stems removed
2 garlic cloves, peeled
2 teaspoons dried rosemary, lightly crushed
2 anchovy fillets, rinsed and patted dry
½ teaspoon salt
⅛ teaspoon pepper
¼ cup water
2 tablespoons white wine vinegar
⅓ cup extra-virgin olive oil
2 tablespoons minced fresh parsley

Pulse red peppers, cherry peppers, garlic, rosemary, anchovies, salt, and pepper in food processor until finely chopped, 15 to 20 pulses. Add water and vinegar and pulse briefly to combine. Transfer mixture to medium bowl and slowly whisk in oil until fully incorporated. Stir in parsley.

MINT PERSILLADE
MAKES ABOUT I CUP

You can substitute 1½ teaspoons of anchovy paste for the fillets, if desired.

I cup fresh mint leaves
I cup fresh parsley leaves
3 garlic cloves, peeled
3 anchovy fillets, rinsed and patted dry
I teaspoon grated lemon zest plus
  I tablespoon juice
½ teaspoon salt
⅛ teaspoon pepper
⅓ cup extra-virgin olive oil

Pulse mint, parsley, garlic, anchovies, lemon zest, salt, and pepper in food processor until finely chopped, 15 to 20 pulses. Add lemon juice and pulse briefly to combine. Transfer mixture to medium bowl and slowly whisk in oil until fully incorporated.

Chicken and Sausage Gumbo

The depth and body of this Louisiana mainstay largely depend on a humble pantry staple: flour. We rethought its treatment—from how it is cooked to how it is incorporated.

⇒ BY ANNIE PETITO ⇐

Like any folk recipe, gumbo has hundreds of variations. The flavor, texture, and even the provenance of this legendary dish—a symbol of melting-pot cooking—are all fodder for debate.

There are, however, some characteristics that all gumbos share. Some are brothy, while others are thick. A pot typically holds seafood, poultry, or wild game, along with andouille sausage or some type of cured smoked pork. The proteins are simmered with the "holy trinity" of celery, bell pepper, and onion while seasonings such as garlic, cayenne, paprika, thyme, and bay leaves provide complexity. This mix is thickened slightly, sometimes with okra or ground dried sassafras leaves, known as filé ("fee-LAY") powder. Last, and perhaps most important, is the roux—a slow-cooked mixture of flour and fat that gives the gumbo its deep brown color, a bit of body, and a toasty flavor.

Inspired by the late Louisiana chef Paul Prudhomme's dark, meaty, poultry-centric gumbo, I decided to develop my own recipe featuring just chicken and andouille. I also opted to omit okra and filé—okra is more typical of shrimp- and tomato-based gumbos, and filé's distinct, earthy flavor can be polarizing.

Roux-minating

I started with the roux. In classic French cuisine, roux can be cooked to shades ranging from blondish white to the color of peanut butter. But Cajun and Creole chefs push the roux much further—to a deep, dark brown or even just short of black—to develop the toasty, nutty flavor that characterizes gumbo. To guard against burning, the roux is stirred constantly over low heat, meaning it can take an hour or more of hands-on attention to make.

That said, there are renegade techniques for making dark roux that don't require stirring at the stove for long (if at all). I found methods using the microwave or the oven, as well as a quick one that involved

▶ Watch Every Step
A step-by-step video is available at CooksIllustrated.com/feb17

Gumbo doesn't always include shrimp. Our version pairs shredded chicken thighs with slices of garlicky andouille sausage.

heating the oil on the stovetop until smoking and then adding the flour.

Working with the typical 1:1 ratio of all-purpose flour to vegetable oil—½ cup of each for now—I first tried the quick method of adding flour to smoking oil. This produced a superdark roux in a mere 10 minutes, but the flour was more burnt than deeply toasted. The microwave wasn't much more hands-off than the stove, as I had to stir the roux frequently between short bursts of heating. However, in the dry, even heat of a 425-degree oven, a roux required stirring just every 20 minutes. The downside was that it took 1¼ hours to reach the proper dark chocolate color.

Still, I pressed on. In the roux, I sautéed onion, celery, and green bell pepper. I then poured in 6 cups of chicken broth and added a couple of pounds of boneless, skinless chicken thighs and some sliced andouille. I kept the seasonings simple for now: cayenne, bay leaves, and thyme sprigs. I simmered the gumbo until the chicken was tender, at which point I removed it, shredded it for easy eating, and added it back to the pot. This version boasted just the right

toastiness from the roux, but the seasonings needed tweaking.

I'd address those later. For now, I wanted to deal with the fact that the roux had taken more than an hour to make. Plus, my gumbo was thin, with a thick slick of grease that had to be skimmed off the surface. That wasn't surprising: The fat in a typical roux coats its flour particles, making it easier for them to disperse in a hot liquid without forming lumps. At the same time, the starch chains in the flour are becoming hydrated and thickening the hot liquid. But browning the flour for a gumbo's roux weakens its ability to trap (and thereby thicken) liquid as well as its ability to keep the fat in it from separating and pooling on the surface. This is where okra and filé powder—secondary thickeners—usually come in, but I stuck to my decision to keep them out of the pot.

At this point, I considered a less-common approach that I had initially dismissed: a dry roux, where the flour is toasted without fat. The benefits were clear: no hot oil-flour paste to stand over, no skimming, and—while it hadn't been my original goal—a gumbo with less fat overall. What, if anything, would I be losing if I ditched the oil?

To find out, I would need to produce a dry roux comparable in color to the wet roux I'd been using. Dry roux can be made on the stovetop or in the microwave, but each method has the same challenges as a wet roux does, so I stuck with the oven. Conveniently, a hands-off dry roux cooked faster than the wet kind, clocking in at about 45 minutes. That's because a hot pan transfers heat more rapidly to dry flour than to oil-coated flour, as oil is a much poorer conductor of heat energy than hot metal is.

I moved forward, making two batches: one with a dry roux and one with a wet roux. Happily, the dry-roux gumbo boasted a dark color, rich flavor that compared favorably to the wet-roux gumbo, and a minimal grease slick. What's more, thanks to the dark-meat chicken and sausage, the dish didn't taste lean, even though I'd cut out ½ cup of oil. Satisfied, I shifted my focus to the gumbo's consistency.

The most obvious way to make the gumbo thicker was to increase the amount of roux. I gradually added more flour until I hit a full cup. It helped, but it wasn't enough (see "The Thick (and Thin) of It"). Rather than up the roux amount even more, which might have overwhelmed the dish, I decided to compensate by decreasing the amount of broth. After a few tests, I found that using just 4 cups finally gave me the perfect ratio of liquid to dark roux, yielding a rich, glossy, emulsified gumbo with body that coated the back of a spoon.

So Efficient

My gumbo was coming along and, at this point, took just under 2 hours from start to finish. I wondered if I could speed things along by adding the roux at the end of cooking instead of the beginning. That way I could prep my other ingredients and start cooking while the flour toasted.

Whisking the roux directly into the simmering broth made it difficult to incorporate without clumping, so I decided to reserve half the broth used for cooking the chicken to make a paste with the flour, allowing me to break up any lumps beforehand. Bingo: The paste whisked seamlessly into the remaining broth. Now I had rich, dark, luscious gumbo in just under 90 minutes.

All that was left to do was enliven the flavors. I stirred in ground black pepper, paprika, and minced garlic to mimic and highlight the seasonings in the andouille. I also incorporated some sliced scallions, a common garnish. The gumbo needed acidity to lift its rich, meaty flavor, but rather than add hot sauce (the usual final flourish), I stirred in clean-tasting white vinegar, letting my guests choose whether to add hot sauce to their own portions.

As I ladled my gumbo over a pile of white rice, I was satisfied with my recipe, and as I watched it disappear from the pot, I knew everyone else was, too.

CHICKEN AND SAUSAGE GUMBO
SERVES 6

This recipe is engineered for efficiency: Start toasting the flour in the oven before prepping the remaining ingredients and beginning to cook. We strongly recommend using andouille, but in a pinch, you can substitute kielbasa, if desired. In step 3, be sure to whisk the broth into the toasted flour in small increments to prevent lumps from forming. The saltiness of the final dish may vary depending on the brand of andouille you use, so liberal seasoning with additional salt before serving may be necessary. Serve over white rice.

- 1 cup (5 ounces) all-purpose flour
- 1 tablespoon vegetable oil
- 1 onion, chopped fine
- 1 green bell pepper, chopped fine
- 2 celery ribs, chopped fine
- 1 tablespoon minced fresh thyme
- 3 garlic cloves, minced
- 1 teaspoon paprika
- 2 bay leaves
- ½ teaspoon cayenne pepper
    Salt and pepper
- 4 cups chicken broth, room temperature
- 2 pounds boneless, skinless chicken thighs, trimmed
- 8 ounces andouille sausage, halved and sliced ¼ inch thick
- 6 scallions, sliced thin
- 1 teaspoon distilled white vinegar
    Hot sauce

1. Adjust oven rack to middle position and heat oven to 425 degrees. Place flour in 12-inch skillet and bake, stirring occasionally, until color of ground cinnamon, 40 to 55 minutes. (As flour approaches desired color, it will take on very nutty aroma that will smell faintly of burnt popcorn, and it will need to be stirred more frequently.) Transfer flour to medium bowl and let cool. (Toasted flour can be stored in airtight container in cool, dark place for up to 6 months.)

2. Heat oil in Dutch oven over medium heat until shimmering. Add onion, bell pepper, and celery and cook, stirring frequently, until softened, 5 to 7 minutes. Stir in thyme, garlic, paprika, bay leaves, cayenne, ¼ teaspoon salt, and ¼ teaspoon pepper and cook until fragrant, about 1 minute. Stir in 2 cups broth. Add chicken in single layer (chicken will not be completely submerged in liquid) and bring to simmer. Reduce heat to medium-low, cover, and simmer until chicken is fork-tender, 15 to 17 minutes. Transfer chicken to plate.

3. Slowly whisk remaining 2 cups broth in small increments into toasted flour until thick, smooth, batter-like paste forms. Increase heat to medium and slowly whisk paste into gumbo, making sure each addition is incorporated before adding next. Stir in andouille. Simmer, uncovered, until gumbo thickens slightly, 20 to 25 minutes.

4. Once cool enough to handle, shred chicken into bite-size pieces. Stir chicken and scallions into gumbo. Remove pot from heat, stir in vinegar, and season with salt to taste. Discard bay leaves. Serve, passing hot sauce separately. (Gumbo can be refrigerated in airtight container for up to 3 days.)

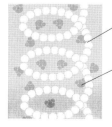
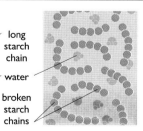

Weeknight Bolognese

Half a dozen meats and hours of pot watching make a lush, deeply savory version of this Italian ragu. We wanted those results with fewer ingredients in half the time.

⇒ BY ANNIE PETITO ⇐

Six years ago we published a recipe for *ragu alla Bolognese*, the lavish, long-cooked meat sauce named for the northern Italian city from which it hails. It's an "ultimate" version, loaded up with not just ground beef but also ground pork, veal, pancetta, mortadella, and chicken livers. The meats simmer gently with a *soffritto* (softened chopped onion, carrot, and celery), broth, wine, and a goodly amount of tomato paste for about 1½ hours, by which time the sauce is silky, deeply savory, and thick enough that a wooden spoon leaves a trail when dragged along the bottom of the pot. When tossed with eggy ribbons of tagliatelle or pappardelle, it's about as satisfying as a bowl of pasta can get.

Because Bolognese is a long-cooked sauce, it's a perfect project for a winter weekend when I don't mind lingering in the kitchen. But often I don't have the time or patience to make a proper version. That's when I wish I could whip up a streamlined sauce that would closely approximate the meaty depth and richness of the real deal. In fact, I've tried a few recipes called "quick" or "simple" Bolognese that cut the number of meats down to just one (ground beef) and come together in no more than an hour, but none was worth repeating. The most common flaw of these recipes was that they were too tomatoey and acidic—more like meaty marinara than true Bolognese, which actually contains relatively little tomato. Most also lacked the traditional sauce's velvety consistency and ultrasavory flavor; in other words, they tasted like the shortcut sauces they were.

Was it possible to have it both ways—a rich, complex-tasting meat sauce that didn't require half a dozen meats and an afternoon of pot watching? I was about to find out.

Where's the Beef?

I wanted to use ground beef—and only ground beef—as the meat in my sauce. But instead of searing it hard to develop deep color and flavor, which would turn it dry and pebbly, I tossed 1 pound of 85 percent lean ground beef with a little water and

Rich, meaty, and deeply savory, our sauce has all the appeal of a long-cooked Bolognese with about an hour's work.

baking soda. Odd as it sounds, this has been our routine first move when braising ground beef since we discovered that the alkaline baking soda can raise the meat's pH, helping it retain moisture (without affecting the sauce's flavor).

While the beef soaked, I sautéed finely chopped carrot, onion, and celery in a Dutch oven with a little oil and butter until much of their moisture had evaporated. Then came the tomato component—paste, not canned tomatoes, since I wanted to add savory depth to the sauce and not bright, fruity acidity. I cooked the paste until it developed a rusty hue, an indication that it had caramelized, and then added the meat, which I cooked just until it lost its raw pink color. In went some red wine to deglaze the pot, followed by a cup of beef broth. Some cooks would add dairy at this point; depending on who you ask, it's either an essential component, lending further richness and supposedly tenderizing the long-cooked meat, or it has no place in the sauce whatsoever. I opted not to, lest the dairy mute the meat's flavor. Instead, I simply simmered the mixture briefly to evaporate some of the liquid before reducing the heat and letting the sauce gurgle gently for about 30 minutes until it thickened up a bit; I then tossed it with the boiled pasta.

This sauce, while not bland, wasn't nearly as meaty-tasting as Bolognese should be. It was also greasy, but that was an easy fix: I switched to 93 percent lean ground beef. Ordinarily, such lean meat can be tough, but the baking soda treatment kept the beef moist and tender.

▶ **Annie Shows You How**
A step-by-step video is available at CooksIllustrated.com/feb17

SHOPPING Not All Egg Noodles Are Created Equal

Our recipe calls for dried tagliatelle, an Italian egg pasta that's the classic choice for Bolognese. Dried pappardelle, a wider Italian egg pasta, is a fine substitute. Do not use short egg noodles, such as those from Pennsylvania Dutch or Manischewitz, in this recipe. Their smooth surfaces are far less effective at gripping sauce than the rough-hewn, porous surfaces of good-quality Italian pasta (from brands such as De Cecco and Bionaturae). Only such traditionally made pasta will soak up enough liquid from our sauce to give it the right consistency. (For more details, see "Why Some Pasta Absorbs More [or Less] Sauce" on page 28.)

BUY THIS
Strands of good-quality Italian egg pasta have a rough-hewn, highly absorbent surface.

DON'T BUY THIS
Most non-Italian egg noodles are smoother and less absorbent than Italian egg pasta.

But what could I do to beef up the flavor? I was still reluctant to brown the ground meat, so I tried another unusual technique we've used in recipes for gravy and shepherd's pie: deeply browning the aromatic vegetables. I sautéed the carrot, onion, and celery for about 10 minutes, which gave me a visibly dark, rich flavor base, and then I finished building the sauce. It was meatier for sure—but still not meaty enough to be called Bolognese.

At this point, I reconsidered my initial ban on other meats. I didn't have to go whole hog, but it would be easy enough to add back something like pancetta, which is widely available and often used in small quantities to flavor Italian braises and sauces. The key would be chopping it very fine so that there would be a lot of surface area for browning and so it could thoroughly integrate into the sauce. I processed 6 ounces in the food processor, and while I was at it, I threw in the aromatic vegetables, too, again to maximize surface area for browning and to save myself the knife work. Once the mixture was paste-like, I spread it into a thin layer in the pot and cooked it.

This was the best-tasting sauce to date, but I had one other ingredient to try: Parmesan cheese. Garnishing each serving with a couple of spoonfuls is the classic way to season Italian pasta dishes with an extra jolt of salty, tangy richness, so why not add some directly to the pot? Sure enough, when I stirred a generous ½ cup into the sauce along with the broth, the final sauce was complex and seriously savory. It wasn't no-holds-barred Bolognese, but it was a convincingly close second.

Through Thick and Thin

The sauce tasted great and boasted a thick, velvety consistency that I thought would coat the tagliatelle beautifully. But instead the noodles sucked up all the liquid, leaving the sauce dry and scant.

The problem was that the rough surface of the tagliatelle soaks up a lot of liquid. I needed to make the sauce looser so that by the time the tagliatelle absorbed the liquid, the sauce's consistency would tighten up just enough. I would need to scale up the liquid volume without diluting the sauce's now-meaty flavor. I was able to easily accomplish this by reducing 4 cups of beef broth down to 2 cups, which took just 15 minutes and could be done while the beef soaked in the baking soda solution and the vegetables browned.

When I added the concentrated broth to the sauce, I feared I had increased the amount of liquid too much: The sauce looked thin even after cooking for 30 minutes—not a consistency I'd equate with Bolognese. It wasn't until I tossed the sauce with the noodles and they soaked up just enough of the liquid that the sauce looked appropriately thick and clung beautifully to the pasta (see "Looks Wrong, But It's Right").

Barely an hour had passed before I was sitting down to a bowl of tagliatelle Bolognese with a savory depth and richness that rivaled long-cooked versions but came together in about half the time.

WEEKNIGHT TAGLIATELLE WITH BOLOGNESE SAUCE
SERVES 4 TO 6

If you use our recommended beef broth, Better Than Bouillon Roasted Beef Base, you can skip step 2 and make a concentrated broth by adding 4 teaspoons paste to 2 cups water. To ensure the best flavor, be sure to brown the pancetta-vegetable mixture in step 4 until the fond on the bottom of the pot is quite dark. The cooked sauce will look thin but will thicken once tossed with the pasta. Tagliatelle is a long, flat, dry egg pasta that is about ¼ inch wide; if you can't find it, you can substitute pappardelle. Substituting other pasta may result in a too-wet sauce.

1	pound 93 percent lean ground beef
2	tablespoons water
¼	teaspoon baking soda
	Salt and pepper
4	cups beef broth
6	ounces pancetta, chopped coarse
1	onion, chopped coarse
1	large carrot, peeled and chopped coarse
1	celery rib, chopped coarse
1	tablespoon unsalted butter
1	tablespoon extra-virgin olive oil
3	tablespoons tomato paste
1	cup dry red wine
1	ounce Parmesan cheese, grated (½ cup), plus extra for serving
1	pound tagliatelle

1. Toss beef with water, baking soda, and ¼ teaspoon pepper in bowl until thoroughly combined. Set aside.

2. While beef sits, bring broth to boil over high heat in large pot (this pot will be used to cook pasta in step 6) and cook until reduced to 2 cups, about 15 minutes; set aside.

3. Pulse pancetta in food processor until finely chopped, 15 to 20 pulses. Add onion, carrot, and celery and pulse until vegetables are finely chopped and mixture has paste-like consistency, 12 to 15 pulses, scraping down sides of bowl as needed.

4. Heat butter and oil in large Dutch oven over medium-high heat until shimmering. When foaming subsides, add pancetta-vegetable mixture and ¼ teaspoon pepper and cook, stirring occasionally, until liquid has evaporated, about 8 minutes. Spread mixture in even layer in bottom of pot and continue to cook, stirring every couple of minutes, until very dark browned bits form on bottom of pot, 7 to 12 minutes longer. Stir in tomato paste and cook until paste is rust-colored and bottom of pot is dark brown, 1 to 2 minutes.

5. Reduce heat to medium, add beef, and cook, using wooden spoon to break meat into pieces no larger than ¼ inch, until beef has just lost its raw pink color, 4 to 7 minutes. Stir in wine, scraping up any browned bits, and bring to simmer. Cook until wine has evaporated and sauce has thickened, about 5 minutes. Stir in broth and Parmesan. Return sauce to simmer; cover, reduce heat to low, and simmer for 30 minutes (sauce will look thin). Remove from heat and season with salt and pepper to taste.

6. Rinse pot that held broth. While sauce simmers, bring 4 quarts water to boil in now-empty pot. Add pasta and 1 tablespoon salt and cook, stirring occasionally, until al dente. Reserve ¼ cup cooking water, then drain pasta. Add pasta to pot with sauce and toss to combine. Adjust sauce consistency with reserved cooking water as needed. Transfer to platter or individual bowls and serve, passing extra Parmesan separately.

A New Cauliflower Gratin

Who says a gratin needs to be stodgy and rich to be satisfying? The unique attributes of cauliflower put a fresh spin on this old standby.

> BY ANNIE PETITO

Cauliflower gratin should be a lighter alternative to the rich, starchy classic made with potatoes. Yet most of the recipes I've tried model themselves on that heavy, potato-based template: Cauliflower florets (which have been either boiled or steamed first) are arranged in a baking dish and inevitably buried under a stodgy, flour-thickened, cheesy cream sauce. I had an entirely different dish in mind: a cauliflower gratin with tender florets covered in a velvety sauce that boasted clean cauliflower flavor and was satisfying without the heft.

Trim and Fit

I started by figuring out the best way to prepare the florets. Cauliflower florets with some of their stem left on look pretty but cook unevenly because the stem is more dense than the floret. Fortunately, I had an easy way to trim the stems and create same-size florets. I first removed the core from the head of cauliflower and then cut the head into ½-inch-thick slabs. This made it easy to trim the stems, leaving flat florets about 1½ inches tall. These florets would cook evenly and, because of their flat shape, would also layer neatly in the gratin dish. I found that it took a full two heads' worth of cauliflower to fill a standard 13 by 9-inch baking dish.

Precooking the florets is typical of most recipes and for good reason; cooking them through from start to finish in the sauce would take far too long. In fact, the actual goal of baking the casserole is not to cook the cauliflower but to marry the flavors of sauce and cauliflower. But what was the best method of precooking them? Boiling the delicate florets was too aggressive; the jostling made them fall apart. I also gave roasting a try. While this approach imparted a nice toasted, nutty flavor, once I combined the florets with the sauce (a placeholder version for now) and baked the dish for about 15 minutes, I found that the nuttiness detracted from the clean flavor profile

▶ **Witness Cauliflower's Duality**
A step-by-step video is available at CooksIllustrated.com/feb17

A light, crispy Parmesan-panko topping gives our gratin texture and flavor while a sprinkling of chives adds color.

I wanted—not to mention that the browned pieces muddied the gratin's appearance. And so I settled on the gentle technique of steaming. I simply loaded my cauliflower florets into a steamer basket and cooked them in a pot over simmering water until a paring knife slipped in and out of them with no resistance.

Cauliflower Power

It was time to move on to the bigger challenge: the sauce. I continued to search for recipes that didn't

call for heavy or rich thickeners, such as a béchamel or lots of eggs, and at last found a few unique approaches to try. One featured a sauce made simply of cream thinned with chicken broth in a 2:1 ratio. It sounded lighter than the flour- or egg-thickened sauces, but sadly it was too thin (and too chicken-y). Another skipped liquids altogether and opted to combine the florets with just cheese and spices, plus a bread-crumb topping. The flavor was clean like I wanted, but the dish didn't come together into a cohesive gratin.

Out of ideas, I began browsing cauliflower recipes beyond gratins. A dish from chef Dan Barber of Blue Hill at Stone Barns in New York caught my eye. It featured pan-roasted cauliflower nestled in a sauce made of nothing more than cauliflower cooked in milk and water and then pureed with some of the cooking liquid. His recipe takes advantage of the fact that, unlike most vegetables, cauliflower is relatively low in fiber, particularly the insoluble fiber that is resistant to breaking down. This gives cauliflower the unique ability to blend into an ultracreamy puree without any cream (see "The Silky Side of Cauliflower").

What if cauliflower became my sauce, too? It would be creamy but not too rich, with the benefit of adding another layer of the starring vegetable's flavor. Furthermore, it occurred to me that I wouldn't need to buy a third head; I could likely use the stems and cores I had been throwing out. Even if I augmented these scraps with a couple of cups of florets, I would still have plenty of florets for the casserole.

I simmered the stem-core-floret mixture in a few cups of water until soft, and then I poured the pot's

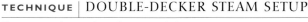

TECHNIQUE | DOUBLE-DECKER STEAM SETUP

To minimize the number of pots needed and to maximize the efficiency of the recipe, we place the cauliflower stems and cores and other sauce ingredients in the bottom of the Dutch oven to simmer and arrange the steamer basket with the florets on top before adding the lid.

We use two entire heads of cauliflower in our gratin. The florets make up the bulk of the dish while the cores and stems (and a small portion of florets) create the sauce. Here's the most efficient way to cut up the vegetable to allow for more evenly cooked florets.

1. PREP CORE Cut out each core, halve it lengthwise, and slice it thin crosswise. Reserve for sauce.

2. CUT SLABS Slice each head into ½-inch-thick slabs.

3. PREP STEMS Cut stems from slabs to create flat, 1½-inch-tall florets. Slice stems thin and reserve with sliced cores for sauce.

contents into a blender and pureed them until silky-smooth. I poured this sauce over the steamed florets layered in the dish and baked the gratin just until the sauce bubbled around the edges.

I was off to a good start, but the sauce was a bit thin and (not surprisingly, given that the cooking liquid was water) tasted too lean. Adding a little cornstarch improved the consistency. As for amping up the richness without muting flavor or making the sauce too heavy, I found that 6 tablespoons of butter added to the simmering cauliflower and water —this was the simplest approach, and it all would get blended together anyway—improved matters greatly, and the butter's sweet flavor complemented the cauliflower perfectly.

But there was still room for a little more depth and creaminess. I feared that adding cheese might move the sauce into the heavy, gloppy category, but I was happy to discover that ½ cup of grated Parmesan, which I added to the blender, lent a complementary salty richness without weighing the dish down. For more complexity, I added dry mustard, cayenne, and nutmeg. Tossing the florets with the puree so they were fully and evenly coated before they went into the baking dish ensured that there was sauce in every bite.

Stacked in My Favor

At this point, all my gratin needed was a classic bread-crumb-and-cheese topping for some texture, flavor, and color, so I toasted panko bread crumbs in butter until they were golden and then tossed them with some Parmesan. A sprinkling of minced chives over the finished gratin enlivened its appearance.

Before I was done, I made one more improvement for efficiency's sake. Did I really need two pots, one to steam the florets and one to simmer the sauce? For my next test, I put the stem-core-floret mixture, water, and butter in a Dutch oven and arranged my steamer basket, filled with the bulk of the florets, right on top of the mixture before adding the lid. When the florets in the basket were cooked through, I removed the basket and replaced the lid

so the sauce mixture could continue to simmer. My double-decker setup was a success.

With that, I had an easy cauliflower gratin that was good enough to require a second helping and light enough to guarantee that there'd be room for it.

MODERN CAULIFLOWER GRATIN
SERVES 8 TO 10

When buying cauliflower, look for heads without many leaves. Alternatively, if your cauliflower does have a lot of leaves, buy slightly larger heads—about 2¼ pounds each. This recipe can be halved to serve 4 to 6; cook the cauliflower in a large saucepan and bake the gratin in an 8-inch square baking dish.

2	heads cauliflower (2 pounds each)
8	tablespoons unsalted butter
½	cup panko bread crumbs
2	ounces Parmesan cheese, grated (1 cup)
	Salt and pepper
½	teaspoon dry mustard
⅛	teaspoon ground nutmeg
	Pinch cayenne pepper
1	teaspoon cornstarch dissolved in 1 teaspoon water
1	tablespoon minced fresh chives

1. Adjust oven rack to middle position and heat oven to 400 degrees.

2. Pull off outer leaves of 1 head of cauliflower and trim stem. Using paring knife, cut around core to remove; halve core lengthwise and slice thin crosswise. Slice head into ½-inch-thick slabs. Cut stems from slabs to create florets that are about 1½ inches tall; slice stems thin and reserve along with sliced core. Transfer florets to bowl, including any small pieces that may have been created during trimming, and set aside. Repeat with remaining head of cauliflower. (After trimming you should have about 3 cups of sliced stems and cores and 12 cups of florets.)

3. Combine sliced stems and cores, 2 cups florets, 3 cups water, and 6 tablespoons butter in Dutch oven and bring to boil over high heat. Place remaining florets in steamer basket (do not rinse bowl). Once mixture is boiling, place steamer basket in pot, cover, and reduce heat to medium. Steam florets in basket until translucent and stem ends can be easily pierced with paring knife, 10 to 12 minutes. Remove steamer basket and drain florets. Re-cover pot, reduce heat to low, and continue to cook stem mixture until very soft, about 10 minutes longer. Transfer drained florets to now-empty bowl.

4. While cauliflower is cooking, melt remaining 2 tablespoons butter in 10-inch skillet over medium heat. Add panko and cook, stirring frequently, until golden brown, 3 to 5 minutes. Transfer to bowl and let cool. Once cool, add ½ cup Parmesan and toss to combine.

5. Transfer stem mixture and cooking liquid to blender and add 2 teaspoons salt, ½ teaspoon pepper, mustard, nutmeg, cayenne, and remaining ½ cup Parmesan. Process until smooth and velvety, about 1 minute (puree should be pourable; adjust consistency with additional water as needed). With blender running, add cornstarch slurry. Season with salt and pepper to taste. Pour puree over cauliflower florets and toss gently to evenly coat. Transfer mixture to 13 by 9-inch baking dish (it will be quite loose) and smooth top with spatula.

6. Scatter bread-crumb mixture evenly over top. Transfer dish to oven and bake until sauce bubbles around edges, 13 to 15 minutes. Let stand for 20 to 25 minutes. Sprinkle with chives and serve.

TO MAKE AHEAD: Follow recipe through step 5, refrigerating gratin and bread-crumb mixture separately for up to 24 hours. To serve, assemble and bake gratin as directed in step 6, increasing baking time by 13 to 15 minutes.

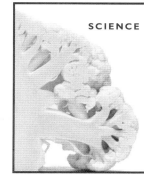

SCIENCE The Silky Side of Cauliflower

All vegetables contain both soluble and insoluble fiber—the soluble kind fully breaks down during cooking, but the insoluble kind does not. Cauliflower has a leg up on other vegetables because it is very low in overall fiber, and only half its fiber is insoluble. This meant we could easily puree cauliflower into a silky-smooth sauce—no need to weigh our gratin down with lots of cream.

Bringing Back Brown Bread

Colonists knew how to mix up batter and steam it over an open fire to make
a remarkably moist whole-grain bread. We think they were onto something.

⇒ BY ANDREW JANJIGIAN ⇐

As a native New Englander, I've always had a thing for Boston brown bread. It's deeply, darkly delicious—sort of a cross between a cake and a quick bread in texture and rich with molasses, raisins, and the complex flavors (and nutrition) of whole grains. When colonists started making this unyeasted, one-bowl bread in the 18th century, most cooking was done over an open hearth—a tricky environment for bread baking. To get around this, brown bread was steamed in lidded tin pudding molds in a kettle of simmering water over an open fire, giving the loaves a distinctive shape and a smooth, crustless exterior—and keeping the whole-grain crumb remarkably moist. Yankees have always paired brown bread with baked beans for supper, but it is equally delicious toasted, with a schmear of cream cheese or butter, for breakfast or as a snack.

To create a brown bread recipe of my own, I turned to one of the best-known recipes for inspiration. It comes from *Fannie Farmer's Boston Cooking-School Cook Book* (1898) and calls for grains that were plentiful and cheap at the time: rye meal, granulated (coarse) cornmeal, and graham flour. The grains are mixed with salt and baking soda, and then molasses and buttermilk are poured in to create a thick, bubbly batter (the baking soda reacts with both the buttermilk and the molasses to help lighten the loaf). The batter is then scooped into a buttered mold, leaving ample space for the bread to expand during cooking. Next, the mold is covered and set in a boiling-water bath until the bread is fully cooked, which takes about 4 hours since the grains require time to tenderize. Finally, the bread is slid out of the mold and allowed to cool before being sliced and served. I followed the recipe as written, except for employing the modern approach of using a coffee can in place of the pudding mold.

Batter Up(date)

Farmer's recipe has stood the test of time—it was quite good—so I decided to use it as a starting point for my own recipe. I evaluated the ingredients one by one. "Rye meal" simply refers to coarsely ground rye; it has a sandy texture similar to that of grits. Most

Rye flour, cornmeal, and whole-wheat flour are the stars of these rich, satisfying loaves.

modern recipes opt for more readily available rye flour, so I followed suit. Using more finely ground, quicker-cooking rye flour helped cut down the long steaming time. For the same reason, I found it best to use finely ground cornmeal rather than coarse. Finally, the graham flour. This is just coarsely ground

whole-wheat flour, so I swapped in much more readily available regular whole-wheat flour. I used equal amounts of these three components so that their flavors would get equal billing.

Farmer called for molasses as the sole sweetener in the bread, but many contemporary recipes also include milder sugars such as brown or white. However, I found that these made the bread sweeter than it really should be and masked the pleasing trace of bitterness that is essential to brown bread. Molasses alone was the way to go, and any type—except for blackstrap, which is far too intensely flavored—worked just fine. (For more information, see "Molasses Morass, Unraveled.")

That said, I did come across a few modern refinements that were worth implementing. Adding a second leavener (baking powder) helped give the bread a lighter texture. And mixing in fat—in the form of a few tablespoons of melted butter—gave the bread a welcome richness and softened its coarse texture.

Full Steam Ahead

Finally, there was the question of cooking the bread in a 1-pound coffee can. Since nowadays few people buy coffee in metal cans and even fewer own pudding molds, it seemed like a good idea to scale the recipe to fit into two 28-ounce tomato cans. BPA-free cans are now available, which alleviates any safety concerns (see "A Newer Approach to Steaming Bread"). To prevent

---

**SKIP THE
BLACKSTRAP**

SHOPPING **Molasses Morass, Unraveled**

Buying molasses can be a confusing experience since bottles may be variously labeled mild, dark, robust, full, or blackstrap. Fortunately, we've found that with the exception of blackstrap, these other products all taste similar, and they all work fine in our recipes. As for blackstrap, this designation indicates that the mixture of sugarcane and sugar beet juice used to make the syrup has been boiled three times, rendering the molasses darker and thicker. In taste tests, this type stood out as strongly bitter, smoky, and much less sweet than other types. When we substituted blackstrap in recipes calling for regular molasses (brown bread, baked beans, and chewy molasses cookies), tasters found the results too intense. Another reason to avoid blackstrap in recipes that don't specifically call for it: a lower sugar and higher calcium content. Cookies made with blackstrap didn't spread appropriately, and bean skins refused to soften completely.

sticking, I greased the interiors; once the cans were loaded with batter, I wrapped their tops with greased aluminum foil.

I came across a few recipes that suggested baking the bread in a gentle oven instead of steaming it, but to prevent the tops of the loaves from getting overly dark and leathery, I had to set the oven so low that they took a very long time to cook through. Steaming on the stovetop by setting the cans in a stockpot of simmering water was faster and ensured that the loaves stayed moist inside and out. (Even though the cans are wrapped tightly and the steam never makes contact with the bread, it prevents the loaves from exceeding 212 degrees.) After 2 hours, I pulled two steamy cylinders of utterly delicious whole-grain bread from the pot, happy to carry on the tradition.

BOSTON BROWN BREAD
MAKES 2 SMALL LOAVES; SERVES 6 TO 8

This recipe requires two empty 28-ounce cans. Use cans that are labeled "BPA-free." We prefer Quaker white cornmeal in this recipe, though other types will work; do not use coarse grits. Any style of molasses will work except for blackstrap. This recipe requires a 10-quart or larger stockpot that is at least 7 inches deep. Brown bread is traditionally served with baked beans but is also good toasted and buttered.

    ¾   cup (4⅛ ounces) rye flour
    ¾   cup (4⅛ ounces) whole-wheat flour
    ¾   cup (3¾ ounces) fine white cornmeal
   1¾   teaspoons baking soda
    ½   teaspoon baking powder
    1   teaspoon salt
   1⅔   cups buttermilk
    ½   cup molasses
    3   tablespoons butter, melted and cooled slightly
    ¾   cup raisins

1. Bring 3 quarts water to simmer in large stockpot over high heat. Fold two 16 by 12-inch pieces of aluminum foil in half to yield two rectangles that measure 8 by 12 inches. Spray 4-inch circle in center of each rectangle with vegetable oil spray. Spray insides of two clean 28-ounce cans with vegetable oil spray.

2. Whisk rye flour, whole-wheat flour, cornmeal, baking soda, baking powder, and salt together in large bowl. Whisk buttermilk, molasses, and melted butter together in second bowl. Stir raisins into buttermilk mixture. Add buttermilk mixture to flour mixture and stir until combined and no dry flour remains. Evenly divide batter between cans. Wrap tops of cans tightly with prepared foil, positioning sprayed side of foil over can openings.

3. Place cans in stockpot (water should come about halfway up sides of cans). Cover pot and cook, maintaining gentle simmer, until skewer inserted in center of loaves comes out clean, about 2 hours. Check pot occasionally and add hot water as needed to maintain water level.

4. Using jar lifter, carefully transfer cans to wire rack set in rimmed baking sheet and let cool for 20 minutes. Slide loaves from cans onto rack and let cool completely, about 1 hour. Slice and serve. (Bread can be wrapped tightly in plastic wrap and stored at room temperature for up to 3 days or frozen for up to 2 weeks.)

An Easy Out
To ensure that the bread releases easily from the cans, we spray the insides with vegetable oil spray. The bread shrinks slightly as it cools, so make sure to let it cool for the full 20 minutes. Giving the can a gentle shake before sliding the loaf onto the rack will also facilitate an easy release.

TESTING Thermal Carafes
Thermal carafes can keep coffee hot (and milk cold) for hours—perfect for brunch or a dessert table. Most models are double-walled and vacuum-sealed, meaning the air between the two stainless-steel walls has been removed (without air, heat transfers much more slowly). To find the best carafe, we put eight models, priced from $21.99 to $72.07 and with capacities from 44 to 68 ounces, through their paces.

To test heat retention, we filled each carafe with 161-degree coffee and recorded its temperature every hour. After 4 hours, the coolest coffee was a tepid 138 degrees. Meanwhile, the coffee in the top performers was still quite hot at 152 degrees. The carafes weren't as adept in our cold-water tests, but they are still mostly fine for keeping milk or cream cold for a few hours.

We preferred models that poured with even streams and had valves that quickly closed the pour spouts. We also liked sturdy handles. Finally, we preferred carafes with wide openings for easy filling and lids that closed smoothly and securely. Ultimately, the Zojirushi Stainless Steel Vacuum Carafe won top marks. For complete results, go to CooksIllustrated.com/feb17. –Kate Shannon

HIGHLY RECOMMENDED
ZOJIRUSHI Stainless Steel Vacuum Carafe 
MODEL: SH-HB15
PRICE: $57.51
COMMENTS: This model is the only carafe that has extra insulation in addition to the standard double-wall vacuum seal, and it received high marks for maintaining the temperature of hot and cold liquids. It boasts a comfortable handle, and it pours with a steady stream.

RECOMMENDED (BEST BUY)
GENUINE THERMOS BRAND 51-Ounce Vacuum Insulated Stainless Steel Carafe 
MODEL: TGS1500SS4
PRICE: $42.70
COMMENTS: This carafe nearly kept pace with our favorite in temperature tests. Minor quibbles: The twist-on lid was a bit tricky to attach, especially when it was wet, and it sometimes took an extra try to close the carafe properly.

▶ **Andrew Bakes the Bread**
A step-by-step video is available at CooksIllustrated.com/feb17

TECHNIQUE | A NEWER APPROACH TO STEAMING BREAD

The colonists steamed their brown bread in tin pudding molds; modern cooks took to using empty coffee cans. But these days, few cooks buy their coffee in cans, so we turned to empty 28-ounce tomato cans, which we wrapped in foil and steamed in a covered stockpot for 2 hours. We made sure to select cans labeled "BPA-free." BPA is a controversial chemical used in the linings of some cans that could leach into the bread when exposed to prolonged heat. Today, many companies use BPA-free cans.

New England Baked Beans

The transformation of a few humble ingredients into a rich, deeply flavorful dish is a tradition worth continuing. But does it have to take all day?

⇒ BY ANNIE PETITO ⇐

In early New England, Puritans baked bread in communal ovens on Saturdays. When the last loaf was pulled from the hearth, the town baker collected bean pots and set them to cook in the residual heat. After bubbling away all afternoon, the beans were served for supper; leftovers were on the table again for breakfast on Sunday. It all worked out to be quite convenient, as cooking was forbidden from sundown on Saturday through sundown on Sunday as part of Sabbath customs.

Today, baked beans are still all about patience: Recipes call for 6, 8, or even 10 hours of cooking to transform modest ingredients—dried beans, smoky pork, bittersweet molasses, mustard, and sometimes onion and brown sugar—into a pot of creamy, tender beans coated in a lightly thickened, sweet, and savory sauce. Delicious, indeed. But must they take so long? I wanted to create the best possible version of this American classic but hopefully without hours and hours of cooking.

Bean Basics

White navy beans, which boast a mild flavor and a dense, creamy texture, are typically used for New England baked beans. Step one was to soak them overnight in salty water—an adjustment we make to the usual plain-water soak because we've learned that sodium weakens the pectin in the beans' skins, reducing the number of ruptured beans. That's a good thing, since when beans burst, they spill their starchy innards, creating a sticky, unappealing texture. Soaked beans also cook faster than unsoaked and seem to absorb water more evenly, so the result is creamier.

To my pot of drained, brined beans, I added some standard flavorings: a cup each of molasses and dark brown sugar, plus dry mustard, black pepper, and a bay leaf. For the pork element, some cooks use bacon, but traditionalists swear by salt pork, and I agreed: It would add meaty depth without

Chunks of salt pork add meatiness to the sweet, earthy beans.

▶ Behold the Baking Beans
A step-by-step video is available at CooksIllustrated.com/feb17

the distracting smokiness of bacon. Sticking to the ultrasimple old-fashioned approach, I skipped browning and tossed a few raw chunks of salt pork straight into the pot, where their fat would melt into the beans.

Now, about the long cooking time. The test kitchen has plenty of recipes in which dried beans are fully cooked after simmering in water for only an hour. Baked beans take longer because adding acid to the mix via brown sugar and molasses firms the cell structure of legumes and slows down their cooking—but by how much?

To find out, I added enough water to cover the beans by a couple of inches. Then, to jump-start the cooking process, I brought the pot to a boil on the stovetop before placing a lid on it and transferring it to a 300-degree oven. It took 3 hours for the beans to turn perfectly creamy. Longer cooking times, it seemed, were just a holdover from the low-temperature hearth cooking of yesteryear.

Holding back the acidic brown sugar and molasses until the beans had softened could save time, but would there be a flavor sacrifice? I

added the molasses and brown sugar to separate batches of beans after 15, 30, and 45 minutes of cooking, tracking how much longer the beans took to soften once the acidic ingredients were added. The results were eye-opening: Adding the molasses and brown sugar at 45 minutes resulted in tender beans in just over an hour, while the 15- and 30-minute batches took twice as long.

The problem was that the longer I waited to add the flavorings, the less they penetrated, leaving the beans pale and bland. Even the batches where the ingredients were added just 15 minutes into simmering didn't compare to the deeply bronzed beans flavored from the get-go. (For more information, see "A Shortcut That Wasn't Worth It.") I would have to live with a 3-hour cooking time—still quite a bit shorter than what most recipes call for.

Simple Tweaks

My next tests involved thickening the sauce, which was too soupy. I eventually determined that covering the beans by just ½ inch of water at the start would keep them submerged during cooking and still create a more viscous sauce. But I wanted it even more reduced. Removing the lid for the last hour of cooking helped the sauce cook down just below the beans, creating an attractive browned crust on top and a rich, velvety liquid underneath.

I also needed to adjust the beans' overt sweetness. I cut the molasses in half and reduced the brown sugar to just 2 tablespoons. I also threw a halved yellow onion into the pot. Tasters loved the mild, partly sweet, partly savory note it lent the beans as it softened in the oven (no need to sauté it beforehand).

The beans were now really good, but I felt they needed just a bit more character, so I stirred in a tablespoon of umami-rich soy sauce. My tasters (even the traditionalists) approved of the way it elevated the flavor.

Finally, to capture every last bit of goodness, I made sure to scrape the fond from the pot's inside edge and stirred it into the beans. Tender, creamy, hearty, and glazed in a lightly sweet sauce, these baked beans had it all—in a modest amount of time.

1. USE LESS WATER Four cups of water cooks down into a thick, savory sauce in 3 hours.

2. UNCOVER POT Removing the lid for the last hour of cooking helps the sauce rapidly reduce.

3. ADD FLAVOR BOOST Soy sauce replicates the depth produced by longer cooking times.

NEW ENGLAND BAKED BEANS
SERVES 4 TO 6

You'll get fewer blowouts if you soak the beans overnight, but if you're pressed for time, you can quick-salt-soak your beans. In step 1, combine the salt, water, and beans in a large Dutch oven and bring them to a boil over high heat. Remove the pot from the heat, cover it, and let it stand for 1 hour. Drain and rinse the beans and proceed with the recipe.

    Salt
1 pound (2½ cups) dried navy beans, picked over and rinsed
6 ounces salt pork, rinsed, cut into 3 pieces
1 onion, halved
½ cup molasses
2 tablespoons packed dark brown sugar
1 tablespoon soy sauce
2 teaspoons dry mustard
½ teaspoon pepper
1 bay leaf

1. Dissolve 1½ tablespoons salt in 2 quarts cold water in large container. Add beans and let soak at room temperature for at least 8 hours or up to 24 hours. Drain and rinse well.

2. Adjust oven rack to lower-middle position and heat oven to 300 degrees. Combine beans, salt pork, onion, molasses, sugar, soy sauce, mustard, pepper, bay leaf, ¼ teaspoon salt, and 4 cups water in large Dutch oven. (Liquid should cover beans by about ½ inch. Add more water if necessary.) Bring to boil over high heat. Cover pot, transfer to oven, and cook until beans are softened and bean skins curl up and split when you blow on them, about 2 hours. (After 1 hour, stir beans and check amount of liquid. Liquid should just cover beans. Add water if necessary.)

3. Remove lid and continue to cook until beans are fully tender, browned, and slightly crusty on top, about 1 hour longer. (Liquid will reduce slightly below top layer of beans.)

4. Remove pot from oven, cover, and let stand for 5 minutes. Using wooden spoon or rubber spatula, scrape any browned bits from sides of pot and stir into beans. Discard onion and bay leaf. (Salt pork can be eaten, if desired.) Let beans stand, uncovered, until liquid has thickened slightly and clings to beans, 10 to 15 minutes, stirring once halfway through. Season with salt and pepper to taste, and serve. (Beans can be refrigerated for up to 4 days.)

RECIPE TESTING   A Shortcut That Wasn't Worth It

Our baked beans cook for 3 hours—quicker than many recipes but still a time investment. We wondered if we could shorten the simmering time by adding the molasses and brown sugar after we started cooking the beans, since these acidic ingredients firm up the cell structure of the beans and prolong cooking time. While the beans became tender more quickly, they also were progressively lighter in flavor and color. Only when the molasses and brown sugar were added at the start of cooking did the beans fully absorb their flavors.

ADDED AT THE START: FULL FLAVOR

ADDED AFTER 30 MINUTES: MODERATE FLAVOR

ADDED AFTER 45 MINUTES: MILD FLAVOR

Bean Basics

CHECKING BEANS FOR DONENESS

Not sure if your beans are done? Blow on them. The skins of properly cooked beans will wrinkle and curl back when you blow.

HOW BRINING SOFTENS BEANS

The pectin molecules in bean skins are tightly bound by calcium and magnesium ions. When beans are soaked in salted water, sodium replaces some of these ions, causing the pectin to weaken and leading to skins that are less likely to burst during cooking.

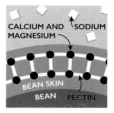 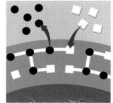

TOUGH SKIN
At the start of brining, the pectin molecules in the skin are tightly bound by calcium and magnesium ions.

SOFTER SKIN
Sodium ions replace the calcium and magnesium ions, weakening the pectin, for skin that's less prone to bursting.

HARD WATER? BRINE YOUR BEANS.

Cooking beans in hard water (which has a relatively high mineral content) purportedly can cause them to cook up with tougher skins and firmer interiors than beans cooked in soft water. To confirm this, we compared batches of navy beans soaked and cooked in soft tap water from our Brookline, Massachusetts, offices; in moderately hard water from the nearby town of Natick; and in distilled water with calcium chloride added to approximate what the U.S. Geological Survey defines as hard water (121 to 180 mg/L calcium carbonate).* After an hour, we found that beans cooked in hard water had noticeably tougher skins and firmer interiors than the soft-water batch, while those cooked in moderately hard water had slightly tougher skins.

We repeated this experiment, this time brining and then cooking the beans in each type of water. After an hour, we found that they all softened with minimal differences among them. **BOTTOM LINE:** If your water is hard, all the more reason to brine your dried beans before cooking. *Note: Calcium carbonate is not very soluble in water, so we used calcium chloride, adjusting the amount to equal the calcium carbonate concentration in hard water.

Cooking in—and Caring for—Cast Iron

Game for any recipe from seared steak to fried eggs to apple pie, a cast-iron skillet can be the most versatile piece of cookware in the kitchen. BY ELIZABETH BOMZE

A CHEMICAL-FREE, DURABLE, AFFORDABLE WORKHORSE

Since its inception in fifth-century BCE China, cast iron has been a favorite cookware material across the globe. In the United States, early settlers took advantage of its high-heat compatibility for open-fire cooking. Though it fell out of favor in the mid-20th century when Teflon became widely available, it's recently regained popularity as an alternative to both traditional and nonstick cookware. Here's what it offers.

➤ **EXCEPTIONAL HEAT RETENTION** Though it transfers heat very slowly compared with aluminum or stainless steel, cast iron retains heat much more effectively than these materials, making it ideal for browning, searing, and shallow frying.

➤ **NATURALLY NONSTICK SURFACE** Whereas most chemically coated cookware deteriorates over time, cast iron only gets better, gradually developing a slick patina, or "seasoning," which releases food easily—and with no harmful chemicals involved.

➤ **UNBEATABLE DURABILITY AND VALUE** Cast iron is virtually indestructible and is easily restored if mistreated. Plus, a good skillet can be had for well under $50 and should last for generations.

A 10-inch cooking surface provides plenty of room for good browning.

A helper handle makes the heavyweight frame easy to lift.

The preseasoned interior is smooth right out of the box.

TRADITIONAL FAVORITE
Lodge Classic Cast-Iron Skillet, 12" ($33.31)

The Other Cast Iron: Enameled

Enameled cast-iron skillets are coated inside and out with the same kind of porcelain finish found on enameled cast-iron Dutch ovens. They cost more than traditional cast-iron skillets, but they have certain advantages: They never have to be seasoned, their coating prevents rust and doesn't interact with acid, and they can be cleaned much like other pots and pans.

ENAMELED FAVORITE
Le Creuset Signature 11¾" Iron Handle Skillet ($179.95)

TWO USEFUL ACCESSORIES

➤ **LIDS**
Lodge 12-Inch Tempered Glass Cover ($25.81)
Why We Like It: Lightweight, stay-cool handle; good visibility; ovensafe to 400 degrees
RSVP Endurance Stainless-Steel Universal Lid with Glass Insert ($19.99)
Why We Like It: Vent to release steam, heat-resistant handle, usable with other pans

➤ **CHAIN-MAIL SCRUBBER**
Knapp Made Small Ring CM Scrubber ($19.98)
Why We Like It: Fine rings scour grooves with ease, won't damage pan's finish (don't use on enameled cast iron), doesn't rust

COMMON MYTHS, BUSTED

After testing dozens of skillets, we upended these common misconceptions about cast iron.

MYTH: You should never wash cast iron with soap.
REALITY: A few drops of dish soap are not enough to interfere with the polymerized oil bonds that comprise the surface of a well-seasoned pan. In fact, a little soap can help rid the pan of excess greasiness.

MYTH: It's bad to cook with acidic ingredients in cast iron.
REALITY: It's OK to cook with acidic ingredients, but keep the cooking time to 30 minutes and remove the food immediately after cooking. Longer exposure can damage the seasoning and cause trace amounts of metal to leach into the food, imparting metallic flavors.

MYTH: Metal utensils will scratch the seasoning.
REALITY: The seasoning on a cast-iron pan is chemically bonded to the surface, and it will not scratch off. When we slashed the surface of our favorite Lodge skillet with a chef's knife and scraped it repeatedly with a metal spatula, it survived with nary a mark.

MYTH: If a cast-iron pan rusts, it's ruined.
REALITY: It takes a lot to kill a cast-iron skillet. If yours does rust, first try scrubbing with a nonabrasive pad. If this doesn't work, strip and reseason the pan (see "Servicing Your Skillet"). Only if the pan has literally rusted through is it time to throw it out.

MYTH: Cooking fatty meats, such as bacon, in cast iron is the best way to season it.
REALITY: Fat from animal proteins will lubricate the pan's surface but won't season it. These highly saturated fats don't polymerize as well as highly unsaturated oils like sunflower, soybean, and corn. (For more information, see "The Science of Seasoning.")

THE SCIENCE OF SEASONING

When fat or cooking oil is heated to its smoke point in cast iron, its fatty acids oxidize and reorganize (or "polymerize") into a new plastic-like layer of molecules. This layer becomes trapped within the pitted surface of the pan and bonds to the metal itself, creating the slick coating known as seasoning. Repeated exposure to smoking hot oil continues to build on this coating, making it more slippery and durable. That's why even though most skillets these days come with a factory seasoning, the surface will become even more nonstick with repeated use.

WHAT DOES "WELL SEASONED" MEAN? FRY AN EGG TO FIND OUT

A well-seasoned skillet will have a dark, semiglossy finish and won't be sticky or greasy to the touch. It won't have any rust or any dull or dry patches.

➤ An easy way to test a skillet's seasoning is to fry an egg (heat 1 tablespoon vegetable oil in skillet over medium heat for 3 minutes, then add egg). If your pan is well seasoned, you should not experience any major sticking.

USE THE RIGHT OIL

The more polyunsaturated the fat, the more readily it will oxidize and polymerize. We have found that flaxseed oil, which oxidizes and polymerizes faster than other vegetable oils, forms a particularly durable seasoning. But cheaper oils such as sunflower and soybean also work fine.

	BEST	GOOD, LOWER-COST CHOICES				WORST
OIL	Flaxseed	Sunflower	Soybean	Corn	Canola	Bacon Fat
% SATURATED	9%	10%	16%	13%	7%	39%
% MONOUNSATURATED	18%	20%	23%	28%	63%	45%
% POLYUNSATURATED	68%	66%	58%	55%	28%	11%

SERVICING YOUR SKILLET

Caring for a cast-iron skillet is like caring for a car: Service it regularly and it will last a long time; use it hard (or neglect it) and it will need more heavy-duty repair work. These care guidelines will bring your skillet back to life, no matter what condition it's in. **Use the fried egg test (above) to test your skillet's seasoning.**

➤ **LEVEL 1: ROUTINE MAINTENANCE**
1. Clean after every use: Wipe interior surface of still-warm skillet with paper towels to remove any excess food and oil. Rinse under hot running water, scrubbing with nonmetal brush or nonabrasive scrub pad to remove any traces of food. (Use small amount of soap if you like; rinse well.) Go to CooksIllustrated.com/cleaning for more cleaning tips.
2. Lightly oil after each cleaning: Dry skillet thoroughly (do not drip-dry), then heat over medium-low heat until all traces of moisture have evaporated. Add ½ teaspoon oil to pan and use paper towels to lightly coat interior surface with oil. Continue to wipe surface with oiled paper towels until it looks dark and smooth and no oil residue remains. Let pan cool completely.

➤ **LEVEL 2: MINOR SERVICE**
Stovetop repair: Heat skillet over medium-high heat. Using paper towels dipped in 2 tablespoons oil and held with tongs, wipe surface until oil smokes and there is no remaining oil residue. Repeat oil application 3 to 5 times, making sure oil smokes and letting skillet cool slightly after each application.
Oven repair: Heat oven to 500 degrees. Using paper towels, rub 1 tablespoon (for 12-inch skillet) or 2 teaspoons (for 10-inch skillet) oil over surface. Using clean paper towels, thoroughly wipe out excess oil (surface should look dark and smooth). Place skillet in oven for 1 hour. Using potholders, remove skillet from oven and let cool completely.

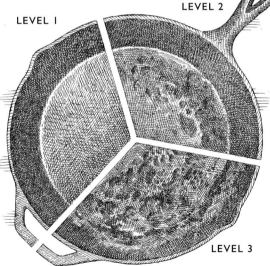

LEVEL 1

LEVEL 2

LEVEL 3

➤ **LEVEL 3: MAJOR SERVICE**
Over the lifetime of a cast-iron skillet, you'll usually just need to maintain or touch up its seasoning. But if the seasoning becomes very dull or damaged or if the pan badly rusts (it can't be scrubbed away), you'll need to give it an overhaul by stripping and reseasoning the surface. (Go to CooksIllustrated.com/stripping for detailed instructions.) Once the skillet's seasoning has been stripped away, follow the oven repair directions, repeating the process six times or until the skillet has a dark, smooth finish.

HACK YOUR SKILLET

MAKESHIFT FLAME TAMER
Place skillet over low flame and place your pot or saucepan in skillet. Skillet will moderate heat.

PANINI WITHOUT A PANINI PRESS
Set cast-iron skillet over medium-high heat and place assembled sandwiches in middle. Place smaller cast-iron skillet on top of sandwiches to press. (If you have only 1 cast-iron pan, place sandwiches in traditional skillet and weigh them down with cast-iron skillet.) Cook until bottoms of sandwiches are golden brown; flip and repeat on other side.

IN-A-PINCH PIE PLATE
A seasoned cast-iron skillet can be a handy pie plate alternative as long as your skillet is 9 or 10 inches in diameter to keep the volume and baking times consistent.

TROUBLESHOOTING

PROBLEM: Lingering fishy odors
SOLUTION: Bake in 400-degree oven for 10 minutes. High heat eliminates fishy-smelling compounds called trialkylamines and oxidized fatty acids.

PROBLEM: Stuck-on food
SOLUTION: Rub skillet with nonabrasive scrub pad; wipe clean. Heat ¼ inch oil over medium-low flame for 5 minutes. Off heat, add ¼ cup kosher salt. Using potholder to grip handle, scrub skillet with paper towels (held with tongs). Rinse with hot water; dry well. Repeat if necessary (no need to lightly reseason).

Warm Winter Salads

For tender, lightly wilted greens, forget the salad bowl and get out your Dutch oven.

⇒ BY STEVE DUNN ⇐

Spinach is the typical choice for tossing with a warm vinaigrette, but there are plenty of other contenders. I wanted to build a satisfying main-course wilted-green salad featuring a few lettuces that don't get as much attention: frisée, the curly star of French bistro salad; ruffled escarole; and frilly chicory. I hoped that each (or a combination thereof) would soften under a hot dressing and be a unique, robust canvas for all sorts of bold, flavorful ingredients.

When drizzling a hot vinaigrette over the greens wasn't enough to wilt them, I wondered if I could take the unorthodox step of warming the greens with the dressing. But I needed a vessel big enough for 10 cups of greens. That's when I pulled out my roomy Dutch oven. I warmed the dressing in the pot, but by the time I had tossed in all the greens, some leaves were not just wilted but were cooked. I had a better idea: Warm up the pot by sautéing at least one mix-in (such as carrots or fennel), let it cool briefly, and then add the greens off the heat. After a few turns of my tongs, the greens had just the right slightly softened texture.

All that was left was to incorporate other ingredients with contrasting yet complementary tastes and textures: nuts for crunch, cheese for fat and salt, and fruit for sweetness, all tied together with a tangy mustard vinaigrette.

BITTER GREENS, CARROT, AND CHICKPEA SALAD WITH WARM LEMON DRESSING
SERVES 4

The volume measurement of the greens may vary depending on the variety or combination used. Our recipe for Bitter Greens and Fig Salad with Warm Shallot Dressing is available for free for four months at CooksIllustrated.com/feb17.

Vinaigrette
- 2 tablespoons extra-virgin olive oil
- 1 tablespoon grated lemon zest plus 6 tablespoons juice (2 lemons)
- 1 tablespoon Dijon mustard
- 1 tablespoon minced shallot
- ½ teaspoon ground cumin
- ½ teaspoon ground coriander
- ¼ teaspoon smoked paprika

▶ **Watch: It Really Works**
A step-by-step video is available at CooksIllustrated.com/feb17

Residual heat from the Dutch oven wilts the greens.

- ¼ teaspoon cayenne pepper
- ¼ teaspoon salt
- ¼ teaspoon pepper

Salad
- 1 (15-ounce) can chickpeas, rinsed Salt and pepper
- 1 tablespoon extra-virgin olive oil
- 3 carrots, peeled and shredded
- ¾ cup raisins, chopped
- ½ cup slivered almonds
- 12 ounces (10–12 cups) bitter greens, such as escarole, chicory, and/or frisée, torn into bite-size pieces
- ⅓ cup mint leaves, chopped
- 1½ ounces feta cheese, crumbled (⅓ cup)

1. FOR THE VINAIGRETTE: Whisk all ingredients in bowl until emulsified.

2. FOR THE SALAD: Toss chickpeas with 1 tablespoon vinaigrette and pinch salt in bowl; set aside. Heat oil in Dutch oven over medium heat until shimmering. Add carrots, raisins, and almonds and cook, stirring frequently, until carrots are wilted, 4 to 5 minutes. Remove pot from heat and let cool for 5 minutes.

3. Add half of remaining vinaigrette to pot, then add half of greens and toss for 1 minute to warm and wilt. Add remaining greens and mint followed by remaining vinaigrette and continue to toss until greens are evenly coated and warmed through, about 2 minutes longer. Season with salt and pepper to taste. Transfer greens to serving platter, top with chickpeas and feta, and serve.

BITTER GREENS, FENNEL, AND APPLE SALAD WITH WARM PANCETTA DRESSING
SERVES 4

The volume measurement of the greens may vary depending on the variety or combination used.

Vinaigrette
- ¼ cup red wine vinegar
- 2 tablespoons extra-virgin olive oil
- 1 tablespoon Dijon mustard
- 1 tablespoon minced shallot
- 1 teaspoon minced fresh thyme
- ¼ teaspoon salt
- ¼ teaspoon pepper

Salad
- 3 ounces pancetta, cut into ¼-inch pieces
- 1 small fennel bulb (8 ounces), stalks discarded, bulb halved, cored, and sliced thin
- 1 cup walnuts, chopped coarse
- 12 ounces (10–12 cups) bitter greens, such as escarole, chicory, and/or frisée, torn into bite-size pieces Salt and pepper
- 1 Fuji apple, cored, halved, and sliced thin
- 2 ounces blue cheese, crumbled (½ cup)

1. FOR THE VINAIGRETTE: Whisk all ingredients in bowl until emulsified.

2. FOR THE SALAD: Cook pancetta in large Dutch oven over medium heat until browned and fat is rendered, 7 to 8 minutes. Using slotted spoon, transfer pancetta to paper towel–lined plate. Pour off all but 1 tablespoon fat from pot. Add fennel and walnuts to fat left in pot and cook over medium heat, stirring occasionally, until fennel is crisp-tender, 5 to 7 minutes. Remove pot from heat and let cool for 5 minutes.

3. Add half of vinaigrette to pot, then add half of greens and toss for 1 minute to warm and wilt. Add remaining greens followed by remaining vinaigrette and continue to toss until greens are evenly coated and warmed through, about 2 minutes longer. Season with salt and pepper to taste. Transfer greens to serving platter, top with apple, sprinkle with blue cheese and pancetta, and serve.

The Easiest Carrot Side Dish

It's time to get reacquainted with a neglected cooking method.

≥ BY ANDREA GEARY ≤

We all should eat more carrots. They're nutritious, inexpensive, and available year-round, and their cheery color brightens any plate. But if eating carrots means roasting them for 45 minutes or grating a pile of them for a salad, most of us are unlikely to prepare them often. That's why I decided to make something that, at first blush, seems deeply unfashionable: boiled carrots.

Before you scoff, let me extol the virtues of boiling. First, it requires minimal equipment: saucepan, lid, and burner. Second, it's fast—about 25 percent faster than steaming. That's because boiling water transfers heat to the carrots faster than steam does, thus breaking down pectin more quickly so the carrots soften more quickly. And the clincher? Salt in the cooking water seasons the carrots as they cook, which makes them tastier than carrots that have received a superficial postcook sprinkle.

But is a recipe required for something as simple as boiled carrots? Pretty sure I could just wing it, I brought 2 cups of water (minimal water would mean minimal time wasted) and ½ teaspoon of salt to a boil and added 1 pound of peeled, trimmed carrots that I had cut into chunky rods. Seven minutes later, I drained them. The carrots were beautifully tender throughout, but they were also underseasoned and boring. A simple recipe would be helpful after all.

First, the seasoning. I recalled a culinary instructor who used to stride through the kitchen bellowing, "Cooking water should be salty! Salty like the SEA!" He never explained it, but it turns out there's a scientific reason: Boiling vegetables in unsalted water causes them to lose some of their natural salts and sugars (read: flavor). Boiling them in water that has the same salt concentration as seawater, about 3 percent, helps the vegetables retain that flavor. As a bonus, vegetables cooked in heavily salted water soften more quickly than those cooked in unsalted water. (This is because the sodium ions in salt displace some of the calcium ions that give strength to the vegetable's pectin network.)

Carrots cooked in a 3 percent solution (1 tablespoon salt to 2 cups water) were a little too salty for me, but the science was right: The high salt concentration boosted the flavor and decreased the cooking time by more than a minute. I compromised with 2 cups of water, 2 teaspoons of salt, and a 6-minute cooking time.

From there, I developed five flavor variations that could be matched with different types of meals. Each

Boiling is a faster cooking method than steaming, and it allows you to season the carrots as they cook.

variation had either butter or oil to provide a bit of sheen and richness and help the flavorings cling and either citrus juice or vinegar to balance the carrots' natural sweetness. Some chopped fresh herbs countered the carrots' earthiness, and a bit of spice added interest.

Have you heard about the latest fashion in vegetables? It's boiled carrots.

BOILED CARROTS WITH LEMON AND CHIVES
SERVES 4

For even cooking, it is important that the carrot pieces are of similar size. This recipe was developed using carrots with a diameter between 1 and 1½ inches at the thick end. If you are using larger carrots, you may have to cut them into more pieces. Our recipe for Boiled Carrots with Scallions and Ginger is available for free for four months at CooksIllustrated.com/feb17.

- 1 pound carrots, peeled
- 2 teaspoons salt
- 1 tablespoon unsalted butter, cut into 4 pieces
- 1 teaspoon lemon juice, plus extra for serving
- ⅛ teaspoon pepper
- 1 tablespoon chopped fresh chives

1. Cut carrots into 1½- to 2-inch lengths. Leave thin pieces whole, halve medium pieces lengthwise, and quarter thick pieces lengthwise.

2. Bring 2 cups water to boil in medium saucepan over high heat. Add carrots and salt, cover, and cook until tender throughout, about 6 minutes (start timer as soon as carrots go into water).

3. Drain carrots and return them to saucepan. Add butter, lemon juice, and pepper and stir until butter is melted. Stir in chives. Season with extra lemon juice to taste, and serve.

BOILED CARROTS WITH CUMIN, LIME, AND CILANTRO

Substitute extra-virgin olive oil for butter; ½ teaspoon grated lime zest plus 1 teaspoon lime juice for lemon juice; ½ teaspoon cumin seeds, crushed (use mortar and pestle or spice grinder to crush) for pepper; and cilantro for chives.

BOILED CARROTS WITH FENNEL SEEDS AND CITRUS

Substitute extra-virgin olive oil for butter; ½ teaspoon fennel seeds, crushed (use mortar and pestle or spice grinder to crush) for pepper; and parsley for chives. Add ½ teaspoon grated orange zest to carrots with lemon juice.

BOILED CARROTS WITH MINT AND PAPRIKA

Substitute sherry vinegar for lemon juice, ½ teaspoon paprika for pepper, and mint for chives.

TECHNIQUE | MAKE IT SALTY

Boiling the carrots in very salty water has a number of benefits: It seasons them, allows them to retain more of their own natural sugars and salt for even better flavor, and—most interesting—speeds up cooking. How? The sodium ions in salt displace some of the calcium ions that give strength to the carrots' pectin network, weakening it and allowing the carrots to soften more quickly.

○ **Look: Easiest Is Best**
A step-by-step video is available at CooksIllustrated.com/feb17

French Butter Cake

Hailing from France's Brittany coast, gâteau Breton boasts a bright jam filling and a rich, dense texture, which elevate this rustic cake to a first-class confection.

⋟ BY STEVE DUNN ⋞

I first encountered gâteau Breton years ago while living in France, and I was smitten from my first bite. As its name implies, the cake hails from the Brittany region of France, which lies on the western edge of the country, abutting the Atlantic Ocean. It's a simple yet pretty cake, rich in butter, with a dense, tender crumb that falls somewhere between shortbread cookies and pound cake. In my favorite versions, the cake camouflages a thin layer of jam or fruit filling baked into its center, which delivers a vein of sweet acidity that balances the cake's richness. The cake's firm structure allows it to be cut into thin wedges for nibbling with an afternoon cup of tea, but in my experience, a portion so small is never enough.

When I tried my hand at gâteau Breton by baking five existing recipes, I quickly learned that there are plenty of ways to go wrong. One cake, made with buckwheat flour (an ancient tradition from the days when wheat flour was unavailable in Brittany), was dry enough for a colleague to liken it to "compressed sawdust." The center of another was so wet and gummy that folks were convinced it included gooey marzipan. As for the fillings, most tasted flat and were thin and runny; spreading them evenly over the sticky batter proved to be quite a challenge. I wanted a cake with a crumb to rival the very best I had enjoyed in France, along with a lively filling with a workable consistency.

Beau Gâteau

Most modern recipes call for four main ingredients: all-purpose flour, salted butter, sugar, and egg yolks. (Since the test kitchen almost exclusively uses unsalted butter for baking, I would investigate later whether salted butter was worth a special purchase.) I used one of the better recipes from my first round of testing as a starting point. It was pleasantly dense but a little too wet and greasy, so I spent a few

The rich, dense texture of gâteau Breton lies somewhere between shortbread and pound cake.

▶ **Steve Explains It All**
A step-by-step video is available at CooksIllustrated.com/feb17

afternoons in the test kitchen, baking gâteau after gâteau and slowly increasing the amount of dry ingredients and decreasing the amount of butter until I got a cake I liked.

I also examined the technique. Most recipes call for creaming the butter and sugar before incorporating the yolks and flour, and some specify upwards of 10 minutes of creaming. But extensive creaming incorporated too much air into the batter and resulted in a light, fluffy crumb—just the opposite of what I wanted. Ultimately, I landed on creaming two sticks of butter with a little less than 1 cup of sugar in a stand mixer for only 3 minutes, adding 5 yolks one at a time, and finally mixing in 2 cups of flour. This produced an ultrathick batter that baked up with the trademark firm yet tender crumb that I was after.

With the cake nailed down, I dug deeper into the butter issue. Bretons insist that their local butter made with sea salt is key to this cake, so I arranged a head-to-head comparison of cake made with the test kitchen's favorite salted butter, Lurpak (a cultured

butter from Denmark), and cake made with our favorite unsalted sticks, from Land O'Lakes (with some salt stirred into the batter to compensate). Not surprisingly, tasters found that the European butter delivered a slightly more complex cake, but in the end I decided that the difference wasn't enough to warrant the extra cost or trip to the market.

I did, however, want to explore other ways to add complexity. In France, liquor is often used as a flavor enhancer for this cake, so why not add some to mine? I experimented with kirsch and Calvados before finally settling on dark rum for its rich caramel notes. I also added vanilla extract for even more depth.

In a Jam

I'd produced a rich, flavorful cake with just the right dense texture. Now it was time to address the filling. A prune puree is traditional, and while I did end up developing a prune variation, I preferred to showcase a version with a brighter, bolder filling. I'd seen recipes featuring chocolate, date, or apricot fillings, and apricot seemed like the ideal foil to my buttery cake.

Unfortunately, store-bought apricot jam was too sweet and dull; plus, it was too thin and runny to work well as a filling. You see, when constructing this cake, you first spread half the thick batter in the bottom of a buttered cake pan, and then you layer on the filling before finally spreading the rest of the batter on top and baking the cake. If the filling is too thin, it'll either get picked up and mixed in with the batter or leak from the sides of the cake as it bakes, creating a real mess.

I thought that reducing the jam might concentrate its flavor and give me the consistency I wanted, but ultimately I decided to craft my own filling from dried apricots so that I could achieve the exact flavor and consistency I wanted.

Too bad my first batch didn't taste very good. I had made the puree with dried Turkish apricots, and they just didn't have enough oomph. Using dried California apricots remedied this weakness in a hurry: Their concentrated sweet-tart flavor delivered a bright, fruity zing (for more information, see "Dried Apricots"). I chopped up the apricots, tossed them into a blender with enough water to

QUICK CHILL FOR EASIER ASSEMBLY

To make gâteau Breton, a fruit filling is baked between two layers of batter. To facilitate the process, we briefly freeze the first layer of batter so it stays put when the filling is added. We then return the pan to the freezer so the filling doesn't budge when a second layer is spread on top.

A HOT MESS
If the batter isn't chilled before the filling is added, the two components will smear together instead of remaining distinct.

engage the blade, and whizzed them until smooth. After cooking the puree in a skillet with sugar until it thickened and darkened slightly, I squeezed in a bit of fresh lemon juice. Now I had a thick, fruity puree to highlight the rich, buttery cake.

To make the assembly of the cake foolproof, I experimented with what a fellow test cook called a "jam dam," a lip of batter at the edge of the pan designed to hold the filling in place and keep it from oozing out the sides of the cake during baking. It worked well enough in that regard but did little to keep the jam from mixing with the cake batter. Ultimately, I solved the problem with a bakery trick: quickly chilling the first layer of batter by sliding the cake pan into the freezer. Given the high concentration of butter in this cake, just 10 minutes of chilling did the trick: The batter became so firm that it didn't budge when I spooned on the apricot puree. Putting the pan back into the freezer for 10 minutes once the jam layer was on ensured that everything stayed put when the remaining batter was added.

All that was left to do was pretty up the cake

Using room-temperature butter makes the creaming process faster. Let the sticks sit at room temperature for about an hour to soften. Alternatively, cut the butter into 1-tablespoon chunks. By the time you've preheated the oven and measured the remaining ingredients, the pieces should be near 65 degrees, the right temperature for creaming.

IS IT SOFT ENOUGH?
A stick that's ready for creaming bends easily.

---

with a simple egg wash and decoration. Here, I didn't deviate at all from tradition. I first brushed the cake with an egg yolk beaten with a teaspoon of water (this would give it a slight sheen) and then gently dragged the tines of a fork across the cake's surface in a crisscrossing diamond pattern. This branded my dessert as a classic gâteau Breton and was the final step in ensuring that my beautiful, buttery cake held true to its roots.

GÂTEAU BRETON WITH APRICOT FILLING
SERVES 8

We strongly prefer the flavor of California apricots in the filling. Mediterranean (or Turkish) apricots can be used, but increase the amount of lemon juice to 2 tablespoons. This cake is traditionally served plain with coffee or tea but can be dressed up with fresh berries, if desired. Our free recipe for Gâteau Breton with Prune Filling is available for four months at CooksIllustrated.com/feb17.

Filling

⅔	cup water
½	cup dried California apricots, chopped
⅓	cup (2⅓ ounces) sugar
1	tablespoon lemon juice

Cake

16	tablespoons unsalted butter, softened
¾	cup plus 2 tablespoons (6⅛ ounces) sugar
6	large egg yolks (1 lightly beaten with 1 teaspoon water)
2	tablespoons dark rum
1	teaspoon vanilla extract
2	cups (10 ounces) all-purpose flour
½	teaspoon salt

1. FOR THE FILLING: Process water and apricots in blender until uniformly pureed, about 2 minutes. Transfer puree to 10-inch nonstick skillet and stir in sugar. Set skillet over medium heat and cook, stirring frequently, until puree has darkened slightly and rubber spatula leaves distinct trail when dragged across bottom of pan, 10 to 12 minutes. Transfer filling to bowl and stir in lemon juice. Refrigerate filling until cool to touch, about 15 minutes.

2. FOR THE CAKE: Adjust oven rack to lower-middle position and heat oven to 350 degrees. Grease 9-inch round cake pan.

3. Using stand mixer fitted with paddle, beat butter

CALIFORNIAN VERSUS TURKISH

Turkish apricots are cheaper than the Californian variety, but we found that they lack the intensely sweet-tart flavor of those grown domestically. Turkish apricots are the Malatya variety, which has a less concentrated flavor than the Patterson and Blenheim varieties prevalent in California. In addition, Turkish apricots are "slip-pitted": The pit is removed from whole slit fruit, rather than the fruit being halved and pitted as apricots are in California. Slip-pitting results in more moisture retention, which dilutes flavor.

TURKISH	**CALIFORNIAN**
Dull flavor	Bright flavor

SULFURED VERSUS UNSULFURED

Both Turkish and Californian apricots are often treated with sulfur dioxide to prevent browning, oxidation, and flavor changes. When we prepared the apricot filling for our gâteau Breton with sulfured and unsulfured apricots, we preferred the deeply fruity flavor and bright color of the former. (That said, the unsulfured type was acceptable.)

on medium-high speed until smooth and lightened in color, 1 to 2 minutes. Add sugar and continue to beat until pale and fluffy, about 3 minutes longer. Add 5 egg yolks, one at a time, and beat until combined. Scrape down bowl, add rum and vanilla, and mix until incorporated, about 1 minute. Reduce speed to low, add flour and salt, and mix until flour is just incorporated, about 30 seconds. Give batter final stir by hand.

4. Spoon half of batter into bottom of prepared pan. Using small offset spatula, spread batter into even layer. Freeze for 10 minutes.

5. Spread ½ cup filling in even layer over chilled batter, leaving ¾-inch border around edge (reserve remaining filling for another use). Freeze for 10 minutes.

6. Gently spread remaining batter over filling. Using offset spatula, carefully smooth top of batter. Brush with egg yolk wash. Using tines of fork, make light scores in surface of cake, spaced about 1½ inches apart, in diamond pattern, being careful not to score all the way to sides of pan. Bake until top is golden brown and edges of cake start to pull away from sides of pan, 45 to 50 minutes. Let cake cool in pan on wire rack for 30 minutes. Run paring knife between cake and sides of pan, remove cake from pan, and let cool completely on rack, about 1 hour. Cut into wedges and serve.

do this because baking soda changes the meat's pH and makes it more tender. The meat in my previous pie was plenty tender, but the higher pH would also boost browning, deepening the color and flavor of my gravy.

Worried that some of the limited moisture would evaporate before the meat cooked, I covered the Dutch oven with foil before putting on the lid and moving the pot to the oven. After 1 hour, I stirred the meat. It was almost tender, but the cooking liquid was still a little thin, so I replaced the lid but not the foil and returned the pot to the oven for 30 minutes more. After a total of 1½ hours of oven time, the meat was beautifully tender and the gravy was a deep, glossy brown, thick enough to coat the meat generously—no reducing or thickening required. And the fond, extra mushrooms, beer, thyme, and garlic had done wonders for the flavor. It was time for the crust.

The test kitchen's Foolproof Pie Dough (September/October 2010) is my go-to for fruit pie, but its high moisture and fat content made it too soft to place on a warm filling. For a dough that was sturdy yet flaky, I chose a dough we've used for chicken pot pie that includes an egg for strength; it also substitutes sour cream for some of the fat. Less butter meant less fat that would melt with heat, so I was able to place this dough on the warm filling with no problems. And how did it bake? Beautifully. The edge held its attractive crispness, and the crust was flaky but substantial. Now that I've got this recipe in my back pocket, I'm looking forward to the next chilly day.

PUB-STYLE STEAK AND ALE PIE
SERVES 6

Don't substitute bone-in short ribs; their yield is too variable. Instead, use a 4-pound chuck-eye roast, well trimmed of fat. Use a good-quality beef broth for this recipe; the test kitchen's favorite is Better Than Bouillon Roasted Beef Base. If you don't have a deep-dish pie plate, use an 8 by 8-inch baking dish and roll the pie dough into a 10-inch square. We prefer pale and brown ales for this recipe.

Filling

3	tablespoons water
½	teaspoon baking soda
3	pounds boneless beef short ribs, trimmed and cut into ¾-inch chunks
½	teaspoon salt
½	teaspoon pepper
2	slices bacon, chopped
1	pound cremini mushrooms, trimmed and halved if medium or quartered if large
1½	cups beef broth
1	large onion, chopped
1	garlic clove, minced
½	teaspoon dried thyme
¼	cup all-purpose flour
¾	cup beer

Crust

1	large egg, lightly beaten
¼	cup sour cream, chilled
1¼	cups (6¼ ounces) all-purpose flour
½	teaspoon salt
6	tablespoons unsalted butter, cut into ½-inch pieces and chilled

1. FOR THE FILLING: Combine water and baking soda in large bowl. Add beef, salt, and pepper and toss to combine. Adjust oven rack to lower-middle position and heat oven to 350 degrees.

2. Cook bacon in large Dutch oven over high heat, stirring occasionally, until partially rendered but not browned, about 3 minutes. Add mushrooms and ¼ cup broth and stir to coat. Cover and cook, stirring occasionally, until mushrooms are reduced to about half their original volume, about 5 minutes. Add onion, garlic, and thyme and cook, uncovered, stirring occasionally, until onion is softened and fond begins to form on bottom of pot, 3 to 5 minutes. Sprinkle flour over mushroom mixture and stir until all flour is moistened. Cook, stirring occasionally, until fond is deep brown, 2 to 4 minutes. Stir in beer and remaining 1¼ cups broth, scraping up any browned bits. Stir in beef and bring to simmer, pressing as much beef as possible below surface of liquid. Cover pot tightly with aluminum foil, then lid; transfer to oven. Cook for 1 hour.

3. Remove lid and discard foil. Stir filling, cover, return to oven, and continue to cook until beef is tender and liquid is thick enough to coat beef, 15 to 30 minutes longer. Transfer filling to deep-dish pie plate. (Once cool, filling can be covered with plastic wrap and refrigerated for up to 2 days.) Increase oven temperature to 400 degrees.

4. FOR THE CRUST: While filling is cooking, measure out 2 tablespoons beaten egg and set aside. Whisk remaining egg and sour cream together in bowl. Process flour and salt in food processor until combined, about 3 seconds. Add butter and pulse until only pea-size pieces remain, about 10 pulses. Add half of sour cream mixture and pulse until combined, about 5 pulses. Add remaining sour cream mixture and pulse until dough begins to form, about 10 pulses. Transfer mixture to lightly floured counter and knead briefly until dough comes together. Form into 4-inch disk, wrap in plastic, and refrigerate for at least 1 hour or up to 2 days.

5. Roll dough into 11-inch round on lightly floured counter. Using knife or 1-inch round biscuit cutter, cut round from center of dough. Drape dough over filling (it's OK if filling is hot). Trim overhang to ½ inch beyond lip of plate. Tuck overhang under itself; folded edge should be flush with edge of plate. Crimp dough evenly around edge of plate using your fingers or press with tines of fork to seal. Brush crust with reserved egg. Place pie on rimmed baking sheet. Bake until filling is bubbling and crust is deep golden brown and crisp, 25 to 30 minutes. (If filling has been refrigerated, increase baking time by 15 minutes and cover with foil for last 15 minutes to prevent over-browning.) Let cool for 10 minutes before serving.

RECIPE TESTING **Four Not-So-Humble Pies**

The roots of meat pies run as far back as medieval times. While eating a pie's crust in those days was questionable (its primary purpose was serving as a baking vessel), the crusts for four more modern versions we tried were most certainly edible. However, the quality of both crust and filling ran the gamut, and all fell short of our ideal.

SCORCHED
The puff pastry topping burned and turned soggy while the gravy was thin and the meat dry.

ALL LOOKS
This impressive-looking crust was tough to eat. Too many onions made the filling sweet.

BONE TO PICK
The decorative bone was striking, but marrow added to the crust turned it "overwhelmingly rich."

SLOW GOING
Our favorite of the group, this pie was flavorful (if a bit salty) and took hours to prepare.

Easiest-Ever Macaroni and Cheese

We set out to make a smooth, creamy, cheesy sauce without the bother of a béchamel or custard. Making the whole dish in just 20 minutes was a bonus.

> BY ANDREA GEARY <

I've always made mac and cheese the traditional way, and though the final product is comforting and delicious, getting there is a bit of a slog: I first cook flour in melted butter, whisk in milk, and simmer until the sauce, known as a béchamel, thickens. It's this béchamel that allows me to then add flavorful aged cheeses, such as extra-sharp cheddar, which are prone to breaking down and separating into a greasy, lumpy mess when heated (more later on why some cheeses "break"). Sometimes I add eggs for an even richer, more custardy result. Finally, I combine the cheese sauce with cooked macaroni, transfer it to a buttered baking dish, top it with bread crumbs, and bake it until it's bubbly. Creamy and cheesy? Yes. Fast? Definitely not.

So when I heard of an ultramodern recipe for the creamiest, cheesiest macaroni and cheese ever, I was curious. When I heard that it was also the fastest ever, I knew I had to try it. Modernist Cuisine, a research group at the forefront of the molecular gastronomy movement, devised a four-ingredient recipe said to have an extraordinarily smooth texture without relying on a béchamel. The key? An ingredient called sodium citrate, which isn't as scary as it sounds. It's an additive that's used as an emulsifier or preservative in foods such as gelatin desserts, jam, ice cream, and candy. Its downside is that it's a mail-order item—and therefore a nonstarter for the quick, pantry-ready recipe I hoped to produce. But I did get my hands on some just to see how it works. Following the Modernist recipe, I dissolved a tiny bit of sodium citrate in water, which I then brought to a simmer. Next, I used an immersion blender to incorporate handfuls of shredded crumbly, mature cheddar cheese (though subsequent tests showed that simply whisking did the job just as well)—a true test of the smoothing properties of the sodium citrate because the more aged and dry a cheese is, the more likely it is to break.

We cook the macaroni in water and milk and then stir two types of shredded cheese directly into the pot.

Dubious as I'd been, this sauce was remarkably creamy and homogeneous. I stirred it into cooked elbow macaroni, tasted it, and had to admit: It wasn't just fast (coming together in just 5 minutes)—it really was the smoothest and cheesiest, too.

In fact, with no milk, flour, or eggs to dilute it, this sauce was actually too cheesy and salty for me; I'd have to tame it a bit or I wouldn't be able to eat a whole serving. And though I loved the quick prep time, I missed that crispy top that you get on a baked mac and cheese. But these issues were easily fixable. The real hurdle would be making a quick, smooth, richly flavored batch of macaroni and cheese without using sodium citrate.

Ugly Breakup

Back to why cheese breaks when heated: Cheese is an emulsion of fat and water bound up in a protein gel. When it's exposed to heat, the fat liquefies. As it gets even hotter, the protein network begins to break apart, the emulsion breaks down, the fat and water begin to separate out, and the cheese begins to

melt and flow. Then the protein molecules find each other again and begin to regroup, this time in clumps or strings rather than in that tidy gel formation. The result is melted cheese with a pasty, lumpy texture and pools of fat.

Most cooks prevent breaking the same way I did in my classic mac and cheese: by adding flour in the form of a béchamel. When combined with melting cheese, the starch granules in the flour release elongated threads of amylose, which then wrap around the proteins, preventing them from squeezing out fat and recombining into unpleasant curds. But making a béchamel adds work.

Sodium citrate works differently. It doesn't simply adhere to the cheese proteins; it changes them. When you add it to a cheese sauce, the calcium ions in the cheese proteins are replaced with sodium ions. This changes the structure of the protein in such a way that the protein itself becomes a stabilizing gel, holding the fat and water together so the sauce remains supersmooth.

In fact, the glossy flow of the sauce made with sodium citrate reminded me of the molten American cheese on a cheeseburger, and it turned out that this was no coincidence. So-called process cheeses, like American and Velveeta, contain "emulsifying salts" to keep them smooth when melted (see "Why We Can Skip the Béchamel").

So if I used process cheese instead of my usual cheddar, could I skip the sodium citrate? While I boiled macaroni in one saucepan, I whisked 2 cups of shredded American cheese into 1 cup of simmering milk in another saucepan, where it melted smoothly to form a sauce. I stirred the sauce into the drained macaroni and, to simulate the crispy top of a baked macaroni and cheese, sprinkled some toasted, buttered bread crumbs (made from white sandwich bread) on top.

Fast and Fuss-Free

Our macaroni and cheese isn't just quick—it cooks entirely on the stovetop. And instead of using separate pots to boil the macaroni and to make a cheese sauce, we do both simultaneously in the same vessel.

▶ **Watch: It's Amazing**
A step-by-step video is available at CooksIllustrated.com/apr17

Why We Can Skip the Béchamel

Most versions of macaroni and cheese achieve a smooth consistency by starting with a béchamel, the classic sauce made by combining a flour-and-fat paste with milk. When combined with aged cheese, which is prone to breaking, the starches in the béchamel release elongated threads of amylose, which then wrap around the cheese's casein proteins, preventing them from squeezing out fat and recombining into curds. By using American cheese, we're able to skip the béchamel. Thanks to its emulsifying salts, American cheese stays smooth when melted and acts as a stabilizing agent for aged cheeses such as the extra-sharp cheddar in our recipe.

SHARP CHEDDAR ALONE = GRAINY
Without any stabilizing agent, the protein network in cheese breaks down when heated, fat breaks out, and proteins regroup in clumps. Aged (and thus drier) cheese is even more prone to breaking.

SHARP CHEDDAR + AMERICAN = SMOOTH
American cheese contains emulsifying salts that replace calcium ions in dairy with sodium ions, stabilizing the cheese sauce so that it doesn't form curds and fat stays emulsified.

Crumb topping aside, it looked exactly like macaroni and cheese made from a box mix. The sauce was almost unnaturally shiny, but it sure was smooth. The flavor was as bland as one would expect, and the pairing of buttered bread crumbs and American cheese made it taste like a grilled cheese sandwich.

But this test showed that the emulsifying salts in process cheese were more than sufficient to prevent my quick cheese sauce from breaking. The trick would be to use a more flavorful cheese and supplement with enough process cheese to keep the sauce smooth.

One-Pot Wonder

I went back to the extra-sharp cheddar I'd started with and tested it with various ratios of American cheese. A 1:1 ratio of cheddar to American was sufficient to maintain the smooth texture of the sauce, but it still tasted a touch bland, so I doctored it with a bit of Dijon mustard and a dash of cayenne pepper. I mixed the sauce with the cooked and drained macaroni, transferred it to a serving dish, and sprinkled the top with a new version of the crumb topping.

To minimize the grilled cheese sandwich associations, I substituted panko bread crumbs for the sandwich bread, and instead of toasting the crumbs in butter, I used olive oil. A bit of grated Parmesan sprinkled onto the still-warm crumbs reinforced the cheesy flavor of the dish and added some extra crunch.

The dish was everything I wanted: creamy, cheesy, and fast. But it occurred to me that I could make it even faster. The next time around, I cooked the macaroni in a mere 1½ cups of water and the 1 cup of milk I was already using in the sauce. After about 7 minutes, the macaroni was fully cooked, but instead of draining it, I simply stirred in the American cheese, mustard, and cayenne. Then I removed the saucepan from the heat and stirred in the cheddar until it was just distributed throughout. I let it sit, covered, so the cheese could melt gently in the residual heat while I made the topping. A final stir and a sprinkling of crumbs and I was done.

I was so delighted with the results that I immediately set about making a slightly more sophisticated version that calls for Gruyère and blue cheese in place of the cheddar. I'll welcome the variety because, with a recipe this easy and fast, there's a lot of macaroni and cheese in my future.

SIMPLE STOVETOP MACARONI AND CHEESE
SERVES 4

Barilla makes our favorite elbow macaroni. Because the macaroni is cooked in a measured amount of liquid, we don't recommend using different shapes or sizes of pasta. Use a 4-ounce block of American cheese from the deli counter rather than presliced cheese.

1½	cups water
1	cup milk
8	ounces elbow macaroni
4	ounces American cheese, shredded (1 cup)
½	teaspoon Dijon mustard
	Small pinch cayenne pepper
4	ounces extra-sharp cheddar cheese, shredded (1 cup)
⅓	cup panko bread crumbs
1	tablespoon extra-virgin olive oil
	Salt and pepper
2	tablespoons grated Parmesan cheese

1. Bring water and milk to boil in medium saucepan over high heat. Stir in macaroni and reduce heat to medium-low. Cook, stirring frequently, until macaroni is soft (slightly past al dente), 6 to 8 minutes. Add American cheese, mustard, and cayenne and cook, stirring constantly, until cheese is completely melted, about 1 minute. Off heat, stir in cheddar until evenly distributed but not melted. Cover saucepan and let stand for 5 minutes.

2. Meanwhile, combine panko, oil, ⅛ teaspoon salt, and ⅛ teaspoon pepper in 8-inch nonstick skillet until panko is evenly moistened. Cook over medium heat, stirring frequently, until evenly browned, 3 to 4 minutes. Off heat, sprinkle Parmesan over panko mixture and stir to combine. Transfer panko mixture to small bowl.

3. Stir macaroni until sauce is smooth (sauce may look loose but will thicken as it cools). Season with salt and pepper to taste. Transfer to warm serving dish and sprinkle panko mixture over top. Serve immediately.

GROWN-UP STOVETOP MACARONI AND CHEESE

Increase water to 1¾ cups. Substitute ¾ cup shredded Gruyère cheese and 2 tablespoons crumbled blue cheese for cheddar.

American Cheese

Though it's hardly an exemplar of America's cultured dairy achievements, American cheese—the key to our sauce's remarkably velvety texture—is real cheese. It's

BUY A BLOCK
Only American cheese from the deli case will do.

what the U.S. Food and Drug Administration calls "pasteurized process cheese," made by combining one or more mild cheeses with dairy, water, and emulsifying salts that keep its texture smooth when melted. We buy a 4-ounce block from the deli counter, which is easy to shred for the sauce.

There are two products you want to avoid, both of which are typically sold in packages of individually wrapped slices. The first are products such as Kraft Singles, which are technically considered American cheese since they contain 51 percent real cheese but are bland and contain added whey that made our cheese sauce too thick. The second is known as "imitation cheese food." These slices aren't cheese at all; they're a vegetable oil–based product loaded with stabilizers and thickeners and are more chemically related to plastic than to cheese. In our cheese sauce, they weren't just bland; they didn't even melt and instead formed large orange clumps.

SAY NO TO SINGLES
The added whey in cheese products such as Kraft Singles made the sauce too thick.

PASS ON THE IMITATION CHEESE
Products that list oil and starch among their primary ingredients don't even melt.

Perfect Poached Eggs

The most vexing problem with poached eggs is keeping the whites neat and tidy. Gimmicky methods abound, but a few simple tricks and tools are all you need.

> BY ANDREW JANJIGIAN <

You could argue that poaching eggs is an ambitious goal from the start. Drop a delicate raw egg, without its protective shell, into a pot of simmering water in the hope that it will emerge perfectly cooked. That means a tender, fully set white—no ring of gelatinous, translucent goo surrounding the yolk—and a yolk that's fluid but thickened, almost saucy. Equally important: The white must not be raggedy or wispy at the edges and must boast a plump, ovoid flying-saucer shape that's ideal for nestling atop an English muffin or a bed of salad greens.

Since a raw egg cooked in simmering water wants to spread out in all directions before it sets, it's this latter issue that's the trickiest to overcome. I was determined to figure out a solution, and I would have plenty of help: There are dozens of recipes, essays, and videos claiming to produce perfect results. I would try them all and see where I landed.

Down the Drain

First I experimented with the more novel suggestions I found. These ranged from poaching eggs in a muffin tin in the oven to microwaving each egg individually in a small bowl of shallow water to parcooking them in the shell before releasing them directly into the simmering water. I wasn't too surprised when most of these ideas proved to be dead ends. (See "Poaching Approaches That Didn't Pan Out.") Conventional methods worked better, but they also had their limitations. The most common trick was to swirl the water around the eggs to create a vortex that kept the white from spreading, all the while folding any loose stragglers back on the yolk. The whirlpool worked, but it meant I could only poach one or two eggs a time. Another approach involved lowering an egg into the water in a large metal spoon and keeping it there while using a second spoon to block the loose white from straying too far. The results were perfect—but who wants to juggle

▶ **Perfect Poaching Demo**
A step-by-step video is available at CooksIllustrated.com/apr17

Great poached eggs have the same fluid yolks as soft-cooked eggs, but their whites are more moist and plump from direct contact with water.

spoons like that to cook a single egg?

The most useful trick I found didn't try to corral the white during cooking but instead started by draining the raw eggs in a colander. At first I found this step counterintuitive—wouldn't all the white just drain off through the holes? It turns out that every egg contains two kinds of white, thick and thin. The thicker portion clings more tightly to the yolk, while the thinner portion is looser and can break away and slip through the colander holes. It is this thinner white that is most prone to spreading out into wispy tendrils in the water, so eliminating it went a long way toward fixing this issue. I also found that starting with the freshest eggs possible increased the chance that more of the white was thick, so less of it would drain away (see "Fresh Eggs = Thick Whites" for more information), leaving me with a plumper poached egg.

Acid Test

I next tried a common method targeted at a different issue: ensuring that the yolks stay runny while the whites, which solidify at a much higher temperature,

reach the right degree of tender firmness. This approach calls for adding a few splashes of vinegar to the simmering water before slipping in the eggs. Acid lowers the water's pH, which makes the proteins in the white set faster. The only issue? For the vinegar to be effective, you have to add so much that it gives the eggs a sour taste. I found that the upper limit was ½ teaspoon per cup of water, which wasn't enough to be much help. But there was something else I could add that also makes egg proteins bond faster: salt. Using vinegar and salt together meant I didn't need much of either one. After a few tests, I worked out my formula: 1 tablespoon vinegar and 1 teaspoon salt to 6 cups water.

Testing the Waters

But there was still more I could do to keep the whites tidy—I could get the eggs into the water as gently as possible. Gingerly sliding them into the water from bowls held close to the water's surface, as many recipes suggest, kept the white contained, but pouring multiple bowls at once—I was poaching four eggs to serve 2 people—was awkward. Cracking all the eggs into a 2-cup liquid measuring cup and pouring them in one by one at different spots in the water was easier. Plus, I could retrieve them in the order they were added, so they cooked to the same degree. It made sense at this point to switch from a large saucepan to a broader Dutch oven, which made bringing the measuring cup close to the water easier.

PHOTOGRAPHY: CARL TREMBLAY

TEST 1
POACH IN MUFFIN TIN
Method: Poach eggs in 350-degree oven in muffin tin with 1 tablespoon water added to each muffin cup.

Results: Whites stayed neat, but eggs cooked unevenly, setting faster in the outside cups.

TEST 2
POACH IN MICROWAVE
Method: Place each egg in small glass bowl with ¼ cup water. Microwave for 1 to 2 minutes.

Results: Whites stayed contained, but cooking time and heat level would need tinkering for every microwave.

TEST 3
PARCOOK IN SHELLS
Method: Briefly boil eggs in shells, then scoop each parcooked egg out of shell into water.

Results: Too involved; eggs must be cool before removing from shells, which was messy and tended to break up white.

TEST 4
CREATE VORTEX
Method: Swirl water vigorously around eggs to create whirlpool.

Results: Effective at keeping whites neat but too fussy and only works for one or two eggs at a time.

TEST 5
ENCLOSE IN SPOONS
Method: Lower 1 egg at a time into boiling water in large metal spoon, using smaller second spoon to keep loose white from straying too far.

Results: Effective but fussy and only works for one egg at a time.

After bringing the water to a boil, I added the vinegar and salt, deposited the drained eggs around the water's surface, and then considered whether to lower the heat to a bare simmer or shut it off completely and cover the pot, allowing residual heat to do the cooking. I'd seen recipes calling for both methods, and after a quick test, I settled on the latter for two reasons: First, even though it was very gentle, the residual heat was still enough to allow the egg whites to set, and it was extra insurance that the yolk would stay beautifully runny. Second, in the covered environment, steam could cook the white at the very top of the eggs, which can be the most stubborn to set, without constantly turning the egg over in the water. Though timing varied slightly depending on the size of the eggs, I found that it took about 3 minutes for the white, including the top, to become nicely opaque. Plus, one advantage of poaching eggs as opposed to cooking them in their shells is that you can actually see the results and return the eggs to the pot if necessary.

And with that, I really had it: a foolproof recipe for perfect poached eggs. As ambitious as it had seemed at first, poaching eggs now felt like a quick, simple way to add protein to any meal, from eggs Benedict and corned beef hash to a salad or pasta to fried rice to polenta.

PERFECT POACHED EGGS
SERVES 2

For the best results, be sure to use the freshest eggs possible. Cracking the eggs into a colander will rid them of any watery, loose whites and result in perfectly shaped poached eggs. This recipe can be used to cook from one to four eggs. To make two batches of eggs to serve all at once, transfer four cooked eggs directly to a large pot of 150-degree water and cover them. This will keep them warm for 15 minutes or so while you return the poaching water to a boil and cook the next batch. We like to serve these eggs on buttered toast or toasted and buttered English muffins or on salads made with assertively flavored greens.

- 4 large eggs
- 1 tablespoon distilled white vinegar
  Salt and pepper

1. Bring 6 cups water to boil in Dutch oven over high heat. Meanwhile, crack eggs, one at a time, into colander. Let stand until loose, watery whites drain away from eggs, 20 to 30 seconds. Gently transfer eggs to 2-cup liquid measuring cup.

2. Add vinegar and 1 teaspoon salt to boiling water. With lip of measuring cup just above surface of water, gently tip eggs into water, one at a time, leaving space between them. Cover pot, remove from heat, and let stand until whites closest to yolks are just set and opaque, about 3 minutes. If after 3 minutes whites are not set, let stand in water, checking every 30 seconds, until eggs reach desired doneness. (For medium-cooked yolks, let eggs sit in pot, covered, for 4 minutes, then begin checking for doneness.)

3. Using slotted spoon, carefully lift and drain each egg over Dutch oven. Season with salt and pepper to taste, and serve.

Fresh Eggs = Thick Whites

A raw egg white (albumen) has two consistencies, thick and thin. The ratio of the two consistencies depends on the egg's age: In the freshest eggs, 60 percent of the white is thick, but as the egg ages, it drops to 50 percent and below. In most cooked egg applications, the albumen ratio won't be noticeable because the white is either scrambled, browned in a pan, or cooked in the confines of the shell. A poached egg is the exception since the thin white is able to freely flow away from the thick white and cooks up ragged and wispy, not plump and tidy.

Our recipe gets around the issue of egg freshness by draining off the loose, watery white in a colander before poaching. But for the plumpest results, it's best to use the freshest eggs you can find. (For tips on how to tell, see "Determining the Age of Eggs," page 28.)

FRESH   **OLD**

TOOLS FOR SUCCESS

Besides adding salt and vinegar to the poaching water, which helps the whites set at a lower temperature off the heat before the faster-cooking yolks get too thick, we use these tools to achieve perfect results.

COLANDER
Draining the eggs before cooking removes the loose whites, preventing messy, wispy tendrils.

LIQUID MEASURING CUP
Pouring the eggs from a measuring cup allows us to add them to the water gently, minimizing jostling.

DUTCH OVEN WITH LID
Covering the pot allows residual heat to finish cooking the eggs, even the gooey white at the top.

Greek Chicken and Rice Soup

Egg and lemon give *avgolemono* a velvety consistency and a bright taste. We perfected these qualities while ensuring that every shred of chicken was tender and juicy.

> BY LAN LAM <

When beaten eggs and fresh lemon juice are whisked together with a little hot chicken broth, the duo is transformed into the classic Greek sauce known as *avgolemono* (egg-lemon). Increase the amount of broth (homemade if you've got it) and throw in a handful of rice, and avgolemono becomes a creamy, comforting first-course soup punctuated with lemony tang. The chicken from which the broth is made, along with an assortment of vegetables, typically follows as the main course.

As lovely as the classic version of avgolemono is, it's a more practical variation that interests me: Simply shredding the chicken and adding it to the soup, along with increasing the amount of rice, turns this starter into a light yet satisfying meal. I wanted a savory, citrusy soup, velvety with egg and studded with tender bites of chicken—all in a reasonable amount of time.

Chicken Soup with Rice

For the chicken, I chose boneless, skinless breasts. Their milder flavor would fit in better with the fresh, light nature of this soup than thighs would. As a bonus, the breasts would also cook faster than thighs.

Before poaching and shredding, I halved the chicken breasts lengthwise. The benefits of this small move were threefold: First, the extra surface area created would help salt penetrate more uniformly. Second, the smaller pieces of chicken would cook more quickly. Third, halving the muscle fibers ensured that the shreds of chicken would be short enough to fit neatly on a spoon. (I let the salted meat sit while I got the soup going, giving the salt time to both season the chicken and change its protein structure, which would help it stay juicy when cooked.)

My plan was to cook the chicken and rice in tandem to save time, but I knew that just dropping the chicken into simmering broth wouldn't work. That's because water simmers at approximately

We puree some of the rice to give our soup its full, lush body (egg yolks help, too). And the chicken stays moist because it's off the heat.

⊙ **Watch Lan Make the Soup**
A step-by-step video is available at CooksIllustrated.com/apr17

190 degrees, and when a chicken breast hits this hot liquid, the exterior quickly overshoots the target doneness temperature of 160 degrees. The result? Dry, chalky meat.

The test kitchen's solution to this problem is to submerge the chicken in subsimmering water and then shut off the heat. The water immediately drops in temperature when the chicken is added; the chicken then cooks very gently with no risk of overshooting the 160-degree mark.

I brought 8 cups of broth and 1 cup of rice to a boil and then let the pot simmer for just 5 minutes. In went the prepared breasts, at which point

I put a lid on and shut off the heat. After 15 minutes, the chicken was almost—but not quite—cooked through and the rice was al dente. I removed the breasts from the broth, shredded them, and returned the pieces to the pot, where they quickly finished cooking. Just as I expected, the shreds remained supermoist and tender.

In the Thick of It

Having achieved perfectly poached chicken, I turned to avgolemono's namesake egg-lemon mixture, which thickens the soup. It's the egg proteins that do the work: They uncoil, entangle, and form an open mesh that prevents water molecules from moving freely, thus increasing viscosity. Before being whisked into the soup, the egg mixture is typically tempered, meaning it is combined with a portion of the hot broth to prevent the eggs from curdling when they make contact with the rest of the liquid in the pot. Some Greek cooks so fear a curdled soup that they are known to chant the "avgolemono prayer"—"please don't curdle, please don't curdle"—or make a kissing sound while adding the eggs to magically ensure smooth results. I saw no need for such extreme measures, but I was curious and felt that some testing was in order. We found that tempering worked not because it raised the temperature of the eggs but rather because it diluted the egg proteins (see "Do You Need to Temper Eggs?" on page 31 for more information).

The tempering step safeguarded against curdling, but I had another issue to deal with. As the proteins in egg whites unwind, they unleash hydrogen sulfide, a compound that can give off a lightly sulfurous aroma. To limit this smell while getting the same thickening power, I mixed 6 tablespoons of lemon juice with two eggs and two yolks (diluted with a little broth) instead of three eggs. This mixture

A Neat Fit—and Well Seasoned, Too

We start by cutting each chicken breast in half lengthwise and salting it for 30 minutes. The increased surface area of the pieces allows the salt to penetrate the meat uniformly. The halved pieces cook more quickly; plus, they make it easier to shred the chicken after cooking to create bite-size pieces that fit neatly on a spoon.

Maximizing the Lemon Flavor in Avgolemono

A trio of ingredients brings multifaceted lemon flavor to the broth: **Lemon zest** provides fruitiness, **coriander seeds** add herbal/citrus notes, and **lemon juice** offers tartness.

---

didn't provide quite as much body as I'd hoped, but I didn't want to add more eggs lest the soup become too rich. Luckily, there was another thickener present: amylose, a starch molecule in rice. Similar to egg proteins, it increases viscosity by entangling and forming a matrix that slows the movement of water. To put this starch to work, I simply needed to release it from the rice grains. And I knew just the way to do it: I'd puree some of the rice.

I went back to the stove and prepared another batch of soup, this time using 1 cup of cooked rice from the soup to dilute the eggs. I put the rice into the blender jar along with the eggs, yolks, and lemon juice. After a minute of processing, I had a starchy egg-lemon-rice puree to stir into the broth. And there it was, a soup with exactly the luxurious creamy consistency I wanted.

But there's more. Reheating avgolemono is typically a no-no because the eggs will curdle when they are cooked a second time. In this version, though, because the rice has enough starchy bulk even after being pureed to physically interrupt the egg proteins from interacting with each other, the proteins had a hard time forming curds, even when the soup was reheated—a nice bonus.

Flavor Bundle

The sumptuous consistency of the soup was right where I wanted it, but its flavor needed attention. Although it was tart from the lemon juice, it needed some tweaking if it was to also boast more complexity. I chose garlic, black peppercorns, and lemony coriander seeds to add depth, along with dill for an herbal note. I also used a vegetable peeler to strip the zest from a couple of lemons. The intensely flavored oils in the zest would boost the fruity, citrusy notes without making the soup overly sour.

The complexity imparted by the herb bundle, in combination with the creamy soup and tender chicken, made this avgolemono outshine all the rest.

GREEK CHICKEN AND RICE SOUP WITH EGG AND LEMON (AVGOLEMONO)
SERVES 4 TO 6

If you have homemade chicken broth such as our Classic Chicken Broth, we recommend using it in this recipe, as it gives the soup the best flavor and body. Our preferred commercial chicken broth is Swanson Chicken Stock. Use a vegetable peeler to remove strips of zest from the lemons.

1½	pounds boneless, skinless chicken breasts, trimmed
	Salt and pepper
12	(3-inch) strips lemon zest plus 6 tablespoons juice, plus extra juice for seasoning (3 lemons)
2	sprigs fresh dill, plus 2 teaspoons chopped
2	teaspoons coriander seeds
1	teaspoon black peppercorns
1	garlic clove, peeled and smashed
8	cups chicken broth
1	cup long-grain rice
2	large eggs plus 2 large yolks

1. Cut each chicken breast in half lengthwise. Toss with 1¾ teaspoons salt and let stand at room temperature for at least 15 minutes or up to 30 minutes. Cut 8-inch square of triple-thickness cheesecloth. Place lemon zest, dill sprigs, coriander seeds, peppercorns, and garlic in center of cheesecloth and tie into bundle with kitchen twine.

2. Bring broth, rice, and spice bundle to boil in large saucepan over high heat. Reduce heat to low, cover, and cook for 5 minutes. Turn off heat, add chicken, cover, and let stand for 15 minutes.

3. Transfer chicken to large plate and discard spice bundle. Using two forks, shred chicken into bite-size pieces. Using ladle, transfer 1 cup cooked rice to blender (leave any liquid in pot). Add lemon juice and eggs and yolks to blender and process until smooth, about 1 minute.

4. Return chicken and any accumulated juices to pot. Return soup to simmer over high heat. Remove pot from heat and stir in egg mixture until fully incorporated. Stir in chopped dill and season with salt, pepper, and extra lemon juice to taste. Serve.

Go Ahead, Reheat It

Most recipes for *avgolemono* warn against reheating the soup lest the eggs curdle. But our avgolemono won't produce curdled threads of egg if you reheat it gently. That's because the starchy rice that's blended with the eggs physically interrupts the proteins, making it much harder for them to curdle.

The soup will thicken substantially during refrigeration. Thin it out with a little broth and reheat it over medium-low heat, stirring frequently. Then reseason it with lemon juice, salt, and pepper.

Hands-off Chicken Broth

This classic approach to making chicken broth calls for gently simmering a mix of chicken backs and wings in water for several hours but requires almost no hands-on work. The long, slow simmer helps the bones and meat release both deep flavor and gelatin. –Keith Dresser

---

CLASSIC CHICKEN BROTH
MAKES 8 CUPS

If you have a large pot (at least 12 quarts), you can easily double this recipe to make 1 gallon.

4	pounds chicken backs and wings
3½	quarts water
1	onion, chopped
2	bay leaves
2	teaspoons salt

1. Heat chicken and water in large stockpot or Dutch oven over medium-high heat until boiling, skimming off any scum that comes to surface. Reduce heat to low and simmer gently for 3 hours.

2. Add onion, bay leaves, and salt and continue to simmer for 2 hours longer.

3. Strain broth through fine-mesh strainer into large pot or container, pressing on solids to extract as much liquid as possible. Let broth settle for about 5 minutes, then skim off fat.

SCIENCE To Reduce Egginess, Ditch the White

To create just the right rich, velvety texture in our soup, we use two eggs plus two yolks. But there's another reason to ditch some of the whites: They're largely responsible for the "eggy" flavor of eggs. Though the whites are typically regarded as bland, they contain sulfur compounds that release hydrogen sulfide when the eggs are exposed to heat, producing that characteristic eggy taste. We tested this premise in our recipe for French Toast (January/February 2009), dipping bread into milk mixed with whole eggs and yolks alone. The toast dipped into the yolks-only soaking liquid tasted significantly less eggy and more custard-like. Similarly, *avgolemono* made with three whole eggs had an overt egginess that was absent when we switched to two whole eggs and two yolks.

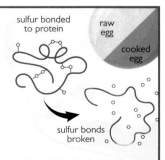

WHY WHITES TASTE EGGY
As egg whites cook, their sulfur bonds break, releasing eggy flavor.

Classic Deli Rye at Home

Rye flour contributes little structure to bread and soaks up water like a sponge. So how do you make a tender loaf strong enough to hold up under a pile of sandwich fixings?

≽ BY ANDREW JANJIGIAN ≼

Ask people what they think is the epitome of a deli sandwich, and I'd bet most would say pastrami on rye. I'd agree that it's one of the best uses of rye out there, but deli rye is also great for grilled cheese or even just spread with butter and sprinkled with flaky salt. But a good loaf isn't always easy to come by.

Unlike German and Scandinavian rye breads, which are dark, crumbly, and dense, American deli rye relies on the addition of wheat flour to make a loaf that is lighter in both color and texture. A great loaf should have a fine, even crumb and a tender-yet-sturdy texture that will hold up under sandwich fillings. It's usually a torpedo-shaped free-form loaf, but unlike the crust on a rustic loaf, this loaf's crust should be soft and pliable. And what about the flavor? Caraway seed's anise-like flavor is strongly associated with deli rye, but try a loaf without caraway and you'll notice that rye's flavor is actually fairly similar to that of very fresh wheat flour, but it's sweeter and lacks the bitter edge.

I tried a handful of recipes, most of which produced bread that was either too dense, dry, or crumbly, or too light on rye flavor and more like regular white or wheat bread. Some loaves were also far too small for sandwich-making.

We brush the loaf with a cooked cornstarch wash after baking. The starch provides sheen while the moisture softens the crust.

Flour Power

To fashion my own recipe, I combined 2 cups of bread flour, 1 cup of medium rye flour (see "Sorting out Rye Flours" on page 29 for more information), yeast, water, and molasses in a stand mixer. I kneaded this until a loose dough formed, and then I let it sit for 20 minutes. This resting stage, known as an autolyse, helps a dough build structure. I figured I needed the insurance since the test loaves I had made were in need of more. I then added the salt and continued kneading until a smooth dough formed. I took it out, gave it a few more kneads and shaped it into a ball, and transferred it to a bowl to proof for a couple of hours, until it had doubled in size. I shaped it into a log, covered it, and allowed it to proof again until it had nearly

Rye's True Taste

Caraway's anise-like flavor has become so strongly associated with rye bread that many mistakenly think that's what rye tastes like. But leave out the caraway and you'll discover rye's true flavor: sweet and almost wheaty but without the bitterness.

doubled. I scored it with a sharp knife every inch or so across the top and baked it in a 375-degree oven for about an hour.

This loaf wasn't horrible, but it was a bit light on rye flavor, the slashes were too deep, and the crumb was a bit tight. In addition, the crust lacked an appealing sheen and was somewhat tough, and the loaf was too narrow.

My first change was increasing the proportion of rye flour to wheat flour. But as the percentage of rye flour increased, the density and dryness of the loaf did, too. Here's the thing about working with rye flour: It doesn't contain the proteins that exist in wheat flour that form gluten, the elastic network that gives bread structure and allows it to hold the carbon dioxide produced during fermentation. On top of that, rye does contain carbohydrates called arabinoxylans, which you don't find in wheat flour. They allow rye flour to absorb four times as much water as wheat flour.

You might think this would make a loaf more moist, but in reality more water gets bound up by the flour, producing a loaf that tastes drier. This explains why German- and Scandinavian-style rye breads, made with 100 percent rye flour, are so dense and why wheat flour is key in deli rye.

For a moister loaf, the fix is obvious: Add more water. But there's a limit; you can add only so much water before the gluten is too dilute and the loaf lacks structure. After tinkering with the amounts, I hit the limit: $13\frac{1}{3}$ ounces of water and $8\frac{1}{4}$ ounces of rye flour (at least 10 percent more than most recipes call for) with $12\frac{1}{2}$ ounces of bread flour.

Now my bread was moist and had nice rye flavor, but the crumb was a bit too chewy. In many breads, this can be attributed to the formation of too much gluten. Bread flour is comparatively high in gluten, and I didn't want to change my proportion of wheat flour to rye flour, so I tried swapping an equal amount of lower-protein all-purpose flour for the bread flour. This was too far in the other direction—now the loaf didn't have enough structure. King Arthur all-purpose flour, which lands midway between most all-purpose flours and bread flours in terms of gluten, was just right. To further tenderize the loaf, I also added a little vegetable oil.

Shaping Up

To fix the narrow width of my loaf, I reevaluated the shaping process. Instead of rolling the dough up like a carpet to form a log, which produced small tapered ends, I came up with an approach that relied on a series of folds to produce a loaf of even size from end to end (see "How to Shape a Loaf of Deli Rye").

Slashing a loaf before baking allows it to expand evenly in the oven, so the fact that the slashes remained as gouges in the finished bread meant the crumb wasn't expanding much. I looked at factors that might affect oven spring, the rapid rise in volume that yeast breads experience when they enter a hot oven. First, I added steam by pouring boiling water into a preheated pan at the bottom of the oven. The steam, which transfers heat to the loaf more quickly than dry air does, keeps the loaf's exterior soft during the initial stages of baking so that it can expand easily.

Most recipes shape the dough in a way that results in tapered ends. We press it into an oval and then make a few folds for a sandwich-worthy loaf from end to end.

1. With short end facing edge of counter, fold top left and right edges of dough diagonally into center and press to seal.

2. Fold point of dough toward center and press to seal. Rotate 180 degrees and repeat folding and sealing.

3. Fold dough in half toward you to form 8 by 4-inch crescent shape. Using heel of your hand, press seam closed.

4. Roll loaf seam side down. Tuck ends under loaf to form rounded torpedo shape.

Second, I looked at the oven temperature; I decided to increase it from 375 to 450. With these changes, the slashes smoothed out considerably and the crumb opened up, giving me a less dense interior. Adding the extra oomph of a preheated baking stone was all it took to finish the job.

As for the dull, tough crust, many recipes call for brushing the loaf with an egg wash before baking. This produces an attractive sheen, but the crust will still be tough. I used an alternative approach: a cooked cornstarch wash brushed on after baking. The starch produced a good sheen, and because it was brushed on after baking, the moisture helped soften the crust.

With a top-notch deli rye at the ready, I just needed to find some worthy pastrami.

More Heat = Better Spring

For a well-risen loaf with an open crumb and a smooth crust, it's crucial to maximize oven spring, the rapid rise in volume that yeast breads experience when they first go into a hot oven. We found that three adjustments made all the difference.

USE A BAKING STONE
The stone acts as a heat source beneath the bread.

INCREASE OVEN TEMPERATURE
We pushed the dial from 375 degrees to 450 degrees.

ADD STEAM
Steam (from a pan of boiling water) conducts heat better than dry air does; it also helps keep the crust soft so it expands more easily.

DELI RYE BREAD
MAKES 1 LOAF

We prefer King Arthur all-purpose flour for this recipe; if you have trouble finding it at your supermarket, you can use any brand of bread flour instead. Any grade of rye flour will work in this recipe, but for the best flavor and texture we recommend using medium or dark rye flour. Do not use blackstrap molasses here; its flavor is too intense.

- 2½ cups (12½ ounces) King Arthur all-purpose flour
- 1½ cups (8¼ ounces) rye flour
- 1 tablespoon caraway seeds
- 2½ teaspoons instant or rapid-rise yeast
- 1⅔ cups (13⅓ ounces) plus ½ cup (4 ounces) water, room temperature
- 1 tablespoon vegetable oil
- 2 teaspoons molasses
- 1½ teaspoons salt
- 4 teaspoons cornstarch

1. Whisk all-purpose flour, rye flour, caraway seeds, and yeast together in bowl of stand mixer. Whisk 1⅔ cups water, oil, and molasses in 4-cup liquid measuring cup until molasses has dissolved.

2. Fit stand mixer with dough hook; add water mixture to flour mixture and knead on low speed until cohesive dough starts to form and no dry flour remains, about 2 minutes, scraping down bowl as needed. Cover bowl tightly with plastic wrap and let dough rest for 20 minutes.

3. Add salt to dough and knead on medium-low speed until dough is smooth and elastic and clears sides of bowl, about 5 minutes.

4. Transfer dough to lightly floured counter and knead by hand to form smooth, round ball, about 30 seconds. Place dough seam side down in lightly oiled large bowl, cover tightly with plastic, and let rise until doubled in size, 1½ to 2 hours.

5. Transfer dough to lightly floured counter and gently press into 8-inch disk, then fold edges toward middle to form round. Cover loosely with plastic and let rest for 15 minutes.

6. Adjust oven racks to middle and lowest positions, place baking stone on upper rack, and heat oven to 450 degrees. Line overturned rimmed baking sheet with parchment paper and dust lightly with rye flour. Gently press and stretch dough into 12 by 9-inch oval, with short end of oval facing edge of counter. Fold top left and right edges of dough diagonally into center of oval and press gently to seal. Fold point of dough into center of oval and press seam gently to seal. Rotate dough 180 degrees and repeat folding and sealing top half of dough.

7. Fold dough in half toward you to form rough 8 by 4-inch crescent-shaped loaf. Using heel of your hand, press seam closed against counter. Roll loaf seam side down. Tuck ends under loaf to form rounded torpedo shape. Gently slide your hands underneath loaf and transfer, seam side down, to prepared sheet.

8. Spray sheet of plastic with vegetable oil spray and cover loaf loosely. Let loaf rise until increased in size by about half and dough springs back minimally when poked gently with your knuckle, 45 minutes to 1¼ hours.

9. Place empty loaf pan on bottom oven rack. Using sharp paring knife or single-edge razor blade, make six to eight 4-inch-long, ½-inch-deep slashes with swift, fluid motion across width of loaf, spacing slashes about 1 inch apart. Pour 2 cups boiling water into empty loaf pan in oven.

10. Slide parchment and loaf from sheet onto baking stone. Bake until deep golden brown and loaf registers 205 to 210 degrees, 25 to 30 minutes, rotating loaf halfway through baking. Transfer loaf to wire rack.

11. Whisk cornstarch and remaining ½ cup water in bowl until cornstarch has dissolved. Microwave, whisking frequently, until mixture is thickened, 1 to 2 minutes.

12. Brush top and sides of loaf with 3 tablespoons cornstarch mixture (you will have extra cornstarch mixture). Let cool completely, about 3 hours, before slicing and serving.

▶ **Watch: Deli-Style Magic**
A step-by-step video is available at CooksIllustrated.com/apr17

Buying and Cooking Salmon

High in fat and flavor, with lush meat and skin that crisps, salmon is one of America's most-consumed fin fish. Here's our guide to cooking it right. BY ELIZABETH BOMZE

A great choice for pan searing, grilling, roasting, poaching, smoking, and curing, salmon is one of the most versatile fish you can buy. If you're buying it fresh, it should look moist and shiny, not dull, and should smell of the sea rather than overtly fishy. And don't shy away from buying frozen salmon. If it's been vacuum-sealed and the label indicates that it was flash-frozen immediately after harvest, it may taste fresher than the fish behind the counter (which is often flash-frozen fish that's been thawed).

WHAT MAKES SALMON DIFFERENT?

Skin That Crisps: As salmon's abundant fat renders during cooking, its skin browns and crisps as nicely as chicken skin.

Marbled Fat: Unlike most varieties of whitefish, which store fat in the liver, salmon's fat is marbled throughout its flesh, making it taste rich and silky.

Moist Flesh: Salmon's thick muscle fibers can hold more water than those of whitefish, making salmon particularly moist.

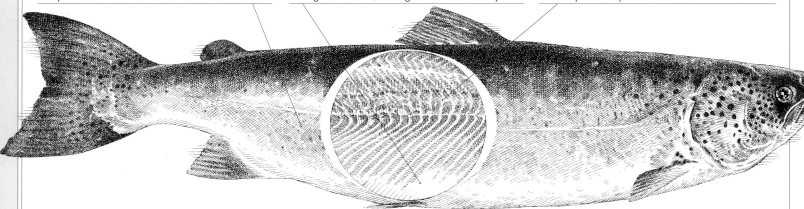

WILD
Alias: Pacific
Species: Chinook (king), chum (dog or silverbrite), coho (silver), masu (cherry), pink (humpy or humpback), sockeye (red)
Flesh color: Deep pink due to compound called astaxanthin from crustacean-based diet
Texture: Firm and meaty
Availability: Late spring to early fall

FARMED
Alias: Atlantic
Origin: Raised on farms primarily in Norway, Scotland, Chile, and Canada
Flesh color: Naturally gray but dyed pale pink by synthetic astaxanthin and carotenoid pigment in feed
Texture: Soft and buttery
Availability: Year-round

SALMON IS FULL OF (GOOD) FAT

Salmon contains much more fat than whitefish such as cod, halibut, and flounder, but much of it is the healthy omega-3 kind. Generally speaking, farmed salmon is fattier than wild salmons.

SPECIES	TYPE	FAT*
Atlantic	Farmed	13.4 g
Chinook (king)	Wild	11.7 g
Sockeye (red)	Wild	7.3 g
Masu (cherry)	Wild	7.0 g
Coho (silver)	Wild	5.6 g
Pink (humpy/humpback)	Wild	4.4 g
Chum (dog/silverbrite)	Wild	3.7 g

*Fat levels based on 100 grams of salmon

DON'T OVERCOOK WILD SALMON

We've always cooked farmed salmon to 125 degrees, at which point its flesh is ideally firm yet silky. But wild varieties taste dry at this temperature. In our tests, tasters unanimously preferred all varieties of wild salmon cooked to just 120 degrees. Here's why: Wild salmon has naturally firmer flesh because its connective tissue has more chemical cross-links. It also lacks the fat that gives farmed salmon the perception of moistness when cooked. Both of these factors mean that wild salmon can taste overcooked at 125 degrees.

SHOPPING FOR SMOKED SALMON

Most smoked salmon sold in supermarkets is cold-smoked: It's cured to draw out moisture and then smoked at temperatures ranging from 75 to 85 degrees for anywhere from 1 day to 3 weeks to produce a dense, silky, translucent texture. (Hot-smoked salmon, which is far less widely available in supermarkets, is smoked at temperatures ranging from 120 to 180 degrees for 6 to 12 hours to produce a flaky texture.) We tasted five nationally available products and found that neither the type of salmon (farmed or wild) nor the wood used to smoke it affected our preferences. What did matter were the curing method and the thickness of the slices. Our winning salmon was cured with only salt (no sweetener or spices), and we liked thin, nicely tender slices. Our favorite, Spence & Co. Traditional Scottish Style Smoked Salmon ($10.99 for 4 ounces), is "silky," "delicate," and "lush."

Salmon by the Numbers

353,000 Tons consumed annually in United States

70 Percentage of global market salmon that is from aquaculture

13 Percentage of fat in some farmed salmon, which rivals that of some premium ice cream

TIPS AND TECHNIQUES

PLUCK PINBONES

Filleted fish has had the backbone and ribs removed, but the thin, needle-like pinbones must be removed separately. Most fish are sold with the pinbones removed, but they are difficult to see and are sometimes missed by the fishmonger.

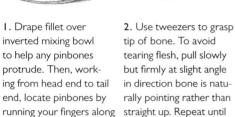

1. Drape fillet over inverted mixing bowl to help any pinbones protrude. Then, working from head end to tail end, locate pinbones by running your fingers along length of fillet.

2. Use tweezers to grasp tip of bone. To avoid tearing flesh, pull slowly but firmly at slight angle in direction bone is naturally pointing rather than straight up. Repeat until all pinbones are removed.

CUT YOUR OWN FILLETS

When making any salmon recipe that calls for fillets, it's important to use fillets of similar thickness so that they cook at the same rate. We find that the best way to ensure uniformity is to buy a large center-cut fillet (1½ to 2 pounds if serving four) and cut it into four equal pieces.

TUCK THE BELLY

If your salmon fillet comes with the belly flap attached, this thinner section will overcook when roasted or seared. To ensure that it cooks on pace with the rest of the fillet, trim away any chewy white membrane on the surface, flip the fillet skin side up, and gently fold the flap over so the skin is facing down. Secure the flap by horizontally inserting a toothpick through it and into the thicker portion of the fillet.

BRINE BRIEFLY

Though it may seem odd to brine something that spent its life in salted water, it's worth doing. Brining salmon helps the flesh stay moist, seasons it, and reduces the presence of albumin, a protein that can congeal into an unappealing white mass on the surface of the fish when heated. Plus, brining works a lot faster on fish than on meat because fish's shorter, looser muscle structure allows the solution to penetrate more rapidly.

Dissolve 5 tablespoons of salt in 2 quarts of water, add 6 fillets, and let them sit for 15 minutes. Dry the fillets well with paper towels just before cooking them.

SKIN IT (IF YOU LIKE)

When well rendered and seared to a crisp, salmon skin can rival great roasted or fried chicken skin. But when you want skinless fillets, you can easily remove the skin before or after cooking.

Before Cooking

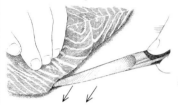

1. Using boning knife or chef's knife, insert blade just above skin about 1 inch from 1 end of fillet. Cut through nearest end, keeping blade just above skin.

2. Rotate fish and grab loose piece of skin. Run slicing knife between flesh and skin, making sure knife is just above skin, until skin is completely removed.

After Cooking

Gently slide thin, wide spatula between flesh and skin and use your fingers of your free hand, if necessary, to help separate skin. It should easily peel off in 1 piece.

The Gray Anatomy

The gray tissue just below a salmon's skin is a fatty deposit rich in omega-3 fatty acids and low in the pink pigments found in the rest of the fish. Many sources claim that it tastes fishier than the rest of the fillet and recommend removing it, but our tasters could barely detect a difference between fillets with the gray tissue attached and fillets with the gray tissue removed. If you do choose to remove it, simply peel the skin off the cooked fillet and scrape it away with the back of a knife.

REHEAT GENTLY

Reheating salmon can make it smell even stronger since heat oxidizes its abundant fatty acids into aldehydes. But reheating it gently will minimize the oxidation.

Place fillets on wire rack set in rimmed baking sheet, cover with aluminum foil (to prevent exteriors from drying out), and heat in 275-degree oven until fish registers 125 to 130 degrees, about 15 minutes for 1-inch-thick fillets (timing varies according to fillet size).

WHY IS SALMON STINKY?

Virtually all fish contain the compound TMAO, which transforms into a fishy-smelling compound called TMA when the fish are killed and can be detected when the fish is raw or cooked. But cooked salmon produces an even more pungent fishy odor for a different reason: Its highly unsaturated fat oxidizes when exposed to heat. To minimize fishy odor, consider choosing leaner wild salmon.

PUT IT ON ICE

Salmon can last up to twice as long if stored closer to 32 degrees, rather than at the typical home refrigerator temperature of 40 degrees. Place the fish in a zipper-lock bag on ice in a bowl (or cover it with ice packs) and place it at the back of the fridge, where it's coldest.

Did you know we have free videos on cooking salmon at CooksIllustrated.com? Go online and watch these and other videos for free.
- Pan-Seared Salmon
- Grilled Salmon Fillets
- Oven-Roasted Salmon
- Poached Salmon with Herb and Caper Vinaigrette

Better Hash Browns

How do you make a crispy, creamy shredded potato cake that isn't greasy and is a cinch to flip? It starts with a cake pan.

≽ BY ANDREA GEARY ≼

Hash browns make people crazy, at least according to esteemed 19th-century domestic science expert Mrs. Sarah Tyson Rorer. In an 1892 lecture, she recounted her research visits to psychiatric hospitals, where the patients appeared to be addicted to the fried potato patties they were served, leading her to conclude that the hash browns had caused the inmates' madness. There's an obvious flaw in Mrs. Rorer's logic, but she wasn't completely mistaken: Hash browns do have the power to unhinge.

There's not even consensus on what hash browns are. Some insist the potatoes are diced; others say shredded. Some claim the potatoes go into the skillet raw, while others say they're cooked first. Hash browns must be fried in a large disk. No, they're formed into individual patties. They never contain onions. They always contain onions.

For the purposes of my recipe, hash browns are shredded potatoes fried in a round until crispy and brown on both sides and tender and moist (but not wet) on the inside. The cake is transferred to a plate, cut into wedges, and served. And as far as I'm concerned, they are simply seasoned with salt and pepper—no herbs, no onions.

But settling on these guidelines led to a series of questions. How do you flip a mass of shredded, partially cooked potatoes without it falling apart? How do you ensure that the inner potatoes are cooked through at the exact moment that the exterior has

Molding our hash browns in a cake pan not only makes them easy to handle but also allows you to make them ahead and cook them the next day.

turned crispy and golden? And how do you make the hash browns crispy but not greasy?

Such questions might make you wonder if being a bit unbalanced is a prerequisite for making hash browns at home when, after all, they're available at every diner. But diner hash browns are often soggy and anemic. I prefer to elevate a simple homemade breakfast with ingredients that I always have on hand.

The Big Squeeze

Many recipes call for squeezing the potatoes before frying to remove excess moisture and thus give the cake a crispier outside and fluffier interior. But is it worth it? I made two batches, one with 2½ pounds of shredded russet potatoes that I squeezed dry in a towel and the other with russets that went straight from food processor to skillet. I tossed each batch with a teaspoon of salt and then fried each in a nonstick skillet with ¼ cup of oil, just enough to coat the bottom. To flip the potatoes, I slid the cake onto a plate, inverted it onto another plate, and then slid it back into the skillet with a bit more oil. I did this a second time using Yukon Gold potatoes, a variety with less starch, to see if it made a difference.

All four batches had serious problems. The cakes fell apart when I tried to flip them, and the outsides scorched before the innermost potatoes were fully cooked. All of the samples were underseasoned, and they were also pretty greasy.

The good news was that the squeezing step seemed worthwhile. The potatoes (both varieties) that I had wrung dry produced hash browns with exteriors that were slightly more crispy and brown and interiors that were a bit fluffier than those of the cakes made with unsqueezed potatoes. That said, they were all still a bit gummy and wet. There was also an unforeseen problem: All four batches of potatoes had turned an unappetizing color after shredding; the Yukons were a pinkish brown and the russets a purplish gray.

Saltwater Cure

A coworker had come up against the discoloration problem once, and she found that briefly swishing the shredded potatoes in a saltwater solution kept them pristine. Our science editor explained that when

Flipping Out

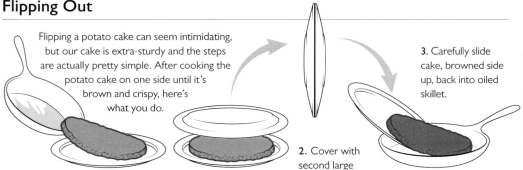

Flipping a potato cake can seem intimidating, but our cake is extra-sturdy and the steps are actually pretty simple. After cooking the potato cake on one side until it's brown and crispy, here's what you do.

1. Slide cake onto large plate.

2. Cover with second large plate; invert.

3. Carefully slide cake, browned side up, back into oiled skillet.

Keeping the Potatoes Pretty

When potato cells are broken and exposed to the air during grating, an enzymatic reaction leads to discoloration. We prevent this by dunking the shreds in salt water, which inhibits the enzyme. (See "Making Better Hash Browns" to learn about another role the salt water plays in our recipe.)

potato cells are broken and exposed to the air during grating, an enzyme called polyphenol oxidase mixes with other compounds in the potatoes, resulting in discoloration. Salt, especially salt in solution, inhibits the enzyme and thus reduces discoloration.

Putting the idea into action, I prepared two batches of salt water made with 4 teaspoons of salt and 2 cups of water. I grated a pound of Yukon Golds and a pound of russets (both were performing equally up to this point) and tossed each in the salt water before wringing them dry. The solution was remarkably effective. Both batches retained their color for more than an hour. Though it was a close call, I settled on Yukon Golds for their buttery, slightly sweet flavor.

The saltwater wash had a couple of additional advantages: The cakes were now seasoned throughout, and the shreds were a bit more cohesive. It turns out that salt decreases the temperature at which potato starch gelatinizes (swells with moisture and bursts). That gelatinized starch acts as a glue that helps the shreds adhere.

Things were looking up, but the cake could have been easier to flip, and the interior was still wet and unevenly cooked. I was not ready to fuss with fully cooking the potatoes by boiling or baking them before frying, but I wondered if a quick stint in the microwave might help.

Stick Together

I transferred a batch of shredded potatoes from their towel to a bowl; after 5 minutes in the microwave, the shreds were steamy and a bit sticky. After 10 minutes they were quite cohesive. I transferred them to the hot skillet and carefully pressed them into a cake.

This batch was easier to flip, and because a lot of moisture had cooked off in the microwave, it also browned more readily. The exterior was crispier, and the inner potatoes were evenly cooked and far less gummy. The only problem? The potatoes had cooked too much and had thus lost the distinctive shredded texture that characterizes hash browns. Inside, they were more like mashed potatoes.

For my next batch, I cooked half the potatoes for 5 minutes, added the remaining potatoes, and then cooked this mixture for another 5 minutes. When I pressed the potatoes into the skillet, the softer, more cooked portion bound the shreds together. This cake had a crispy brown crust and the texture I was after.

But shaping the potatoes into a cake in the hot skillet didn't feel terribly safe, and I wondered if I could make the cake even easier to flip. So instead of transferring the next batch of microwaved potatoes to the skillet, I placed them in a greased 8-inch cake pan. After they had cooled a bit, I pressed them firmly into a smooth disk. After about 20 minutes in the refrigerator the potatoes were completely cool, and I tipped the disk out onto a plate and slid it into the hot skillet.

I discovered that this technique had virtues beyond making the cake easier to handle. This smooth, compact potato cake didn't have as many nooks and crannies, so it wasn't as likely to stick to the skillet, which meant I could fry it in just 2 tablespoons of

1. TOSS the potatoes in a saltwater bath, which allows the potato starch to gelatinize more readily when heated and results in a more cohesive cake.

2. SQUEEZE the potatoes to remove excess moisture and then microwave half of them until almost fully cooked. These sticky shreds bind the cake together.

3. PRESS the potatoes into a cake pan to mold them into a compact, uniform disk with a smooth surface that is less likely to stick to the pan.

oil per side, provided I used a conventional stainless-steel skillet instead of a nonstick one (see "Skip the Nonstick"). Using less oil also meant that the cake was less greasy. Another bonus: make-ahead potential. I found I could leave the potato cake in its pan in the fridge overnight. In the morning all I had to do was flip it out of the pan and fry it.

Mrs. Rorer probably wouldn't endorse my hash browns recipe, and she might even worry for my mental health, but with a recipe this good, I'd be crazy not to make them.

BETTER HASH BROWNS
SERVES 4 TO 6

We prefer using the shredding disk of a food processor to shred the potatoes, but you can use the large holes of a box grater if you prefer.

4	teaspoons salt
2½	pounds Yukon Gold potatoes, peeled and shredded
¼	teaspoon pepper
¼	cup vegetable oil

1. Spray 8-inch round cake pan with vegetable oil spray. Whisk 2 cups water and salt in large bowl until salt dissolves. Transfer potatoes to salt water and toss briefly to coat. Immediately drain in colander. Place 2½ cups potatoes in center of clean dish towel. Gather ends together and twist tightly to wring out excess moisture. Transfer dried potatoes to large bowl. Add pepper and toss to combine. Microwave until very hot and slightly softened, about 5 minutes. Place remaining potatoes in towel and wring out excess moisture. Add to microwaved potatoes and toss with two forks until mostly combined (potatoes will not combine completely). Continue to microwave until potatoes are hot and form cohesive mass when pressed with spatula, about 6 minutes, stirring halfway through microwaving.

2. Transfer potatoes to prepared pan and let cool until no longer steaming, about 5 minutes. Using

When Skipping Nonstick Means Less Oil

Because oil beads up in most nonstick pans rather than coating them evenly, we had to use at least ¼ cup of oil per side to ensure an even coating and thus even browning. A conventional skillet required half as much oil to cover its surface and thus produced an evenly browned potato cake that wasn't greasy.

your lightly greased hands, press potatoes firmly into pan to form smooth disk. Refrigerate until cool, at least 20 minutes or up to 24 hours (if refrigerating longer than 30 minutes, wrap pan with plastic wrap once potatoes are cool).

3. Heat 2 tablespoons oil in 10-inch skillet over medium heat until shimmering. Invert potato cake onto plate and carefully slide cake into pan. Cook, swirling pan occasionally to distribute oil evenly and prevent cake from sticking, until bottom of cake is brown and crispy, 6 to 8 minutes. (If not browning after 3 minutes, turn heat up slightly. If browning too quickly, reduce heat.) Slide cake onto large plate. Invert onto second large plate. Heat remaining 2 tablespoons oil until shimmering. Carefully slide cake, browned side up, back into skillet. Cook, swirling pan occasionally, until bottom of cake is brown and crispy, 5 to 6 minutes. Carefully slide cake onto plate and invert onto serving plate. Cut into wedges and serve.

▶ **See How It Works**
A step-by-step video is available at CooksIllustrated.com/apr17

How to Cook Baby Bok Choy

This vegetable's clean, mild flavor is an asset. We don't muddy it with browning.

⇒ BY SANDRA WU ⇐

To many American home cooks, bok choy, a mainstay in Chinese restaurants, is a bit mysterious. A member of the cabbage family, it's an appealing two-fer. Its crisp, mild-tasting stalks retain some of their texture when cooked, while the leaves wilt and soften. But how do you cook a vegetable with two such disparate parts?

When it comes to the larger heads of mature bok choy, cooking the leaves and stems separately is one solution. But with baby bok choy, it's really a shame to separate the two parts since one of this smaller version's assets is that it offers a lot of visual appeal on the plate when served whole or halved. The stalks of the younger variety are slightly more tender, but it's still not a cinch to deliver perfect crisp-tender stalks and wilted but not mushy leaves. I decided to see what I could do.

I started with a pound of baby bok choy, which meant eight small heads. I considered cooking whole heads but changed my mind when grit remained in the nooks and crannies even after cleaning. I settled on halving the heads, which would also allow for faster cooking.

First, I tried a simple pan-seared approach—cooking the bok choy in a skillet until the leaves had wilted—but the stems didn't fully cook through by the time the leaves were tender. I also found that I didn't love the browning the bok choy picked up, as it muddied the vegetable's flavor.

I suspected that a stint of steaming at the start might ensure more even, thorough cooking of the stems with no browning. The vegetables were a tight fit in the pan at first, but after a few minutes of covered cooking (with some water thrown in to provide enough steam), the leaves began to wilt and cook down. I removed the lid and cooked the bok choy a bit longer; by the time the liquid had evaporated, the stems had just the right texture. Adding minced garlic gave me a simple version perfect for any meal.

For a few variations showcasing flavorful sauces, I came up with some combinations for the base flavors (soy sauce with chili-garlic sauce, oyster sauce with sesame oil, mirin with miso, or fish sauce with pepper flakes) and varied the aromatics (ginger or shallot instead of garlic). A little sugar helped balance the salty flavors of the miso and fish sauce variations, and

▶ **Bok Choy Basics**
A step-by-step video is available at CooksIllustrated.com/apr17

For crisp-tender stems and leaves that are wilted but not mushy, we steam and then sauté.

a mere ½ teaspoon of cornstarch gave all of the sauces just the right consistency. I now had a clutch of sautéed baby bok choy options that were easy to prepare, full of flavor, and an attractive addition to any plate.

SAUTÉED BABY BOK CHOY
SERVES 4

If using heads larger than 2 ounces each, quarter them instead of halving. We spin the bok choy dry after washing to avoid adding too much water to the pan. Our recipes for Sautéed Baby Bok Choy with Miso Sauce and Sautéed Baby Bok Choy with Shallot and Fish Sauce are available for free for four months at CooksIllustrated.com/apr17.

- 4 teaspoons vegetable oil
- 2 garlic cloves, minced
- 8 small heads baby bok choy (1½ to 2 ounces each), halved, washed thoroughly, and spun dry
- 2 tablespoons water
- ¼ teaspoon salt

1. Combine 1 teaspoon oil and garlic in small bowl; set aside.

2. Heat remaining 1 tablespoon oil in 12-inch nonstick skillet over medium heat until shimmering.

Add bok choy and water and immediately cover. Cook, covered, shaking pan occasionally, for 2 minutes. Remove lid, toss bok choy, and then push bok choy to sides of skillet. Add garlic mixture to center and cook, stirring constantly, until fragrant, about 20 seconds. Stir garlic mixture into bok choy, sprinkle with salt, and continue to cook, stirring constantly, until all water has evaporated, stems are crisp-tender, and leaves are wilted, 1 to 2 minutes longer. Transfer to platter and serve.

SAUTÉED BABY BOK CHOY WITH CHILI-GARLIC SAUCE

Whisk 1 tablespoon soy sauce, 1 tablespoon chili-garlic sauce, 1 teaspoon sugar, and ½ teaspoon cornstarch together in small bowl. Before transferring cooked bok choy to platter, add soy sauce mixture to skillet and cook, stirring constantly, until sauce is thickened and coats bok choy, about 15 seconds. Omit salt.

SAUTÉED BABY BOK CHOY WITH OYSTER SAUCE AND GINGER

Omit 1 garlic clove and add 1 tablespoon grated fresh ginger to garlic-oil mixture in step 1. Whisk 2 tablespoons oyster sauce, 2 teaspoons toasted sesame oil, and ½ teaspoon cornstarch together in small bowl. Before transferring cooked bok choy to platter, add oyster sauce mixture to skillet and cook, stirring constantly, until sauce is thickened and coats bok choy, about 15 seconds. Omit salt.

TECHNIQUE |

HOW TO CLEAN BOK CHOY

Bok choy's tightly layered stems can retain a lot of grit. To thoroughly clean them, swish the halved heads in three changes of water. Spinning them dry avoids adding too much water to the pan.

Tuscan Shrimp and Beans

Shrimp and bright flavors transform cannellini beans from winter to all-weather fare.

> BY STEVE DUNN

In Italy, Tuscans living in rural areas were once referred to as *mangiafagioli*, or "bean eaters," a reference to their consumption of economical bean dishes. The most traditional preparation is an ultrasimple wintry one in which dried cannellini beans are simmered with herbs and garlic until tender and then drizzled with olive oil for serving. But recently I came across a dish making the rounds on cooking blogs that pairs cannellini with shrimp, a combination that adds up to a nice springtime stew. Most of the recipes go something like this: Warm several cups of cooked beans in olive oil with a little of their cooking liquid. Meanwhile, sear a pound of shrimp separately, sauté some onion and garlic, and stir in chopped tomatoes. Add the shrimp and some shredded fresh basil, and spoon the mixture over the warmed beans.

I loved the sweet-savory pop of flavor from the shrimp in these versions, but that flavor was confined to the shrimp themselves rather than integrated into the dish. I wanted to bolster that seafood flavor so it permeated the beans, too. I also wanted the dish to be fast, so I decided from the outset to use a couple of cans of cannellini beans rather than dried beans. Since it wasn't yet tomato season, I also determined that I would use canned tomatoes instead of the fresh ones that many recipes called for. For ease, and because they maintain their shape due to the addition of calcium chloride, I would use the diced kind.

My next decision was to borrow a trick from our Shrimp Scampi recipe (January/February 2016) and make a 10-minute concentrated stock from the shrimp shells, which are packed with the savory compounds we associate with shrimp flavor. This required nothing more than browning the shells in oil (which further boosts the flavor they contribute), simmering them in a little bit of water, and straining them before discarding them. I then warmed the beans in this shrimpy liquid for a few minutes.

This change helped make the dish seem more integrated, but I wanted still more complex seafood flavor. The fix was threefold. First, in the same pan I'd used to make the stock, I sautéed two minced anchovies along with other simple aromatics and seasonings; it's an ingredient we often turn to when we want to add deep savoriness to dishes both seafood and otherwise. Second, I added the shrimp stock back to the pan along with the canned tomatoes and then simmered the beans in this mixture for about 20 minutes, which not only concentrated the seafood flavor even more but also helped meld all the flavors. Third, instead of searing the shrimp

separately, I poached them—brined first to season them and help them stay juicy—in the bean mixture over low heat during the final few minutes of cooking. The shrimp flavored the beans, and the beans also insulated the shrimp from direct heat so that they stayed plump and moist.

I freshened up the stew's rich seafood flavor with a bit of lemon zest and juice and made one final tweak: adding the liquid from one can of beans, which contained just enough starchy body so that the stew's consistency was lightly thickened and almost creamy—ideal for eating from a spoon or scooping up with a piece of crusty bread.

Deeply flavorful and on the table in less than half an hour, this was the kind of quick dinner I could whip up on a weeknight and the kind I want to tuck into on a lazy Sunday. I was officially a mangiafagioli, too.

Poaching the shrimp in a concentrated stock together with the beans enhances the flavor of both.

TUSCAN SHRIMP AND BEANS
SERVES 4 TO 6

We prefer untreated shrimp, but if your shrimp are treated with added salt or preservatives like sodium tripolyphosphate, skip brining in step 1 and increase the salt to ½ teaspoon in step 3. Serve with crusty bread.

- 2 tablespoons sugar
  Salt and pepper
- 1 pound large shell-on shrimp (26 to 30 per pound), peeled, deveined, and tails removed, shells reserved
- ¼ cup extra-virgin olive oil
- 1 onion, chopped fine
- 4 garlic cloves, peeled, halved lengthwise, and sliced thin
- 2 anchovy fillets, rinsed, patted dry, and minced
- ¼ teaspoon red pepper flakes
- 2 (15-ounce) cans cannellini beans (1 can drained and rinsed, 1 can left undrained)
- 1 (14.5-ounce) can diced tomatoes, drained
- ¼ cup shredded fresh basil
- ½ teaspoon grated lemon zest plus 1 tablespoon juice

1. Dissolve sugar and 1 tablespoon salt in 1 quart cold water in large container. Submerge shrimp in brine, cover, and refrigerate for 15 minutes. Remove shrimp from brine and pat dry with paper towels.

2. Heat 1 tablespoon oil in 12-inch skillet over medium heat until shimmering. Add shrimp shells and cook, stirring frequently, until they begin to turn spotty brown and skillet starts to brown, 5 to

6 minutes. Remove skillet from heat and carefully add 1 cup water. When bubbling subsides, return skillet to medium heat and simmer gently, stirring occasionally, for 5 minutes. Strain mixture through colander set over large bowl. Discard shells and reserve liquid (you should have about ¼ cup). Wipe skillet clean with paper towels.

3. Heat 2 tablespoons oil, onion, garlic, anchovies, pepper flakes, ¼ teaspoon salt, and ⅛ teaspoon pepper in now-empty skillet over medium-low heat. Cook, stirring occasionally, until onion is softened, about 5 minutes. Add 1 can drained beans, 1 can beans and their liquid, tomatoes, and shrimp stock and bring to simmer. Simmer, stirring occasionally, for 15 minutes.

4. Reduce heat to low, add shrimp, cover, and cook, stirring once during cooking, until shrimp are just opaque, 5 to 7 minutes. Remove skillet from heat and stir in basil and lemon zest and juice. Season with salt and pepper to taste. Transfer to serving dish, drizzle with remaining 1 tablespoon oil, and serve.

▶ **Look: It's Simple**
A step-by-step video is available at CooksIllustrated.com/apr17

Chocolate Sheet Cake

Our cake boasts a deeply chocolaty crumb, plush frosting, and a fuss-free method. Plus, it taught us something new about cocoa powder.

⇒ BY ANNIE PETITO ⇐

Sheet cakes don't require the work that goes into making layer cakes; they are simply spread with a thick coat of frosting and served straight from the pan. When the results are good, a sheet cake yields great reward for the effort. But most versions I've made are dry and crumbly, have barely a whisper of chocolate flavor, or are so dense that they verge on brownie territory. Loose, drippy frostings make cakes too messy to eat out of hand, while stiff, fudgy ones weigh down the crumb; more often than not, they're cloyingly sweet, too.

The kind of chocolate sheet cake I could turn to again and again would boast a tender, moist, sturdy crumb that was seriously chocolaty and a silky chocolate frosting just sweet enough to stand apart from the flavor of the cake. It would come together with baking staples and basic equipment—no mixers or food processors needed.

Cocoa Loco

Some recipes for chocolate cake call for cocoa powder but no bar chocolate, but we've found that using both produces cakes with deeper chocolate flavor. That's because, ounce for ounce, cocoa powder packs more chocolate flavor than any other form of chocolate, while bar chocolate adds complexity, fat, and sugar.

In fact, when I made a series of chocolate cakes to get my bearings, the one with the fullest chocolate flavor contained plenty of both—¾ cup of cocoa powder and 8 ounces of melted bittersweet chocolate. That recipe didn't specify which type of cocoa to use, natural or Dutch-processed, but I used the latter. We reserve Dutch-processed cocoa, which tends to be more expensive, for recipes where cocoa makes up a significant portion of the batter because we've found that its flavor is more complex and balanced than that of natural cocoa; "Dutching" refers to processing the cocoa with an alkali that neutralizes its natural acidity.

To make a basic chocolate cake batter, I melted butter with the chocolate and added the cocoa powder so that its flavor molecules would release fully (or "bloom"). Then I whisked eggs with sugar; added the butter-chocolate-cocoa mixture, milk, and vanilla; and whisked in the dry ingredients (flour, salt, and baking soda) until a smooth batter formed. This "dump-and-stir" method is fast and easy and also produces a

Both the cake and frosting are mixed by hand and come together with no more than a half-hour of active time.

less crumbly cake than the creaming method. In that method, flour is combined with creamed butter and sugar alternately with liquid, so some of the flour

When Chocolate Cake Became Chocolate

American chocolate cake as we know it—one that contains chocolate, cocoa powder, or both—is a relatively young dessert. The term "chocolate cake" originally referred to a yellow or vanilla cake that was served with a chocolate beverage. Only once chocolate became cheaper, around 1940, did home cooks start baking with large amounts of cocoa and recipes for truly chocolaty cakes come about.

HERSHEY'S RECIPES

becomes coated in fat and thus can't interact with water to form gluten. And the less gluten, the more crumbly the cake.

I poured the batter into a greased 13 by 9-inch baking pan, which would produce a higher ratio of cake to frosting than a baking sheet would. I baked it at 325 degrees for about 30 minutes. It wasn't too sweet, but despite loading up the batter with cocoa and chocolate, it lacked the chocolate punch and depth that I was hoping for.

Fortunately, trading the melted butter for vegetable oil solved that; its neutral flavor produced a cleaner-tasting cake that allowed the chocolate to shine. I also saved myself a couple of bowls to wash by mixing the dry and wet ingredients into the saucepan where I'd heated the chocolate mixture.

Before focusing on the frosting, I made the cake with natural cocoa, just to check that it worked. I'd expected this cake to be paler (Dutching raises the pH of cocoa, darkening its color) and a bit less complex in flavor, but what caught me by surprise was its noticeably drier crumb. To be sure that I hadn't overbaked the cake, I made several more, using multiple natural cocoas, and was met with the same dry result each time. It wasn't until I did some digging about cocoa—including talking to Clay Gordon, the creator and moderator of chocolatelife.com, a clearinghouse for chocolate information—that I understood the problem: In addition to being more acidic than Dutch-processed cocoas, most natural cocoas are much lower in fat, which makes them very absorbent. In essence, the low-fat natural cocoas were robbing the cake of moisture (for more information, see "Dry Cake? Check Your Cocoa"). I'd be sticking with the Dutch-processed cocoa for sure.

Icing on the Cake

A simple sheet cake deserves an equally simple frosting—one that can be stirred together while the cake bakes. That eliminated buttercreams, which require hauling out a stand mixer or food processor. For something creamy and spreadable, I considered a ganache. This frosting often takes the form of a pourable glaze of melted chocolate and cream, sometimes gilded with softened butter. But ganache can range from soupy to stiff, depending on the ratio of cream and butter to chocolate, so I would adjust the ratio of those ingredients until I had something thick and creamy.

One recipe I'd tried called for spreading the cake with a milk chocolate ganache, the lighter flavor of which countered the darker cake nicely. Riffing on this idea, I landed on ⅔ cup cream heated with a pound of chocolate; the high proportion of chocolate gave me a thicker ganache than most standard recipes. I then added 2 sticks of softened butter, which lent it body and made it spreadable at room temperature. But waiting for my frosting to cool took 2 to 3 hours, so I refrigerated it, which cooled it down within an hour so that it was ready to use when the cake finished cooling. Then I gave the mixture a good whisk, which made it smooth and creamy, before slathering a thick layer of it over the cake.

The dark, complex cake and milky-sweet, satiny frosting was a combination that I knew would tempt both milk and dark chocoholics alike. And since it comes together with baking staples and an unfussy, appliance-free mixing method, this is a chocolate cake built for any cook and any occasion.

CHOCOLATE SHEET CAKE WITH MILK CHOCOLATE FROSTING
SERVES 12

While any high-quality chocolate can be used here, our preferred bittersweet chocolates are Ghirardelli 60% Cacao Bittersweet Chocolate Premium Baking Bar and Callebaut Intense Dark Chocolate, L-60-40NV, and our favorite milk chocolate is Dove Silky Smooth Milk Chocolate. We recommend making this cake with a Dutch-processed cocoa powder; our favorite is from Droste. Using a natural cocoa powder will result in a drier cake.

Cake

1½	cups (10½ ounces) granulated sugar
1¼	cups (6¼ ounces) all-purpose flour
½	teaspoon baking soda
½	teaspoon salt
1	cup whole milk
8	ounces bittersweet chocolate, chopped fine
¾	cup (2¼ ounces) Dutch-processed cocoa powder
⅔	cup vegetable oil
4	large eggs
1	teaspoon vanilla extract

Frosting

1	pound milk chocolate, chopped
⅔	cup heavy cream
16	tablespoons unsalted butter, cut into 16 pieces and softened

1. FOR THE CAKE: Adjust oven rack to middle position and heat oven to 325 degrees. Lightly spray 13 by 9-inch baking pan with vegetable oil spray. Whisk sugar, flour, baking soda, and salt together in medium bowl; set aside.

2. Combine milk, chocolate, and cocoa in large saucepan. Place saucepan over low heat and cook, whisking frequently, until chocolate is melted and mixture is smooth. Remove from heat and let cool slightly, about 5 minutes. Whisk oil, eggs, and vanilla into chocolate mixture (mixture may initially look curdled) until smooth and homogeneous. Add sugar mixture and whisk until combined, making sure to scrape corners of saucepan.

3. Transfer batter to prepared pan; bake until firm in center when lightly pressed and toothpick inserted in center comes out with few crumbs attached, 30 to 35 minutes, rotating pan halfway through baking. Let cake cool completely in pan on wire rack before frosting, 1 to 2 hours.

4. FOR THE FROSTING: While cake is baking, combine chocolate and cream in large heatproof bowl set over saucepan filled with 1 inch barely simmering water, making sure that water does not touch bottom of bowl. Whisk mixture occasionally until chocolate is uniformly smooth and glossy, 10 to 15 minutes. Remove bowl from saucepan. Add butter, whisking once or twice to break up pieces. Let mixture stand for 5 minutes to finish melting butter, then whisk until completely smooth. Refrigerate frosting, without stirring, until cooled and thickened, 30 minutes to 1 hour.

5. Once cool, whisk frosting until smooth. (Whisked frosting will lighten in color slightly and should hold its shape on whisk.) Spread frosting evenly over top of cake. Cut cake into squares and serve out of pan. (Leftover cake can be refrigerated in airtight container for up to 2 days.)

FROSTING CONSISTENCY, BEFORE AND AFTER

Because both chocolate and butter are fluid when warm and solid at room temperature, the frosting consistency will change from start to finish.

At first, the frosting will be pourable and warm.

Once cooled, the frosting will be thicker and stiffer. Giving it a quick whisk after chilling will make it smooth and spreadable.

▶ Watch It Happen
A step-by-step video is available at CooksIllustrated.com/apr17

DUTCHED COCOA
Free moisture does not get bound up with the starches, so the cake is more moist.

NATURAL COCOA
Free moisture gets bound up with the higher level of starches, so the cake is drier.

SCIENCE Dry Cake? Check Your Cocoa

There are two types of unsweetened cocoa powder: natural and what is known as Dutch-processed. The Dutch-processed kind is often more expensive, but in recipes that call for a hefty amount of cocoa powder (more than ½ cup), it is worth seeking out. For one thing, Dutched cocoa has been neutralized with alkali to take away some of the cacao bean's harsher, more acidic notes. But here's another, far less well-known reason: Dutched cocoas typically have far more fat than natural cocoas, sometimes twice as much. Fat adds a perception of moisture in baked goods. In addition, cocoa powders with more fat contain less starch. Why is that important? Starch absorbs free moisture in a batter, so the crumb bakes up drier. In fact, the starches in cocoa powder absorb up to 100 percent of the powder's weight. (Compare that with the starches in flour, which can absorb only 60 percent of the flour's own weight.) This helps explain why we found our cake to be noticeably moister when made with Dutched rather than with natural cocoa powders.

But not just any Dutched cocoa will do, since fat percentages vary. Our recommended cocoa from Droste contains 22 percent fat. Compare that with the 11.9 percent in Equal Exchange Dutch Processed Cocoa Powder, an amount that's similar to those of most natural cocoas. The takeaway: In baked goods that call for a higher proportion of cocoa powder, we'll be calling for higher-fat Dutch-processed cocoas not just for their rounder flavor but for the moist texture they provide.

Premium Extra-Virgin Olive Oil

High-end extra-virgin olive oils offer a world of flavor beyond grocery-store options. But if you want to trade up, where do you begin?

⊰ BY LISA McMANUS ⊱

Extra-virgin olive oil, the lush, vibrant product of fresh olives, is premium by definition. At least, it should be. But as we reported in our story about supermarket olive oils (November/December 2015), most of what you'll find doesn't deserve that prestigious label. The oils are either mislabeled as a higher grade; mishandled so that their bright, complex flavor turns rancid; or even fraudulently blended with other, cheaper oils and passed off as the real deal.

Only one of the oils we sampled in that tasting, from California Olive Ranch, was a cut above the rest—"rich" and "fruity," with a "peppery aftertaste." At $0.59 per ounce, it's one of the pricier supermarket options but costs just a fraction of what you'll spend on a bottle of premium extra-virgin. Which led us to ask: Since the good stuff sells for twice as much as or more than California Olive Ranch does, what are you getting for your money? We decided to find out.

Our supermarket olive oil tasting taught us that freshness is the most important consideration when buying extra-virgin olive oil, since it begins to degrade as soon as it's pressed, and this depreciation

happens even faster when the oil is exposed to air, heat, and light. So we narrowed down the countless number of producers worldwide by first zeroing in on premium oils produced in the Northern Hemisphere; that way, every product we chose would be roughly the same age. Then we carefully purchased oil from only the most recent harvest. The final lineup of 10 included oils priced from $0.94 to $2.13 per ounce (plus shipping) from France, Italy, Spain, Greece, Tunisia, Portugal, and the United States. All of the oils are sold online by reliable retailers; some are also available in gourmet shops or select supermarkets.

Our first step was to sample the oils plain, which made it immediately clear that these oils did indeed taste remarkably fresh. As we then tasted them tossed with butter lettuce and a little salt and finally drizzled over a bowl of warm cannellini beans (a typical application in parts of Italy), we marveled at how each oil seemed as distinct as a fingerprint, with flavors we'd never experienced with supermarket oils: "artichoke," "apples," "flowers," "tomato stems," "watercress," and even "dark wood." They didn't just enliven the lettuce and beans; they elevated the vegetables' flavors to something out of the ordinary.

By the Numbers

The oils tasted top-notch to us, but to be sure that they truly qualified as "extra-virgin," we subjected them to chemical testing and a sensory screening. Olive oils are rated for quality through a two-part evaluation, according to standards set by the International Olive Council, the industry's worldwide governing body. To pass the sensory test, the oil must not only have what experts call "zero defects" but also possess "some fruity flavor." Among the chemical standards, an oil must not exceed certain levels of free fatty acids, peroxides, and other chemical parameters that would indicate olive deterioration, poor processing or storage, or oxidation.

For a sensory perspective, we sent a randomly coded sample of each oil to a group of trained tasters for their expert opinions. In general, the panelists agreed with our assessments of most of the oils and used an array of descriptive terms for distinct flavors such as "artichoke" and "tropical fruit." As for the chemical tests, the premium oils passed most measurements of freshness and quality with flying colors, whereas in our testing of supermarket oils, most of the products barely squeaked by.

So what actually accounts for the dramatic differences in quality between premium and supermarket

IN THE DARK
If your EVOO comes in a light-colored bottle, wrapping it in foil will help protect it from the oxidizing effects of light.

oils? Mostly, it boils down to the control a producer has over the production process—from the quality of the fruit to how quickly and carefully the olives are pressed to how well the freshness of the oil is preserved during bottling, storage, and transport.

To keep costs low, producers of mass-market extra-virgin olive oils usually purchase cheap bulk oils from all over the world and blend them at a facility thousands of miles from where the olives were grown and pressed. This not only suggests that these producers have little to no control over the handling and freshness of their oils but also explains why supermarket extra-virgin olive oils usually lack the distinct flavors that premium oils are known for.

Conversely, the premium oils we tasted are produced in smaller, vertically integrated operations, many of which have run on the same site for hundreds of years. This means the olives are grown, picked, and pressed—and the oil bottled and sold—in a single location or within a strictly defined and limited area, and thus these oils are fresh, distinctly flavorful, and carefully monitored for quality.

Bottom Line

We think these premium oils are worth every penny. And while we singled out one particular crowd-pleaser with "ultrasmooth flavor" (a Greek product called Gaea Fresh), in a break from our usual procedure, we didn't rank the oils. Instead, we categorized them by flavor profile, since choosing the "best" bottle is a matter of personal preference. Think of it as comparing different styles of red wine as opposed to comparing a lineup of Pinot Noirs.

Given the prices of these premium oils, we'll still keep a bottle of our supermarket winner, California Olive Ranch, on hand for day-to-day use. But after tasting that product against a "nicely balanced" crowd-pleaser such as Gaea Fresh and a "complex and bold" powerhouse such as McEvoy Ranch, we were convinced that these oils are something special and are worth the splurge when you want to breathe life into salad greens, punch up a piece of grilled fish, or simply dunk bread in a superb oil.

Hitting All the Right Notes

Olive oil industry experts use spider charts to display flavor nuances in high-quality oils, rating the intensity of 10 flavors on a scale of 0 to 10. Well-balanced oils such as Gaea Fresh (plotted below) hit the full spectrum of flavors in nearly equal measure, confirming our own perceptions of this oil's particular flavors, including nuances of artichoke, grass, and pungency.

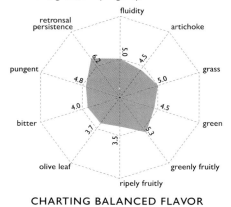

CHARTING BALANCED FLAVOR
The olive oil industry uses spider charts like the one above to plot an oil's flavors.

TASTING PREMIUM EXTRA-VIRGIN OLIVE OIL

We tasted 10 premium extra-virgin olive oils selected from the most recent harvest from a broad selection of countries in the Northern Hemisphere, sampling them plain, tossed with lettuce, and drizzled over warm cannellini beans. We also had the oils tested for quality and freshness at an independent laboratory (an independent group of trained olive oil tasters conducted a separate double-blind tasting of the oils). We obtained information about source, olive varieties, picking and pressing, and filtering from manufacturers. We purchased the oils online and in local stores, where available, and the prices listed are what we paid, not including shipping. We singled out a crowd-pleaser that appealed to all our tasters, but otherwise we didn't rank these oils. Instead, we categorized them by their flavor profiles (from mild to robust) based on our tasters' comments.

RECOMMENDED MEDIUM-ROBUST

GIANFRANCO BECCHINA
Olio Verde Extra Virgin Olive Oil
PRICE: $34.95 for 16.9 fl oz ($2.07 per fl oz)
ORIGIN: Italy OLIVE: Nocellara del Belice
WHERE TO BUY: olio2go.com
TASTERS' COMMENTS: "Smells like fresh-cut green grass" or "artichokes," with a taste of "butter on the front, pepper on the back." "Lively heat sneaks up on you," particularly on a bowl of warm beans.

CASTILLO DE CANENA
Family Reserve Picual Extra Virgin Olive Oil
PRICE: $27.95 for 16.8 fl oz ($1.66 per fl oz)
ORIGIN: Spain OLIVE: Picual
WHERE TO BUY: oliveoillovers.com
TASTERS' COMMENTS: "Intensely fragrant" and "garden-y," like a "bouquet of fresh flowers" or even a "hay loft" with a "spicy and savory" scent. "Rich and complex, with a bite at the end." "Balanced," "bright," and "grassy and green with just enough bitterness."

SCIABICA'S ARBOSANA Fall Harvest
California Extra Virgin Olive Oil
PRICE: $16.00 for 16.9 fl oz ($0.95 per fl oz)
ORIGIN: USA (California) OLIVE: Arbosana (with up to 15% Manzanillo or Mission)
WHERE TO BUY: sunshineinabottle.com
TASTERS' COMMENTS: "Lush," "rich and gently bitter," "ripe," "vegetal," and "robustly spicy" with a "lingering" "peppery" aftertaste.

RECOMMENDED ROBUST

FRESCOBALDI LAUDEMIO Extra Virgin Olive Oil
PRICE: $35.95 for 16.9 fl oz ($2.13 per fl oz)
ORIGIN: Italy OLIVES: Frantoio, Moraiolo, and Leccino
WHERE TO BUY: olio2go.com
TASTERS' COMMENTS: "Superpeppery" with a "clean finish." "Nasal," "wasabi-like heat" is "so bold as to be rough around the edges." "Mouth-coating body—the EVOO equivalent of fatty butter." "Wow! Who knew beans plus good olive oil could be fabulous together?"

McEVOY RANCH Certified Organic
Traditional Blend Extra Virgin Olive Oil
PRICE: $27.00 for 12.7 fl oz ($2.13 per fl oz)
ORIGIN: USA (California) OLIVES: Frantoio, Moraiolo, Leccino, Pendolino, Maurino, Leccio del Corno, and Coratina
WHERE TO BUY: mcevoyranch.com, some supermarkets
TASTERS' COMMENTS: "Aroma" that's "deceptively innocuous." "Complex and bold." Remarkable for its "bracing bitterness" and "peppery wallop." "Slow burner" that "goes all the way up my nose."

LES MOULINS MAHJOUB Organic Extra
Virgin Olive Oil
PRICE: $33.00 for 33.8 fl oz ($0.98 per fl oz)
ORIGIN: Tunisia OLIVE: Chetoui
WHERE TO BUY: zingermans.com
TASTERS' COMMENTS: A powerhouse: "Front notes are fresh and butter-like, but the finish is pungent." "Bold but bitter" and "gives a good kick at the end."

RECOMMENDED MILD

MOULIN CASTELAS CASTELINES
Classic Extra Virgin Olive Oil
PRICE: $29.95 for 16.9 fl oz ($1.77 per fl oz)
ORIGIN: France OLIVES: Salonenque, Aglandau, Grossane, and Verdale
WHERE TO BUY: oliveoillovers.com
TASTERS' COMMENTS: "Ultrasmooth," "mellow," "summery," and "subtle," with "just a hint" of pepper and "afterburn." Scent of "fresh grass cuttings." "Full-bodied," "rounded," and "buttery."

CASA DE SANTO AMARO
Selection Extra Virgin Olive Oil
PRICE: $21.95 for 16.9 fl oz ($1.30 per fl oz)
ORIGIN: Portugal OLIVES: Cobrançosa, Verdeal Transmontana, and Madural
WHERE TO BUY: oliveoillovers.com
TASTERS' COMMENTS: "Green, fresh scent" and "well-balanced," "buttery and silky" flavor. "Good fruit intensity without too much bitterness and pungency." "Love this mild, buttery, sunny-tasting oil. Assertive but not aggressive."

RECOMMENDED MEDIUM

GAEA FRESH
Extra Virgin Olive Oil

> CROWD-PLEASER

PRICE: $18.99 for 17 fl oz ($1.12 per fl oz)
ORIGIN: Greece OLIVE: Koroneiki
WHERE TO BUY: yolenis.com/en-us/, some supermarkets
TASTERS' COMMENTS: "Buttery," "smooth," "lemony and clean," with "sweet" olive fruitiness, aroma like "tomato stems," and a lightly "peppery" aftertaste. "Nicely balanced." Received a thumbs-up from all tasters.

COLUMELA
Original Blend Extra Virgin Olive Oil
PRICE: $19.99 for 17 fl oz ($1.18 per fl oz)
ORIGIN: Spain OLIVES: Picual, Hojiblanca, Ocal, and Arbequina
WHERE TO BUY: Supermarkets
TASTERS' COMMENTS: "Fruity and sweet"-smelling, with notes of "apricot and peach" but also reminiscent of "dark wood" with "bitter and peppery flavors" such as "watercress" or "arugula" that "build." "Really plays well with beans."

How Do You Take Your EVOO?

Identifying other flavors you like can help you pick a premium extra-virgin olive oil that suits your taste.

IF YOU LIKE	CONSIDER	IF YOU LIKE	CONSIDER
Chardonnay		Black espresso	
Lager	Mild to medium EVOO	Bitter IPAs	Medium-robust to robust EVOO
Mild salad greens		Hot chiles	

The Best Silicone Spatula

A spatula should feel like an extension of your arm, nimbly stirring, scraping, and folding any food you put in its path. Why is a good one so hard to find?

⋺ BY KATE SHANNON ⋵

Whether we're baking or cooking, scrambling or sautéing, flipping or folding, a heatproof silicone spatula is one of the busiest tools in our kitchen. Nine years ago, we gave top honors to a heatproof model that is ubiquitous in restaurant kitchens but can sometimes feel too big and unwieldy at home. So we rounded up 10 spatulas priced from $6.95 to $18.67 from the dizzying array available, including our previous winner and a retooled version of our old runner-up. We subjected each to a slew of recipe tests, as well as evaluations of cut resistance, stain and odor resistance, heat resistance, and durability to see which stood out from the pack. With some products, comfort was an issue. Performance was also an issue, with some spatulas failing to reach into the edges of saucepans or leaving pockets of unmixed food. Others left streaks of batter on the sides of bowls.

Heads Above

To understand the differences, we first looked at the spatulas' heads. Models with smaller heads moved less food with each pass, so it took more work to mix cookie dough or stir risotto. But larger heads weren't necessarily better. Two models barely fit inside a food processor bowl or a 1-cup dry measuring cup. In general we found that midsize heads (roughly 4 by 2½ inches) were fast and effective at almost every task.

The shape of the head proved very important, too. Models with sharply angled top edges lacked breadth, so we struggled to empty measuring cups

Bad Spatulas in Action

POOR FIT
Oversized heads, like the one on this Vollrath spatula, can't effectively scrape large measuring cups.

TRAPS WATER
Dishwater dripped out of the crevices in the Cuisinart model.

REAL PUSHOVER
The overly flexible head on the KitchenAid spatula didn't have enough force to push food.

and efficiently stir scrambled eggs. Those with handles that were inserted into the head, much like a Popsicle stick, created annoying ridges on the blade where food got stuck, which prevented thorough mixing and made it difficult to wipe the blade clean.

Thickness and rigidity also mattered. One chubby, stiff-headed model skidded over bowl sides, cut too-wide swaths through food, and threatened to deflate fluffy whipped cream and egg whites. Meanwhile, the flimsy heads on two other models curled up when we gently pushed them against a skillet or bowl. The best options had a fairly straight top edge and one gently curved corner that matched the contours of bowls, and they struck the right balance between rigidity and flexibility.

Hard to Handle

Handles were also key. Narrow handles were uncomfortable to grip. One chunky handle was comfortable only when we gripped it with a fist, which forced us to stir inefficiently and awkwardly. Others were slick and slid around in our hands. A couple of spatulas with short, fatter handles were impossible to grip effectively; another had holes that made for awkward grasping.

Our favorite handles boasted a fairly even width and were neither too hefty nor too narrow. We liked textured silicone handles because they stayed securely in our hands. Most silicone handles also resisted melting when we left them resting on the lip of a hot skillet. (Wood came out unscathed in this test, but plastic handles developed deep grooves.) In terms of length, the best spatula was on the shorter side and also had good affordance, meaning a shape and design that allows for multiple grips.

In general, we preferred models made from one seamless piece of silicone. In one model with a two-piece design, dishwater accumulated in the crevices and later dripped into freshly whipped cream.

Our new all-purpose winner, the di Oro Living Seamless Silicone Spatula ($10.97), has an exceptionally comfortable handle, strikes the right balance between strength and flexibility, and has straight sides that made for thorough scraping. Its head was a bit small for maximum efficiency in folding tasks, which is why we are also recommending our former winner from Rubbermaid ($14.50), whose large head and long handle make it highly effective for use in deep pots and bowls. With these two spatulas on hand, any kitchen will be well equipped.

Fourteen Separate Tests, Four Testers

We put each spatula through a gauntlet of tests in a wide range of kitchen equipment and using a diverse group of testers (short and tall, lefty and righty).

➤ FOLDING
1. Fold whipped egg whites into cake batter in large mixing bowl.
2. Fold fruit puree into whipped cream in stand mixer bowl.

➤ STIRRING
3. Stir mix-ins into thick cookie dough in stand mixer bowl.

4. Stir scrambled eggs in 10-inch nonstick skillet.
5. Stir onions in 4-quart saucepan.
6. Stir risotto in 4-quart saucepan.
7. Stir chopped carrots in Dutch oven.

➤ SCRAPING
8. Scrape scrambled eggs from pan without breaking up curds.
9. Scrape fond from 12-inch traditional skillet.

➤ VERSATILITY
10. Scrape honey from measuring cup and small mixing bowl.

➤ DURABILITY
11. Rest in 450-degree cast-iron skillet for 10 minutes
12. Scrape processor bowl with blade in place; check for cuts.

➤ CLEANUP
13. Submerge in warm tomato sauce, minced garlic, and curry powder for 2 hours; wash.*
14. Wash 35 times in dishwasher or 35 times by hand if not dishwasher-safe.

*washed an additional 12 times by hand throughout testing

RATING SILICONE SPATULAS

We tested 10 silicone spatulas, rating them on their ability to stir, scrape, and fold a wide variety of foods. We also evaluated their compatibility with our favorite pots and pans, mixing bowls, food processor, and stand mixers. A panel of testers evaluated them on general comfort and ease of use. We also rated them on heat resistance and ease of cleanup. All models were purchased online and appear below in order of preference. For complete testing results, go to CooksIllustrated.com/apr17.

HIGHLY RECOMMENDED

BEST ALL-PURPOSE SPATULA
DI ORO LIVING Seamless Silicone Spatula—Large
MODEL: DOL-SS-05
PRICE: $10.97
MATERIALS: Silicone blade, silicone handle, stainless-steel core

CRITERIA
FOLDING: ★ ★
STIRRING: ★ ★ ★
SCRAPING: ★ ★ ★
VERSATILITY: ★ ★ ★
DURABILITY: ★ ★ ★
CLEANUP: ★ ★ ★
HANDLE DESIGN: ★ ★ ★

COMMENTS: This model is firm enough for scraping and scooping but also fit neatly into tight corners. Its straight sides and wide, flat blade ensured that no food was left unmixed. The all-silicone design eliminates any crannies that could trap food. It felt exceptionally comfortable. Its smaller blade fell short in our folding test.

HIGHLY RECOMMENDED

BEST LARGE SPATULA
RUBBERMAID 13.5" High-Heat Scraper
MODEL: FG1963000000
PRICE: $14.50
MATERIALS: Silicone blade, ABS plastic handle, polypropelene core

CRITERIA
FOLDING: ★ ★ ★
STIRRING: ★ ★ ★
SCRAPING: ★ ★ ★
VERSATILITY: ★ ★
DURABILITY: ★ ★ ★
CLEANUP: ★ ★ ½
HANDLE DESIGN: ★ ★

COMMENTS: This model can feel oversized, but the long handle offers good leverage in deep bowls and pots. The large, flat blade makes quick work of folding whipped egg whites, which would suffer from too much agitation. You may not use it every day, but it can't be beat for certain tasks. It lost points for staining, but it eventually did come clean.

RECOMMENDED

TOVOLO Flex-Core Silicone Spatula
MODEL: 81-16705 PRICE: $9.00
MATERIALS: Silicone blade, silicone handle, nylon core
COMMENTS: Efficient, rigid blade but struggled in tight corners

FOLDING: ★ ★ ½
STIRRING: ★ ★ ★
SCRAPING: ★ ★ ★
VERSATILITY: ★ ★
DURABILITY: ★ ★
CLEANUP: ★ ★ ★
HANDLE DESIGN: ★ ★ ½

NOT RECOMMENDED

VOLLRATH NSF Certified, High-Temperature Spatula
MODEL: 52023 PRICE: $15.56
MATERIALS: Silicone blade, glass-reinforced nylon handle
COMMENTS: Blade was too long overall, and its handle was thick and slippery.

FOLDING: ★ ★ ½
STIRRING: ★ ★ ½
SCRAPING: ★ ★
VERSATILITY: ★
DURABILITY: ★ ★ ★
CLEANUP: ★ ★ ★
HANDLE DESIGN: ★

RECOMMENDED WITH RESERVATIONS

STARPACK Premium Silicone Spatula (11.5")
MODEL: n/a PRICE: $6.95
MATERIALS: Silicone blade, silicone handle, steel core
COMMENTS: Scraped and stirred well, but blade's ridge was annoying.

FOLDING: ★ ★
STIRRING: ★ ★ ½
SCRAPING: ★ ★ ½
VERSATILITY: ★ ★
DURABILITY: ★ ★
CLEANUP: ★ ★ ★
HANDLE DESIGN: ★ ★ ★

LE CREUSET Revolution Medium Spatula
MODEL: VB301-2 PRICE: $14.95
MATERIALS: Silicone blade, wooden handle
COMMENTS: Fat, puffy blade required extra effort for all tasks.

FOLDING: ★
STIRRING: ★
SCRAPING: ★
VERSATILITY: ½
DURABILITY: ★ ★ ★
CLEANUP: ★
HANDLE DESIGN: ★ ½

OXO Good Grips Medium Silicone Spatula
MODEL: 1241781V1 PRICE: $8.99
MATERIALS: Silicone blade, silicone handle
COMMENTS: Thin, strong blade could use more flexibility.

FOLDING: ★ ★ ½
STIRRING: ★ ★
SCRAPING: ★ ★ ★
VERSATILITY: ★ ★
DURABILITY: ★ ★
CLEANUP: ★ ★ ½
HANDLE DESIGN: ★ ★ ★

CUISINART Barrel Handle Silicone Spatula
MODEL: CTG-04-SP PRICE: $14.19
MATERIALS: Silicone blade, nylon and stainless-steel handle
COMMENTS: Flimsy blade; two-part design was hard to clean.

FOLDING: ★
STIRRING: ★
SCRAPING: ★
VERSATILITY: ★ ½
DURABILITY: ★ ★
CLEANUP: ★ ½
HANDLE DESIGN: ★

GIR Ultimate Spatula
MODEL: GIRSPU0203RED PRICE: $18.67
MATERIALS: Silicone blade, silicone handle, fiberglass core
COMMENTS: Lost points for too-strong blade and extreme tip angle.

FOLDING: ★ ★
STIRRING: ★ ★ ½
SCRAPING: ★ ★
VERSATILITY: ★ ★
DURABILITY: ★ ★ ★
CLEANUP: ★ ★ ★
HANDLE DESIGN: ★ ★ ½

KITCHENAID Gourmet Series Silicone Scraper Spatula
MODEL: KN031OHERA PRICE: $8.79
MATERIALS: Silicone blade, nylon handle, fiberglass core
COMMENTS: Blade was too small and floppy, and handle was uncomfortable and melted.

FOLDING: ★
STIRRING: ★
SCRAPING: ★
VERSATILITY: ★ ½
DURABILITY: ★
CLEANUP: ★ ½
HANDLE DESIGN: ★ ½

⇒ BY KEITH DRESSER, ANDREA GEARY, ANDREW JANJIGIAN & LAN LAM ⇐

Tasting Firm Tofu

Tofu is trending upward in the United States; Americans spent $274 million on this mild-tasting soybean product in 2013, and sales are increasing annually. To find the best tofu for the home cook, we set our sights on firm tofu—it's the type we call for most often. We tasted five nationally available products, priced from $0.08 to $0.40 per ounce, three ways: plain, coated with cornstarch and fried, and chopped and stir-fried in a filling for Thai basil lettuce wraps. Our panel rated each sample on texture, flavor, and overall appeal.

We liked the flavor of every tofu. Plain and in our recipes, the samples tasted "neutral" and "clean," with subtle "sweet," "nutty" notes. We liked the textures of all the samples, too—save one. Tasted plain, this tofu was so dry, firm, and compact that our tasters compared it to rubber erasers. Its lower moisture level meant that it absorbed cornstarch differently, so the exterior turned pasty and sludgy when fried.

Why was one tofu so different from the others? Because it's pressed more and thus has a denser texture. Our four recommended products contain between 7 and 8 grams of protein per 85-gram serving (about ⅓ cup); the overly dry tofu contains 14 grams of protein. Soy is the only source of protein in tofu, so this dramatic difference indicates that this product contains much more soybean curd per serving. Ultimately, any of the top four products in our lineup will yield successful results in the kitchen. But light, clean Nasoya Firm Tofu ($2.99 for 14 ounces) was our favorite.

–Kate Shannon

RECOMMENDED

NASOYA Organic Firm Tofu
PRICE: $2.99 for 14-oz package ($0.21 per oz)
PROTEIN: 8 g
COMMENTS: Delicate, "clean" soy flavor and "consistent, even texture" earned this tofu high scores throughout the tastings. In both cooked applications, it was "creamy" and "tender" but held its shape and offered just the right amount of chew.

MELISSA'S Organic Tofu (Firm)
PRICE: $2.69 for 18-oz package ($0.15 per oz)
PROTEIN: 7 g
COMMENTS: In every evaluation, tasters liked the "neutral" and mild flavor of this tofu.

HOUSE FOODS Premium Firm Tofu
PRICE: $1.50 for 19-oz package ($0.08 per oz)
PROTEIN: 7 g
COMMENTS: Tasters detected "pleasant," "fresh," and "slightly sweet" flavor in all three tastings.

AZUMAYA Firm Tofu
PRICE: $1.99 for 16-oz package ($0.12 per oz)
PROTEIN: 7 g
COMMENTS: Tasters liked the "clean" flavor and firm and chewy texture of this tofu.

NOT RECOMMENDED

HODO SOY Organic Non-GMO Firm Tofu
PRICE: $4.79 for 12-oz package ($0.40 per oz)
PROTEIN: 14 g
COMMENTS: Flavorwise, this "neutral" and slightly "nutty" tofu hit the right marks. Texture was the problem; it suffered from an ultrafirm and dense consistency that prompted comparisons to rubber erasers.

Protein amounts are based on an 85-gram serving size.

Determining the Age of Eggs

The age of eggs doesn't really matter when you're frying or scrambling, but we prefer the freshest specimens possible for our Perfect Poached Eggs (page 11). To determine the pack date (which is typically the same day that the eggs were laid), check the end of the carton for a three-digit code known as the Julian date; this is often beneath or above the sell-by date when one is provided. The numbers run consecutively, starting with 001 for January 1, so 078 would indicate that the eggs were packed on March 19. (The Julian date may follow a set of numbers beginning with a "P"; this is a code indicating the packing plant.)

While some sources suggest that you can check freshness by putting eggs in a bowl of water—fresher eggs are more likely to sink, while older ones are more likely to float because the air sack expands over time—we found that wasn't a reliable test since eggs didn't float until they were four to six months old. It's a safer bet to just check the Julian date; try to find eggs that are less than three weeks old. –A.J.

DATE CHECK
The three numbers on the second line indicate when the eggs were packed.

Anchovy Alternative

Anchovies typically play one of two roles. In dishes like Caesar salad or pasta puttanesca, these little salt-cured fish provide one of the key flavors and are used generously. But in other cases, from stews to meatballs, we often add just a small amount to provide a meaty, umami boost that isn't identifiably fishy. We wondered if fish sauce, which is made from fermented anchovies, could be substituted in a pinch.

In Caesar dressing, where the flavor of the anchovies plays a dominant role, the fish sauce didn't work. It came across as too fishy and slightly metallic, and it made the consistency too loose and runny. However, it was an acceptable substitute for the anchovies in our Italian-Style Turkey Meatballs, where they give both the tomato sauce and the turkey added meatiness.

So in recipes where anchovies are used to add background flavor, feel free to substitute ½ teaspoon of fish sauce per anchovy fillet. –L.L.

How to Prepare Endive

The crisp, bitter-tasting leaves of endive can provide a bold accent in salads or serve as a counterpoint to dips or fillings. To use the leaves whole for crudités or canapés, pull the leaves off the head one by one, discarding any that are wilted or discolored. To shred endive for salads, first remove the dense, crunchy core: Using a paring knife, halve the endive lengthwise and make two angled cuts along the outside of the core. Pull out and discard the core, and then slice each half on the bias. Note that the cut surfaces of endive can discolor quickly, so it's best to either wait until the last minute before prepping it or soak it in lemon water if you're cutting it in advance. –A.J.

CRUDITÉS: PEEL WILTED LEAVES

SALADS: REMOVE CORE

ILLUSTRATION: JOHN BURGOYNE

Baby Bok Choy

There are two types of baby bok choy. Regular bok choy has white stalks and dark green leaves with a crinkly texture, while Shanghai bok choy boasts wide, jade-colored stalks shaped like soupspoons. While we found that Shanghai has a milder, more celery-like flavor compared to the more mineral-like taste of regular bok choy, both work equally well in our recipes (page 20). –K.D.

REGULAR
Mineral flavor

SHANGHAI
Sweet and mild

Swapping Dried Beans for Canned

Because dried beans offer fuller flavor than canned beans at a fraction of the cost, many of us cook and freeze dried beans to have them at the ready. Some recipes also call for the starchy canned bean liquid, so we also freeze our cooking liquid (separate from the beans, which freeze better when drained). Since our bean cooking liquid isn't as viscous as the canned-bean liquid, we thicken it by adding ½ teaspoon of cornstarch per ½ cup of cooking liquid (the amount in a 15-ounce can). We also season it with salt to taste before freezing it to account for the added salt in canned beans. One 15-ounce can of drained canned beans equals 1½ cups of drained cooked dried beans. –L.L.

How to Make Flavored Salts

Salts infused with herbs or condiments (think mustard or Sriracha sauce) add flair and some crunch when used as a finishing touch. Buying them at specialty stores can be expensive, but it's easy to make them on your own by following a few guidelines.

➤ Combine kosher salt with liquid flavorings and coarser sea salt with herbs and seeds. Herbs and seeds need to be pulsed in a spice grinder with the salt to thoroughly meld. Starting with larger sea salt grains ensures that the salt will still have texture once pulsed. Do not use table salt, as it won't provide any crunch.

➤ Since salt is a powerful seasoning, potent flavorings work best.

➤ The salt needs to be dried out before use and storage; we use the microwave to accelerate the process (if the salt gets too hot, let it cool before proceeding to avoid burning). There are infinite possibilities, but here are five to get you started. –A.G.

LIQUID FLAVORINGS

Mix ½ cup kosher salt and flavoring in small bowl, then spread on large plate and microwave, stirring every 60 seconds, until only slightly damp (salt mixture will continue to dry as it cools).

FLAVORING	MICROWAVE TIME	SUGGESTED USES
⅓ cup Sriracha sauce	6–8 min	Roasted vegetables, sliced or mashed avocado, French fries, broiled fish, fruit (mango, pineapple, melon)
¼ cup grainy mustard + ¼ cup Dijon mustard	6–8 min	Roast beef, salad, grilled meat, homemade pretzels
1 tsp liquid smoke	1–2 min	Enhances grill flavor in quickly grilled food

HERBS AND SEEDS

Combine ⅓ cup coarse sea salt and flavorings in spice grinder and pulse until just combined, about 6 short pulses. Spread on large plate and microwave, stirring every 60 seconds, until only slightly damp (salt mixture will continue to dry as it cools).

FLAVORING	MICROWAVE TIME	SUGGESTED USES
½ cup finely chopped celery leaves + 1 tsp celery seeds	2–3 min	Corn on the cob, rim of a Bloody Mary glass, tuna salad
½ cup finely chopped fresh rosemary	2–3 min	Homemade focaccia, baked potatoes, fresh tomatoes, stirred into olive oil for dipping bread

Gravlax

Compared with its cousins smoked salmon, lox, and nova, which are all usually brined and then smoked, gravlax relies on a one-step process. The name, derived from *gravad lax* (Swedish for "buried salmon"), alludes to covering the fish with a salt-and-sugar cure (and typically dill). We call for skin-on salmon because it makes slicing the cured fish easier. A splash of booze (we use brandy) adds flavor, helps the cure adhere, and assists in the preserving process. Most recipes use granulated sugar, but we opt for brown sugar because its flavor complements the salmon. Pressing the salmon under the weight of a few cans helps it release moisture and gives the fillet a firmer, more sliceable texture. We baste the salmon with the released liquid once a day to help speed up the curing process and to keep it from drying out. Serve it sliced thin on its own or on our Deli Rye Bread (page 15) with cream cheese, shallot, or other accoutrements. –Kate Hartke

GRAVLAX
MAKES ABOUT 1 POUND

To make slicing easier, freeze the gravlax for 30 minutes.

- ⅓ cup packed light brown sugar
- ¼ cup kosher salt
- 1 (1-pound) skin-on salmon fillet
- 3 tablespoons brandy
- 1 cup coarsely chopped fresh dill

1. Combine sugar and salt in bowl. Place salmon, skin side down, in 13 by 9-inch glass baking dish. Drizzle with brandy, making sure to cover entire surface. Rub salmon evenly with sugar-salt mixture, pressing firmly to adhere. Cover with dill, pressing firmly to adhere.

2. Cover salmon loosely with plastic wrap, top with square baking dish or pie plate, and weight with several large, heavy cans. Refrigerate until salmon feels firm, about 3 days, basting salmon with liquid released into dish once a day.

3. Scrape dill off salmon. Remove salmon from dish and pat dry with paper towels before slicing. Gravlax can be wrapped tightly in plastic and refrigerated for up to 1 week; it should be left whole and sliced just before serving.

Sorting out Rye Flours

Rye flour typically comes in light, medium, and dark varieties—these refer to the relative amount of bran and germ each contains—as well as 100 percent whole-grain rye flour, also called "pumpernickel" flour. While light, medium, and dark rye flours are sifted to remove some of the nutrient-rich bran and germ, pumpernickel flour is unsifted and should be made from the entire rye kernel. That said, we've found that labeling is inconsistent among flours. Many companies simply label their product "rye flour" without any mention of type. And because the U.S. Food and Drug Administration doesn't regulate how much "whole grain" a product needs to contain to bear that label, any type of rye flour may bear this description on their label.

Fortunately, all this confusion is a moot point for our Deli Rye Bread (page 15) as well as our Boston Brown Bread (January/February 2017). When we made loaves with each type of flour, they all came out just fine, including the pumpernickel loaf. However, we did observe that the darker the flour, the more intense the rye flavor and the more dense the loaf. Some tasters said that the loaf made with light rye tasted closer to a regular wheat bread. If you have a choice, we recommend using medium or dark rye for the best balance of flavor and texture. –A.J.

COLOR DOES MATTER
Darker flours deliver stronger rye flavor and a denser texture.

KITCHEN NOTES

⇒ BY STEVE DUNN, ANDREA GEARY, LAN LAM & ANNIE PETITO ⇐

WHAT IS IT?

BEL JUBILEE CREAM MAKER

From double to single to clotted, the British love cream. Imagine their delight, then, when this simple gadget was introduced in 1935: the BEL Jubilee Cream Maker. ("Jubilee" refers to the model produced from 1935 to 1939 to celebrate the Silver Jubilee Celebration of King George V). This tool uses pressure to force melted butter and milk together to re-form cream. One reported advantage to owning one was that it allowed the owner to control the amount of fat in the cream.

Putting the cream maker to work, we tried making double cream (which is 48 percent butterfat versus standard heavy cream's 36 percent) according to the manual's instructions. We heated 3 ounces of unsalted butter with 4 ounces of whole milk until the butter melted and then poured the mixture into the hopper on top. Holding the cream maker firmly with one hand, we pumped the handle, forcing the butter-milk mixture through the nozzle and into the lower chamber until it all had been forced through. Not only was this cream luxuriously rich but it also whipped up beautifully (and even held its air overnight). We loved this clever gadget. –S.D.

Cleaning a Rasp-Style Grater

Rasp-style graters are easy to use, but they're not always easy to clean, especially when long, tough ginger fibers get caught in the teeth. We find that the following simple strategy works best.

Be prompt. Cleaning your grater immediately after use makes the job easier. If the grating detritus dries out and bonds itself to the grating surface, soak the grater until the particles are softened before proceeding. When you clean it, rinse it under warm water and then run a wet sponge along the grating surface, moving toward the handle (moving away from the handle will cause bits of sponge to get caught in the teeth). –A.G.

How to Slice Bread

Slicing bread may seem straightforward, but we've seen many a beautiful home-made loaf ravaged by an ill-chosen or carelessly employed knife, even in the test kitchen. Here are some tips to ensure that your sliced bread looks every bit as good as it tastes. –A.G.

LET BREAD COOL The crust of warm bread may be invitingly crisp, but the interior crumb is likely to be soft and gummy, making that warm loaf impossible to slice cleanly. Wait until the loaf is cool, since cooling gives the starches time to set.
USE SERRATED KNIFE The best knife for the job is one with a serrated edge that is at least 9 inches long (our favorite is the Mercer Culinary Millennia 10" Wide Bread Knife, $22.10).
SAW GENTLY Take your time and use the full length of the blade in a gentle horizontal sawing motion. Let the weight of the knife work for you and use minimal downward pressure.

Freeze Your Leftover Fresh Pasta

While testing pasta machines (page 32), we were inundated with fresh noodles, and we wondered if they would hold up better in the fridge or in the freezer. We tossed freshly made fettuccine with flour to help keep the strands separate, put batches in zipper-lock bags, and stored some bags in the fridge and some in the freezer. The refrigerated noodles were fine, but only for 18 hours. After that, the noodles took on a gray-green cast and clumped together. The discoloration is caused by oxidation of the iron in the dough's egg yolks (store-bought fresh pasta is packaged with nitrogen and carbon dioxide and less than 1 percent oxygen to prevent discoloration) and had only a mild effect on the flavor. But even if we closed our eyes to eat these noodles, the clumping would have been a real deal breaker. Caused by water in the noodles migrating outward and moistening the flour coating, it was only exacerbated when we tried cooking the noodles.

Freezing for up to four weeks, however, worked perfectly. We saw no trace of oxidation since freezing slows chemical reactions, and freezing kept the water from migrating outward. –L.L.

How to Carve a Butterflied Chicken

Be sure to let your chicken rest before carving. Once you've found the joints or other points of connection between parts, carving is easy. –L.L.

SEPARATE LEG QUARTERS FROM BREAST Slice through skin connecting leg quarter to breast and lift leg slightly to expose joint connecting thigh to breast. Cut through joint. Repeat on other side.

SEPARATE DRUMSTICKS AND THIGHS Cut through joint, following white line of fat separating drumstick and thigh.

REMOVE BREAST AND WINGS Run tip of knife first along breastbone and then along rib cage, gently pulling meat away from ribs and using ribs as guide as you cut. Cut through joint that connects wings to carcass to separate.

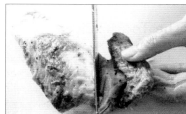

SEPARATE WINGS AND BREAST; HALVE BREAST Locate where wing bone meets breast meat and cut through skin and connective tissue to separate. Halve each breast crosswise.

How to Use a Tapered Rolling Pin

Many home cooks own straight rolling pins, which offer good heft for rolling out dough efficiently. But tapered, or French-style, rolling pins also have their advantages. –A.P.

Quick Correction
If your dough looks amoeba-like, the tapered shape and light weight of this pin make it easy to maneuver and pivot.

Easy Spot Check
Because the pin is in contact with a smaller area of dough, you can focus on one section of it to even its thickness.

Rotate Dough Less
Because the pin's maneuverability means you can focus on specific areas, you don't have to constantly rotate dough like you do with a straight pin.

Use heel of your hand to anchor pin while using your other hand to roll pin in arched motion to fix shape.

Use heel of your hand to anchor pin while pushing it over problem spot with your other hand.

To help prevent sticking, occasionally lift and turn dough.

Grilling on an 18-Inch Kettle Grill

Our winning charcoal grill is a 22.5-inch kettle grill from Weber, and our recipes are designed for its spacious grilling surface. But since home cooks with small outdoor spaces may have smaller grills, we decided to see how our recipes would translate. After cooking our recipes for Peri Peri Grilled Chicken, Sweet and Tangy Grilled Country-Style Pork Ribs, and Smoked Pork Loin on Weber's 18-inch grill, here's what we learned. –L.L.

Don't Grill Large Roasts: A 4-pound pork loin barely fit on the cooking grate, so larger cuts, like a brisket or whole turkey, won't work at all.

Get a Smaller Water/Drip Pan: Instead of using a 13 by 9-inch disposable aluminum pan for catching drippings or holding water (water can help keep meat moist over a long smoking time and also helps moderate the temperature), use a large loaf pan (such as a 7 by 5-inch pan). Reduce the amount of water by 25 percent.

Halve When Necessary: When recipes call for cooking food on only half the cooking grate (i.e. grill-roasting recipes) and thus fitting a lot of food into a limited space, we recommend halving the recipe if using a smaller grill.

Use Less Charcoal: When using a smaller grill, reduce the amount of charcoal by 25 percent to avoid burning food on the exterior before it cooks through.

Don't Cut Back on Wood Chips: If the recipe calls for wood chips, use the full amount. The amount of chips determines how long smoke is present, and that need doesn't change when using a smaller grill. The increased density of smoke may make food taste smokier, but we found the results perfectly acceptable.

The Toothpick Test

To determine if cakes, muffins, and quick breads are done, we often use the toothpick test. For the vast majority of baked goods, we want a toothpick inserted in the center to come out clean, indicating that the crumb is fully set and no excess moisture remains. This ensures that the item will slice neatly and hold together when cool. But when a moist texture is paramount, we deem the cake done when a few moist crumbs still cling to the toothpick. We also want moist crumbs on the toothpick in most chocolate baked goods, sometimes to preserve a very moist texture but also because they taste better: The longer chocolate is exposed to heat, the more its flavor compounds are driven off. But if the toothpick is wet, it's always time for the item to go back into the oven. –A.P.

RAW BATTER   **MOIST TEXTURE**   **FULLY SET**

EXPERIMENT Do You Need to Temper Eggs?

The traditional approach to preparing custards, puddings, and sauces, which rely on eggs for thickening power, requires tempering the eggs. The technique calls for heating the dairy, whisking a portion into the eggs (to which any sugar has usually been added), and then adding this mixture back to the pan with the rest of the hot dairy before cooking the mixture to the final temperature. Conventional cooking wisdom says that tempering prevents the eggs from seizing up into tight curds by allowing them to warm up gradually. We wondered if tempering really is all about temperature, so we set up a test to find out.

EXPERIMENT
We made three batches of crème anglaise, a custard sauce calling for egg yolks, milk, and sugar. For the control batch, we tempered the eggs the traditional way. For the second batch, we warmed the eggs with the sugar before adding them to the heated milk and proceeding as before. For the third batch, we mixed all the ingredients together at the outset and cooked the mixture to the final temperature. In all three cases, once the eggs were in the pot, we stirred the entire time to ensure that the eggs heated evenly from top to bottom.

RESULTS
The second batch, where the eggs were warmed before being combined with liquid, showed signs of curdling as soon as the eggs were stirred into the hot milk. The third batch was identical to the control, with the same smooth consistency and thickness.

EXPLANATION
Tempering doesn't work because of the gradual heating of the yolks; it works because the addition of liquid dilutes the uncooked egg proteins, making it harder for them to link up and form firm clumps when heated. This was borne out by the third batch, where the egg proteins were diluted from the outset. The second batch failed because the eggs had not been diluted before they started cooking; they were able to link up before they could be dispersed throughout the mixture.

TAKEAWAY
The real benefit of tempering is that it reduces the amount of constant stirring necessary since the dairy is already heated by the time the eggs go into the pot, which jump-starts cooking. That said, it does require some back and forth and multiple bowls. If you forgo tempering and choose to put everything in the pot at the same time, just make sure to stir constantly from the outset to prevent the eggs from forming clumps. –L.L.

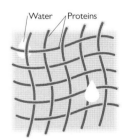
Water   Proteins

UNDILUTED EGGS
Proteins link up, forming clumps.

DILUTED EGGS
Liquid gets in the way of the proteins, making it harder for them to form bonds.

Cool It (Fast)

It happens to all of us: We put a pan of nuts, bread crumbs, or shredded coconut in the oven to toast and then forget about it until it's toastier than intended. The items aren't actually burnt, but the heat of the baking sheet can all too easily accomplish that even after the food is removed from the oven. We recommend quickly dumping the hot nuts/bread crumbs/coconut shreds onto a plate—even the counter will do in a pinch—and spreading them into a thin layer to help them cool rapidly. –A.G.

⇒ BY MIYE BROMBERG, HANNAH CROWLEY & AMY GRAVES ⇐

HIGHLY RECOMMENDED	HIGHLY RECOMMENDED	HIGHLY RECOMMENDED	RECOMMENDED	RECOMMENDED WITH RESERVATIONS
MATFER Steel Non-Stick Fluted Tart Mold MODEL: 332225 PRICE: $27.00	**RÖSLE Fine-Mesh Strainer, Round Handle, 7.9 inches, 20 cm** MODEL: 95260 PRICE: $45.00	**MARCATO ATLAS 150 Wellness Pasta Machine** MODEL: 8845 PRICE: $69.25	**MESSERMEISTER 16.75-Inch Bamboo Knife Magnet** MODEL: KM-16/BB PRICE: $59.95	**FAGOR LUX Multicooker: Pressure Cooker, Slow Cooker, Rice Cooker and Yogurt Maker All-in-One** MODEL: 670041960 PRICE: $159.95

Tart Pans

Shallow, fluted tart pans can give a home baker's quiche or fruit tart a professional look. But does it matter which one you buy? To find out, we made a savory tomato tart with a pat-in-the-pan crust and a lemon tart with a pâte sucrée (traditional French sweet pastry) using five different models (some with traditional and some with nonstick finishes, all with removable bottoms) priced from $8.99 to $27.00.

While traditional-finish pans were slightly easier to work with when patting in the dough, the nonstick pans came out on top. Why? They released tarts more readily, and their dark surfaces made for deeper, more even browning. We also like pans with deeper grooves for more impressive fluted edges. Our winner, the Matfer Steel Non-Stick Fluted Tart Mold, was best in show in all categories. –A.G.

Fine-Mesh Strainers

Fine-mesh strainers are handy for rinsing, washing, straining, and sifting all types of ingredients. But what makes a good one? For starters, it's got to live up to its name. During our testing of six models (priced from $12.28 to $47.02), we found that two models didn't have fine mesh at all; their coarser weaves made for chunky—not smooth—purees and failed to separate the bran from whole-wheat flour. Through our testing, we discovered we preferred stiff mesh to mesh that was loose and floppy, as stiff mesh made it easier to push purees through with ladles or spatulas— a restaurant trick we often employ in the test kitchen. We also liked strainers with a capacity of at least 5 cups and large, durable hooks for full support over bowls and pots. Our favorite was the sturdy 5.5-cup Rösle Fine-Mesh Strainer, Round Handle, 7.9 inches, 20 cm ($45.00). It has very fine mesh, a wide hook that made it sit stably on all sorts of cookware, and a comfortable metal grip. –M.B.

Manual Pasta Machines

You can roll and cut fresh pasta by hand, but pasta machines make the process easier and the results more uniform. Pasta machines come in different sizes, but those built to accommodate pasta sheets that are 150 millimeters (about 6 inches) across are the most common. So we bought four hand-cranked models priced from $32.75 to $69.25 and used them to make fresh pasta sheets for ravioli, fettuccine, and angel hair.

All of the machines were simple to set up, clamped to the counter securely, and produced great pasta. But small design differences affected their ease of use. We preferred machines with knobs that required only one hand to adjust and with clear, accurate thickness markings. And we gave top marks to machines that could roll sheets into a wide range of thicknesses and cut pasta cleanly. One model emerged as our favorite: the Marcato Atlas 150 Wellness Pasta Machine, $69.25. –M.B.

Magnetic Knife Strips

Magnetic knife strips hold knives of all shapes and sizes without taking up valuable drawer or counter space. Since we last tested them, our favorite, from Messermeister, has been redesigned. To find out whether the revamped strip met our standards—and whether it stood up to new competition—we bought seven strips priced from $15.30 to $154.95 (including our redesigned winner), mounted them on a wall, and used them to hold our winning and Best Buy six-piece à la carte knife sets. We focused on strips that were between 15 and 18 inches long, the best size for most collections of essential knives.

A few features separated the best from the rest. First, we liked strips that were easy to install. Once they were mounted, we had a preference for thicker (at least ¾-inch) strips; models with slim profiles kept our knives too close to the wall, making it hard to grab the handles without scraping our knuckles. We liked models whose magnets were strong enough to hold all our knives securely but not so strong that we struggled to pry them off. Lastly, we preferred strips with full magnet coverage and strips that stood up to extended use without too much scuffing and scarring. Our redesigned former winner, the Messermeister Bamboo Knife Magnet, $59.95, came out on top once again. –M.B.

Multicookers

Maybe you've heard the buzz surrounding multicookers, a new category of appliance that promises to do everything your skillet, slow cooker, pressure cooker, and rice cooker can do. Buy one of these, the reasoning goes, and you have no need for any of that other gear. To find out if the buzz is justified, we purchased five such machines priced from $99.99 to $249.95 and tested them against our equipment winner in each category: We slow-cooked pot roast and chicken in sauce; pressure-cooked dried beans and a meaty tomato sauce; made white and brown rice; and sautéed onions. In the end, none of the multicookers produced food that was as good as the food cooked in our winning appliances—and in several cases, the food was awful. What's more, many of the machines had confusing (and sometimes annoying) instructions and controls, further pushing them out of our good graces. We love the idea of multicookers and will monitor the market in hopes that their performance will one day catch up to their promise. We can recommend only one model—but with reservations: The Fagor Lux Multicooker ($159.95) was fairly intuitive to use and performed the best at cooking white and brown rice, but it faltered with pressure cooking and sautéing. –H.C.

For complete testing results, go to CooksIllustrated.com/apr17.

INDEX
March & April 2017

BONUS ONLINE CONTENT
*More recipes, reviews, and videos are available
at* **CooksIllustrated.com/apr17**

RECIPES
Sautéed Baby Bok Choy with Miso Sauce
Sautéed Baby Bok Choy with Shallot and
   Fish Sauce

EXPANDED REVIEWS
Tasting Firm Tofu
Testing Fine-Mesh Strainers
Testing Magnetic Knife Strips
Testing Manual Pasta Machines
Testing Multicookers
Testing Silicone Spatulas
Testing Tart Pans

⏵ RECIPE VIDEOS
Want to see how to make any of the recipes
in this issue? There's a free video for that.

BONUS VIDEOS
Grilled Salmon Fillets
Oven-Roasted Salmon
Pan-Seared Salmon
Poached Salmon with Herb and Caper
   Vinaigrette

FOLLOW US ON SOCIAL MEDIA
facebook.com/CooksIllustrated
twitter.com/TestKitchen
pinterest.com/TestKitchen
google.com/+AmericasTestKitchen
instagram.com/CooksIllustrated
youtube.com/AmericasTestKitchen

Simple Stovetop Macaroni and Cheese, 9

Tuscan Shrimp and Beans, 21

Sautéed Baby Bok Choy, 20

Deli Rye Bread, 15

One-Hour Broiled Chicken and Pan Sauce, 5

Chocolate Sheet Cake, 23

Better Hash Browns, 19

Greek Chicken and Rice Soup with Lemon, 13

Perfect Poached Eggs, 11

Pub-Style Steak and Ale Pie, 7

PHOTOGRAPHY: CARL TREMBLAY; STYLING: MARIE PIRAINO AND SALLY STAUB

Sunflower
Greens

Alfalfa
Sprouts

Mung Bean
Sprouts

Radish
Sprouts

Micro
Arugula

Broccoli
Sprouts

Pea Shoots

Micro Clover

SPROUTS
AND
MICROGREENS

Introducing Risi e Bisi

Brothier than risotto but thicker than soup, this Venetian classic requires a not-so-gentle touch.

⇛ BY STEVE DUNN ⇚

Venetians have a centuries-old tradition of dishing up *risi e bisi* (rice and peas) every April 25, St. Mark's Day, to celebrate spring's first peas and to honor the importance of rice production in the Veneto region. Thinner than a traditional risotto yet thicker than soup, the dish's unique consistency and fresh flavors make it the ideal ambassador for the season: a light and vibrant—yet still satisfying—escape from heavier winter fare.

The classic version is made with arborio rice and fresh spring peas along with onion, garlic, Parmesan cheese, and pancetta. Most recipes adhere to the long-established risotto method of vigorously stirring broth into the rice in multiple additions. Extra broth is then poured in at the end to create something looser than a creamy risotto.

Since my goal was not to create a rich, velvety consistency, I was fairly certain I could jettison the laborious stirring routine and simply cook the dish more like a soup. I was right. I sautéed finely chopped pancetta, onion, and garlic until the meat rendered its fat and the onion turned translucent; added the rice; poured in hot broth all at once; brought the mixture to a boil; and then let it simmer, adding the peas and Parmesan last.

I then focused on the peas. Since fresh pea season is fleeting at best, I'd have to rely on the frozen kind. Stirring them in thawed at the end of cooking, just to warm them through, was key to preserve their texture and verdant color. I also sought out petite peas, which were noticeably sweeter and more tender than full-size peas.

As for the broth, recipes are divided on whether to use chicken or vegetable. I conducted a few tests, ultimately finding that chicken broth diluted with water struck just the right balance of savoriness and lightness. Unfortunately, the consistency of the broth itself was too thin. I tried adding a few pats of butter, but this masked the dish's delicate flavors.

Risi e bisi is the no-fail alternative to risotto.

I realized that my hands-off approach was freeing little starch from the rice. Maybe I needed to stir the rice after all? Indeed, aggressively whisking just before adding the peas and Parmesan loosened just enough starch to lightly thicken the broth.

And with that, I gave this simple supper a final nod to spring, adding a spritz of lemon juice and a sprinkle of minced fresh parsley.

RISI E BISI
SERVES 4 TO 6

We use frozen petite peas here, but regular frozen peas can be substituted, if desired. For the proper consistency, make sure to cook the rice at a gentle boil. Our favorite arborio rice is from RiceSelect.

- 4 cups chicken broth
- 1½ cups water
- 3 tablespoons extra-virgin olive oil
- 2 ounces pancetta, chopped fine
- 1 onion, chopped fine
- 2 garlic cloves, minced
- 1 cup arborio rice
- 2 cups frozen petite peas, thawed
- 1 ounce Parmesan cheese, grated (½ cup), plus extra for serving
- 3 tablespoons minced fresh parsley
- 1 teaspoon lemon juice, plus lemon wedges for serving
   Salt and pepper

1. Bring broth and water to boil in large saucepan over high heat. Remove from heat and cover to keep warm.

2. Cook oil and pancetta in Dutch oven over medium-low heat until pancetta is browned and rendered, 5 to 7 minutes. Add onion and cook, stirring frequently, until softened, 4 to 5 minutes. Add garlic and cook until fragrant, about 30 seconds. Add rice and stir to coat, about 1 minute.

3. Add 5 cups broth mixture, increase heat to high, and bring to boil. Reduce heat to medium-low, cover, and boil gently until rice is tender but not mushy, about 15 minutes, stirring every 5 minutes to ensure that rice is gently boiling.

4. Remove pot from heat and whisk rice vigorously until broth has thickened slightly, 15 seconds. Stir in peas, Parmesan, parsley, and lemon juice. Season with salt and pepper to taste. Adjust consistency with remaining ½ cup broth mixture as needed. Serve, passing extra Parmesan and lemon wedges separately.

Getting the Right Consistency

The consistency of *risi e bisi* is thinner than risotto but thicker than soup: It's lightly thickened yet still fluid. The proper texture is easy to achieve by using a 5:1 ratio of liquid to rice and vigorously whisking toward the end of cooking to free enough starch from the rice to give the broth body.

RISOTTO
Too thick

SOUP
Too thin

RISI E BISI
Just right

▶ **See the Proper Technique**
A step-by-step video is available at CooksIllustrated.com/june17

Olive Oil Cake

Repurpose one of your favorite savory ingredients for a cake that's light yet plush and simple yet sophisticated.

⇒ BY ANDREA GEARY ⇐

New England, where I've lived for most of my life, is not known for its vast and fruitful olive groves. Maybe that's why I only recently learned about olive oil cake, which is commonplace in most traditional olive-producing regions of the world.

That said, I've made plenty of cakes with neutral-flavored vegetable oil. Though most people associate cake with butter, oil is a good choice for simple snack cakes and quick breads because it provides moisture, tenderness, and richness without calling attention to itself. It also makes the mixing process simpler (more on this in a minute). But extra-virgin olive oil, the type I kept seeing called for in recipes for olive oil cake, can be noticeably grassy, peppery, and even a little bitter. That's welcome in a salad, but I was skeptical about how it would work in cake, so I made a few versions.

I happily discovered that the slightly savory notes of olive oil can, in fact, lend appealing complexity to a cake. But there's no definitive version. Some cakes had a lot of oil and a correspondingly assertive flavor and rich, dense crumb; others included only a modest amount of oil and were light and spongy, and the flavor was so faint that they might as well have been made with vegetable oil. Still others had so many additional ingredients—apples, spices, loads of citrus—that the oil's flavor was obscured.

And that's fair enough. I suspect that such recipes originated not to showcase olive oil but because people wanted cake, they needed fat to make it, and the local olive oil was the fat they had on hand. But I have my choice of fats, so if I was going to be using extra-virgin olive oil in my cake, I wanted to be able to taste it, at least a bit. I didn't want sponge-cake austerity or dense decadence but something between the two. I wanted a cake that offered some intrigue but was at the same time simple, something I could enjoy with a cup of tea.

● Andrea Will Demonstrate
A step-by-step video is available at CooksIllustrated.com/june17

This simple, not-too-sweet cake lets the flavor of the olive oil come through, with just a little lemon zest accentuating the oil's fruitiness.

Crumb Quandary

One of the most attractive aspects of making a cake with oil rather than butter is the way it expedites the mixing process: There's no waiting for butter to come to room temperature and then beating it with sugar before you even start to add the rest of the ingredients. With many oil-based cakes, you simply whisk the dry ingredients in one bowl, whisk the wet ingredients in another, and then combine the contents of the two bowls.

So that's where I started. The dry ingredients were all-purpose flour, baking powder, and salt, and the wet ingredients were eggs, milk, the test kitchen's favorite supermarket olive oil (see "Use a Good Oil"), plus the sugar. The batter was ready to go into the oven in 5 minutes flat, and the cake came out just 40 minutes later.

This first attempt was easy to make but not easy to love. The crumb was dry and coarse, and I could detect the olive oil flavor only if I thought about it really, really hard. As for the appearance, I was okay with simplicity, but this cake looked uninvitingly

plain. What I really wanted was the kind of even, fine crumb that the best butter cakes have. The problem? That texture is largely due to their being made with butter.

In a butter cake, air is whipped into the butter before it's mixed with the other ingredients. In the heat of the oven, the baking powder creates carbon dioxide, which inflates those bubbles a bit more. Those tiny bubbles are what make a butter cake fluffy and fine-textured.

But I wasn't without options for producing a similar effect in my oil cake. Although most oil cakes use the "mix wet, mix dry, and combine" method, chiffon cake is an oil cake that's mixed a bit differently. Its light and fluffy texture is achieved by whipping egg whites with some sugar to form a foam, which you then fold into the batter. Might that approach work for my olive oil cake?

I applied the chiffon method to my recipe and, at the same time, implemented a couple of ingredient adjustments: I increased the eggs from two to three for better lift and the olive oil from ½ cup to ¾ cup for more richness and moisture and a more pronounced flavor. The batter was promisingly airy and mousse-like. The cake rose impressively in the oven—but it fell when it cooled. And when I cut it open, there was a line of dense, collapsed cake in the middle.

Don't Panic When It Puffs

Sprinkling sugar on top of this cake creates a crackly-sweet crust once the cake has cooled. It will puff up during baking, but don't worry. This is just air released by the cake batter getting trapped beneath the layer of melted sugar. It will settle once it cools.

It turned out that the batter was too airy to support all the fat; it essentially overextended itself. But I was happy with the more pronounced olive oil flavor, so I was reluctant to back down. Providing more support by switching to a tube pan, the vessel of choice for chiffon cakes, could help, but frankly I didn't want my olive oil cake to be mistaken for chiffon. Instead, I'd adjust the mixing method.

Going All In

If whipped egg whites were too airy, maybe whipping yolks, which aren't as good at holding air, would be better. I did a quick test, but the cake came out dense and squat. Whipping whole eggs, I hoped, would be the solution. I put all three eggs, both whites and yolks, in the mixer bowl with the sugar and whipped the mixture for about 4 minutes, until it was pale and airy. I added the rest of the ingredients, including a tiny bit of lemon zest to accentuate the fruitiness of the olive oil. After pouring the batter into the cake pan, I sprinkled the top liberally with granulated sugar to lend some visual appeal and textural contrast.

The whipped whole eggs did indeed provide just the right amount of lift, creating a crumb that was fine but not dense and light but not spongy. (For more on how whipping eggs impacts cake, see "Aerating Cake with Eggs.") The sugar on top had coalesced into an attractively crackly crust that complemented the cake's plush texture, and the lemon zest supported the olive oil flavor without overwhelming it.

And there's one more advantage to my olive oil cake: Because it's made with liquid fat instead of solid, it will keep longer than its butter-based counterparts (see "A Real Keeper"). It can be stored at room temperature for up to three days—in the unlikely event that it doesn't get eaten right away.

OLIVE OIL CAKE
SERVES 8 TO 10

For the best flavor, use a fresh, high-quality extra-virgin olive oil. Our favorite supermarket option is California Olive Ranch Everyday Extra Virgin Olive Oil. If your springform pan is prone to leaking, place a rimmed baking sheet on the oven floor to catch any drips. Leftover cake can be wrapped in plastic wrap and stored at room temperature for up to three days.

- 1¾ cups (8¾ ounces) all-purpose flour
- 1 teaspoon baking powder
- ¾ teaspoon salt
- 3 large eggs
- 1¼ cups (8¾ ounces) plus 2 tablespoons sugar
- ¼ teaspoon grated lemon zest
- ¾ cup extra-virgin olive oil
- ¾ cup milk

1. Adjust oven rack to middle position and heat oven to 350 degrees. Grease 9-inch springform pan. Whisk flour, baking powder, and salt together in bowl.

2. Using stand mixer fitted with whisk attachment, whip eggs on medium speed until foamy, about 1 minute. Add 1¼ cups sugar and lemon zest, increase speed to high, and whip until mixture is fluffy and pale yellow, about 3 minutes. Reduce speed to medium and, with mixer running, slowly pour in oil. Mix until oil is fully incorporated, about 1 minute. Add half of flour mixture and mix on low speed until incorporated, about 1 minute, scraping down bowl as needed. Add milk and mix until combined, about 30 seconds. Add remaining flour mixture and mix until just incorporated, about 1 minute, scraping down bowl as needed.

3. Transfer batter to prepared pan; sprinkle remaining 2 tablespoons sugar over entire surface. Bake until cake is deep golden brown and toothpick inserted in center comes out with few crumbs attached, 40 to 45 minutes. Transfer pan to wire rack and let cool for 15 minutes. Remove side of pan and let cake cool completely, about 1½ hours. Cut into wedges and serve.

Use a Good Oil
Our goal was a cake with a subtle but noticeable savory, complex flavor imparted by the oil. While there's no need to splurge on a premium extra-virgin olive oil, spring for a good supermarket product such as our favorite from California Olive Ranch. A cheap supermarket EVOO won't deliver enough character.

A Real Keeper
Unlike butter cakes, which start to taste dry just a day after baking, oil-based cakes and tea breads can taste moist for several days. This is an illusion, since over time the starches in both types of cakes retrograde, or stale and harden into a crystalline structure, and this structure traps water within the crystals. A cake made with butter, which is solid at room temperature, will seem drier. But oil, which is liquid at room temperature, acts to retard retrogradation, causing even a days-old cake to seem moist even though it's actually not.

BUTTER CAKE
Dry and crumbly the day after it's baked

OIL CAKE
Seems moist and tender three days after baking

SCIENCE Aerating Cake with Eggs
While butter cakes get their lift from air that's whipped into the butter, our olive oil cake relies on eggs. Whipped whites might be the first thing to come to mind, but you can also whip just yolks or whole eggs. We tried all three in our cake. Whipped whites made it too airy, and our cake collapsed somewhat. Whipped yolks made a squat, dense cake. Whipping whole eggs was the perfect compromise. But why?

The proteins in egg whites are better at unfurling and creating a foam than the proteins in egg yolks are, so whipped whites will be more voluminous than whipped whole eggs and certainly more voluminous than whipped yolks. But the oil in this batter is a factor, too. Oil molecules are able to displace some egg white proteins in whipped whites, which weakens the bubbles. Yolks offer some protection against this; their emulsifiers help keep the oil from interfering with the structure. Thus, whipped whole eggs are the perfect compromise because they provide some lift from the whites as well as a more stable structure from the yolks.

JUST WHITES
Ultrafluffy egg whites made a cake that was too airy and collapsed.

JUST YOLKS
Unable to hold much air, egg yolks made a squat, dense cake.

WHOLE EGGS
Whipping whole eggs provided structure and just enough lift.

Napa Cabbage Slaws

Could we maintain napa cabbage's delicate texture but not end up with a soupy slaw?

≥ BY KEITH DRESSER ≤

While traditional green cabbage has long been the favorite for making coleslaw, napa cabbage is a great alternative. Its crinkly, thin leaves have a more tender texture and a sweeter flavor that can put a new spin on the picnic classic. While our traditional slaw recipes call for salting the cabbage to draw out excess liquid and soften the dense leaves, I wanted to retain napa cabbage's delicate texture. I found that even a brief salting made the shreds too limp, so I decided to skip it. But simply tossing the shredded cabbage with dressing didn't work either; I ended up with a waterlogged, bland slaw. It turns out that what gives napa cabbage its appealing tenderness—thinner, weaker cell walls—is also a liability. It will leach twice as much water as regular cabbage.

To handle the extra moisture, I needed to make a more potent dressing. I mixed up a bracing dressing of 3 parts vinegar to 1 part oil. But when I tossed the shredded cabbage with this mixture, I was surprised to find that the slaw still tasted too watered-down and bland. Our science editor told me what was happening: Vinegar was breaking down the cell walls of the cabbage, causing water to escape and the leaves to wilt.

I had an idea: Why not simmer the vinegar before incorporating it into the dressing? This cooked off some of the vinegar's water so that the water leached by the cabbage would then reconstitute it.

With that in mind, I reduced ⅓ cup of vinegar to 3 tablespoons and proceeded as before. After letting the dressed shreds sit for 5 minutes, I had a slaw that was the best yet. However, simmering had driven off some of the vinegar's volatile compounds, so it tasted a bit flat. Reducing the vinegar even further, to 2 tablespoons, and adding 1 tablespoon of fresh vinegar delivered potent, bright flavor.

I was getting close, but the slaw still seemed too lean. Adding more oil to the dressing would only make it greasy, so I considered add-ins, settling on toasted sesame seeds. They lent a nutty richness that didn't weigh down the slaw. Grated carrots contributed earthy sweetness and color while thinly sliced scallions added another layer of flavor.

From here, I created a few variations so that I'd have a slaw to pair with almost any meal.

▶ **See Our Slaw Solution**
A step-by-step video is available at CooksIllustrated.com/june17

The key to intense, bright flavor is cooking down some of the vinegar.

NAPA CABBAGE SLAW WITH CARROTS AND SESAME
SERVES 4 TO 6

This slaw is best served within an hour of being dressed. For information on shopping for napa cabbage, see page 29. Use the large holes of a box grater to prepare the carrots. Our recipes for Napa Cabbage Slaw with Snow Peas and Mint and Spicy Napa Cabbage Slaw with Red Bell Pepper are available free for four months at CooksIllustrated.com/june17.

⅓ cup white wine vinegar
2 teaspoons toasted sesame oil
2 teaspoons vegetable oil
1 tablespoon rice vinegar
1 tablespoon soy sauce
1 tablespoon sugar
1 teaspoon grated fresh ginger
¼ teaspoon salt
1 small head napa cabbage, sliced thin (9 cups)
2 carrots, peeled and grated
4 scallions, sliced thin on bias
¼ cup sesame seeds, toasted

1. Bring white wine vinegar to simmer in small saucepan over medium heat; cook until reduced to 2 tablespoons, 4 to 6 minutes. Transfer white wine vinegar to large bowl and let cool completely, about 10 minutes. Whisk in sesame oil, vegetable oil, rice vinegar, soy sauce, sugar, ginger, and salt.

2. When ready to serve, add cabbage and carrots to dressing and toss to coat. Let stand for 5 minutes. Add scallions and sesame seeds and toss to combine. Serve.

NAPA CABBAGE SLAW WITH APPLE AND WALNUTS

Omit sesame oil and increase vegetable oil to 4 teaspoons. Omit soy sauce and ginger. Substitute cider vinegar for rice vinegar. Decrease sugar to 2 teaspoons and increase salt to ¾ teaspoon. Substitute 2 celery ribs, sliced thin on bias, and 1 grated Fuji apple for carrots. Substitute 3 tablespoons minced fresh chives for scallions and ½ cup walnuts, toasted and chopped fine, for sesame seeds.

NAPA CABBAGE SLAW WITH JÍCAMA AND PEPITAS

Omit sesame oil and increase vegetable oil to 4 teaspoons. Omit soy sauce. Substitute lime juice for rice vinegar, honey for sugar, and ½ teaspoon ground coriander for ginger. Increase salt to ¾ teaspoon. Substitute 1 seeded and minced jalapeño for ginger. Substitute 6 ounces jícama, peeled and grated, for carrots. Substitute ¼ cup coarsely chopped fresh cilantro for scallions and ½ cup roasted and salted pepitas, chopped fine, for sesame seeds.

TECHNIQUE

HOW TO SLICE NAPA CABBAGE

Unlike the tightly packed heads of regular cabbage, which require coring to release the leaves, napa cabbage leaves come away from the core with just a slight tug.

Trim base. Stack several leaves and cut thin crosswise. Repeat stacking and cutting for entire head.

Testing Fire Extinguishers

When you have only seconds to put out a kitchen fire, you want an extinguisher that's easy to use and effective. We were shocked at how many aren't.

≥ BY LISA McMANUS ≤

Unattended cooking is the primary source of fire-related injuries and household fires in America; more than $1.1 billion in property damages are claimed each year. Neglecting a pan of hot oil or leaving a dish towel too close to a burner are all-too-easy ways to find yourself suddenly facing fire. And fire spreads fast—experts say you have less than 2 minutes before a fire will be out of control.

That's why it's wise to always keep a fire extinguisher within easy reach of your stove. But the big trouble with most fire extinguishers is that you can't practice with them or give them a test run in the store; once the trigger punctures the pressurized canister, they can't be used a second time. So how do you know which one is the best for the job—one that will absolutely easy to use, even with no prior experience, and will work fast when seconds count?

To find out, we bought eight models of home fire extinguishers and drove to a firefighter training facility west of Boston to test them on staged cooking-related fires. Under the supervision of Deputy Chief John F. Sullivan and Captain Robert Hassett of the Worcester Fire Department, we set up shop in the department's "burn building," a blackened concrete structure behind the fire station. With a stack of 10-inch skillets, a dozen cotton dish towels, portable electric burners, and a jug of vegetable oil, we set a series of typical kitchen fires and went about trying to put them out.

Choose Your Weapon

The fire extinguisher market offers a bewildering array of products designed to combat specific types of fires, whether they start in a restaurant deep fryer, in a tractor-trailer, or on a boat. For home cooks, the choice is a little simpler. In this category, fire extinguishers break down into two main types. Those with an "ABC" rating are known as "multipurpose" extinguishers, meaning they can tackle (A) cloth, wood, and paper; (B) flammable liquids and gases, such as grease and gasoline; and (C) electrical fires. "BC"-rated extinguishers cover only the latter two categories. Both types work similarly: When you squeeze the trigger, a chamber inside the pressurized canister is punctured and a spray of fire-suppressing material is propelled. (For more information, see "How to Use a Fire Extinguisher.") For our testing, we chose two ABC and two BC models. The ability to extinguish cloth fires (dish towels, potholders, etc.) is a priority, but BC extinguishers are often sold as "kitchen" extinguishers, which implies that

Clockwise from top left: The Worcester Fire Department's "burn building"; the weak spray of an aerosol-style extinguisher in action; a traditional model creates a huge cloud; starting a fire on our makeshift stovetop; the testing lineup; Lisa McManus with Lt. Annmarie Pickett of the Worcester Fire Department.

they are still up to the task. Plus, a BC extinguisher took first place in our previous testing. We stuck with the smallest size since bigger isn't better—you want something most people can easily lift and use.

Since manufacturers also offer solutions beyond traditional extinguishers, we tried a variety of these, too, including two sprays sold in aerosol-style cans, a fire blanket meant for throwing over and smothering fires, and one "automatic" extinguishing system called the StoveTop FireStop Rangehood, which resembles a pair of Sterno cans that attach via magnet or adhesive to your hood or to the bottom of a cabinet or microwave over your stovetop. When they detect fire, the company claims, the cans automatically burst open, spraying your rangetop with fire suppressant—hands-free, no experience necessary.

If that proved to be true, we reasoned, it could be a great solution.

Fighting Fire

For our first round of tests, we started a grease fire by encouraging a flame to burn in a skillet filled with ¼ cup of vegetable oil. As soon as the flames spread over the pan, I picked up a fire extinguisher and, working as quickly as I could, figured out how to use it and shot it toward the flaming pan. For the second round of tests, we left a cotton dish towel next to an electric burner with one corner just touching the coils. As soon as it caught fire, I went into action.

It took anywhere from 11 seconds to 27 seconds to figure out how to use the products in our lineup. An odd cap on one traditional extinguisher slowed me

How to Use a Fire Extinguisher

Traditional fire extinguishers all work in a similar fashion. Usually a small gauge on top of the extinguisher points to green if the extinguisher has enough pressure to spray. (If the gauge points to red, it's time to buy a new extinguisher.) If a fire breaks out, stand 4 to 6 feet back and PASS.

PULL: Pull the pin.

AIM: Aim low, pointing the extinguisher nozzle (or its horn or hose) at the base of the fire.

SQUEEZE: Squeeze the handle to release the extinguishing agent.

SWEEP: Sweep the spray from side to side to cover the fire until it is out.

Up in Flames: What Went Wrong

We tested several options beyond traditional extinguishers, but none measured up. Here are a few in action.

NO CAN DO
StoveTop FireStop Rangehood
Flames literally had to lick the canister to engage it.

TOO CLOSE FOR COMFORT
FireAway Fire Blanket
You don't know if the fire is out unless you lift the blanket to check.

A FLAIR FOR FLARE-UPS
Fire Gone Fire Suppressant
Flames flared dramatically when hit with this aerosol spray.

---

down. Another can-style model was so covered with colors, busy images, and words that it was impossible to scan quickly for the essential information. A third model's trigger was unmarked. The fire blanket may have been simple—remove from pouch, unfold, walk toward fire, and drop it on—but it was a little scary to get so close to the fire. Our favorite extinguishers had unambiguous, clearly marked, exposed triggers or buttons that we could find and operate without losing time (or getting too close to the fire). As for the automatic canister, our only job was to wait and watch. And wait, and wait. In fact, when used as instructed, this model never went off, despite flames nearly reaching the canister.

Once we had the extinguishers going, effectiveness varied dramatically from model to model. It took anywhere from just 2 seconds to 1 minute and 22 seconds to put out fires. When weak spurts of drippy foam from one can hit the fire, the flames suddenly became a tower several feet high. Though this was terrifying, I stood my ground and kept spraying until the flames finally subsided. One model shut down both types of fire instantly with a powerful, controlled spray, but it filled the room with a choking cloud of chemicals that sent us running for the exit. A few models seemed to put out the fire, but then, seconds later, the flames flickered back to life. One seemingly promising extinguisher quickly and easily put out the grease fire, but when we picked up a fresh copy to put out the burning dish towel, it completely failed to operate. Some models (including one of the BC extinguishers) worked well on grease but didn't fully extinguish the burning towels. The biggest disappointment was the StoveTop FireStop system. Meant to attach to your hood and hang at least 27 inches above the burners, the canisters simply didn't work until we lowered them to a mere 15 inches above the pan and flames literally touched the canisters to ignite the wick, which turns out to be the mechanism for setting them off. At this point, the fire is likely to have spread well beyond the stovetop.

The Best Weapon

After we evaluated each extinguisher's effectiveness on both grease and cloth fires, taking into account how intuitive it was to use and how quickly it put out the fires, we were surprised—and disappointed, given the stakes—that we had only one extinguisher we could highly recommend. The rest we could recommend only with reservations or not at all. Our winner, the Kidde ABC Multipurpose Home Fire Extinguisher ($25.99), was fast and thorough. Its design was simple and obvious, with a basic trigger and nozzle and easy-to-read pressure gauge that clearly shows if your canister is ready to keep you safe. While it created a cloud of fumes (like many other models) and left residue that was a bit harder to clean up than some of the others, we can live with that. It left no question that the fire was out, every time.

We tested eight fire extinguishers, including four traditional pressurized canisters, two aerosol sprays, one fire blanket, and a self-operating canister that attaches to the hood over a stove. In two separate rounds of testing, we allowed vegetable oil to catch fire in a hot skillet and a dish towel to ignite from touching a lit burner. We used the extinguishers to put out these fires, timing the results and rating the extinguishers on ease of use, performance, and, to a lesser extent, cleanup. Scores from both tests were combined to reach our final ranking. Information about fire suppressant material in extinguishers was provided by manufacturers. Models were purchased online and appear in order of preference.

TIME TO UNDERSTAND OPERATION
Time elapsed between when we picked up the product and when we began using it.

TIMES TO PUT OUT GREASE AND TOWEL FIRES
Time elapsed between when we started spraying/smothering the fires and when the fires were extinguished.

EASE OF USE
We evaluated how simple and intuitive the extinguishers were to operate, taking into account that we were working quickly, under pressure, with no preparation (to simulate a real fire emergency).

PERFORMANCE
Models that extinguished both types of fire quickly and thoroughly rated highest.

CLEANUP
Extinguishers that produced less mess and fumes rated higher, although we gave more weight in our ranking to their performance and ease of use.

▶ **Watch Lisa in Action**
A free video available is available at CooksIllustrated.com/june17

TESTING FIRE EXTINGUISHERS

KEY

GOOD ★ ★ ★
FAIR ★ ★
POOR ★

HIGHLY RECOMMENDED

KIDDE ABC Multipurpose Home Fire Extinguisher

MODEL: FA110

PRICE: $25.99

TYPE: ABC

EASE OF USE: ★ ★ ★

PERFORMANCE: ★ ★ ★

CLEANUP: ★ ½

SUPPRESSANT: Monoammonium phosphate

TIME TO UNDERSTAND OPERATION: 15 sec

TIME TO PUT OUT GREASE FIRE: 2 sec

TIME TO PUT OUT TOWEL FIRE: 2 sec

COMMENTS: Fast and very effective, this extinguisher really works. Its powerful spray put out both the grease fire and the towel fire right away, though it left a big cloud of fumes each time. It also left a greenish foam on the burner and pan that took some effort to wipe off.

RECOMMENDED WITH RESERVATIONS

FIRST ALERT Tundra Fire Extinguishing Spray

MODEL: AF400

PRICE: $23.88

TYPE: Aerosol spray

SUPPRESSANT: Potassium lactate

EASE OF USE: ★ ★ ★

PERFORMANCE: ★ ★

CLEANUP: ★ ★

TIME TO UNDERSTAND OPERATION: 11 sec

TIME TO PUT OUT GREASE FIRE: 2 sec*

TIME TO PUT OUT TOWEL FIRE: 3 sec*

COMMENTS: This simple aerosol spray was easy to figure out, and it quickly put out the grease fire. But then, alarmingly, we saw a flare-up after we thought the fire was out, forcing us to spray a second time to eliminate the flames. The same happened with the burning towel. The small cloud of fumes it generated went away fairly quickly, and this lightweight canister is easier to handle than bigger traditional extinguishers, but the spray residue gunked up our stove surface.

AMEREX 2.5 lb ABC Dry Chemical Fire Extinguisher

MODEL: B417

PRICE: $41.13

TYPE: ABC

EASE OF USE: ★ ★ ★

PERFORMANCE: ★ ★ ½

CLEANUP: ★

SUPPRESSANT: Monoammonium phosphate

TIME TO UNDERSTAND OPERATION: 15 sec

TIME TO PUT OUT GREASE FIRE: 2 sec

TIME TO PUT OUT TOWEL FIRE: 5 sec

COMMENTS: While this extinguisher quickly and thoroughly put out the grease fire, it also emitted a cloud of chemical fumes that smelled bad and sent testers running out of the building. One big problem with our second test: The powerful spray knocked the towel right off the stovetop. (Luckily, in our case, it was extinguished first.) Residue stuck to the pan and burner and was difficult to wipe off.

FIREAWAY Fire Blanket

MODEL: 3x3 Small

PRICE: $30.00

TYPE: Blanket

EASE OF USE: ★ ½

PERFORMANCE: ★ ★

CLEANUP: ★ ★ ★

SUPPRESSANT: Fire retardant–coated fiberglass yarn

TIME TO UNDERSTAND OPERATION: 22 sec

TIME TO PUT OUT GREASE FIRE: 11 sec

TIME TO PUT OUT TOWEL FIRE: 1 min, 22 sec

COMMENTS: There's a fear factor to get over when smothering fires with a blanket, but this blanket put out fires, albeit slowly. But you don't really know if the fire is out without lifting the blanket to check, which lets in air that can restart the fire. The blanket was much more effective when it could lie flat over the rim of the burning pan; the lumpy towel continued burning for a long time because air was able to get in. Cleanup was a snap—nearly unscorched, the blanket was ready to use again. It's a good backup to other fire suppression gear, but it's not our top choice.

*Time noted reflects the initial suppression of fire. We didn't time the suppression of surprise flare-ups.

NOT RECOMMENDED

KIDDE RESSP Kitchen Fire Extinguisher

MODEL: RESSP

PRICE: $24.49

TYPE: BC

EASE OF USE: ★ ★

PERFORMANCE: ★ ★

CLEANUP: ★ ★

SUPPRESSANT: Sodium bicarbonate

TIME TO UNDERSTAND OPERATION: 22 sec

TIME TO PUT OUT GREASE FIRE: 4 sec

TIME TO PUT OUT TOWEL FIRE: 5 sec*

COMMENTS: A brief struggle to figure out the trigger wasted some time, but once it was going, this model was very effective on the grease fire and easy to control. But, living up to its BC rating, it didn't work as well on the towel. It extinguished the fire after 5 seconds, so we stopped timing, but the fire reignited a few seconds later. It created a huge cloud and a lot of powder, but residue was easy to clean.

FIRE GONE Fire Suppressant

MODEL: FG-007-102

PRICE: $12.44

TYPE: Aerosol spray, ABC

EASE OF USE: ★ ½

PERFORMANCE: ★

CLEANUP: ★ ★ ★

SUPPRESSANT: AFFF, or aqueous film-forming foam. Water-based.

TIME TO UNDERSTAND OPERATION: 13 sec

TIME TO PUT OUT GREASE FIRE: 9 sec

TIME TO PUT OUT TOWEL FIRE: 5 sec*

COMMENTS: Flames flared up in a terrifying way when we hit them with this spray. We kept spraying, and the fire eventually went out, but it took much longer than with our top performers. Busy, bright labeling slowed us down as we tried to find the instructions; we eventually gave up, sprayed, and hoped for the best. It never fully put out the towel fire. On the plus side, the loose, watery foam was easy to clean up.

FIRST ALERT Kitchen Fire Extinguisher UL Rated 5-B:C

MODEL: KFE2S5

PRICE: $24.72

TYPE: BC

EASE OF USE: ★ ½

PERFORMANCE: ★

CLEANUP: ★ ★ ★

SUPPRESSANT: Sodium bicarbonate, talc, magnesium aluminum silicate, methyl hydrogen polysiloxane, and blue pigment

TIME TO UNDERSTAND OPERATION: 27 sec

TOTAL TIME TO PUT OUT GREASE FIRE: 2 sec

TOTAL TIME TO PUT OUT TOWEL FIRE: Extinguisher failed to work

COMMENTS: An unusual cap slowed us down, but once it was operating, this extinguisher was astonishingly fast (just 2 seconds to put out the grease fire), with a controlled spray. It didn't leave a cloud of fumes, and residue wiped right off. But when we grabbed a fresh copy of this model to put out the towel fire, it would not spray; the brand-new extinguisher had somehow lost pressure and was useless—a fatal flaw.

STOVETOP FIRESTOP Rangehood

MODEL: 679-3D

PRICE: $56.95 for two canisters (need both over a stove)

TYPE: Automatic

EASE OF USE: ★ ★

PERFORMANCE: n/a

CLEANUP: ★

SUPPRESSANT: Proprietary, nontoxic fire-suppressing powder blend (similar to baking soda)

TIME TO UNDERSTAND OPERATION: n/a

TOTAL TIME TO PUT OUT GREASE FIRE: Extinguisher failed to work

TOTAL TIME TO PUT OUT TOWEL FIRE: Extinguisher failed to work

COMMENTS: When we set this device 27 inches above our skillet, the shortest distance recommended, the oil caught fire and burned high, and the FireStop never started. At 24 inches, it still didn't start. After lowering it to just 15 inches above the stovetop, we finally heard a pop after 3 minutes of flames, and a pile of powder dropped into the pan. The dish towel test was also a failure. It turns out that fire must physically light a tiny wick; by the time that happens, the whole house could be in flames.

Another Big Cheese in Our Kitchen

The right Gruyère is buttery and complex, is pleasantly firm and dense, and melts like a champ. If you aren't buying it, you should be.

≥ BY KATE SHANNON ≤

What most Americans think of as "Swiss cheese" is the mild, holey stuff called Emmentaler. That cheese is fine for slicing thin and piling on ham sandwiches, but it bears little resemblance to its fellow citizen, Gruyère. The latter, which has been made in the eponymous alpine region of Switzerland for more than 900 years, is pleasantly firm and dense, slightly crumbly, and boasts that faint crystalline crunch that high-quality aged cheeses such as cheddar and Parmesan are known for. Good versions taste deeply nutty and have sweet, fruity tang; nice salinity; and a good bit of earthy funk. Gruyère is also one of a very few cheeses, Swiss or otherwise, that functions just as well in cooked applications as it does on a cheese plate. Scan the test kitchen's recipe archive and you'll find roughly 100 recipes featuring it—from breads, soufflés, frittatas, and gratins to scrambled eggs, mashed potatoes, fondue, and French onion soup.

As Gruyère's stateside popularity has grown over the years, so, too, has its availability in American supermarkets. When we shopped recently, we found eight nationally available options, priced from $14.99 to $23.99 per pound. Five were Swiss imports bearing the *Appellation d'Origine Protégée* (AOP) seal, meaning they were made according to strict government-mandated rules and quality standards. The other three were domestic facsimiles; two of those, both made by Emmi Roth, stopped calling themselves "Gruyère" several years ago in deference to the Swiss-made cheeses. To find a favorite, we sampled each plain at room temperature, baked in spinach-and-cheese squares, and melted on crostini.

The Swiss Way

Swiss cheesemakers claim that every part of the rigorous AOP-regulated process contributes to Gruyère's unique, deeply complex flavor and dense, crystalline texture, starting with the milk itself. It must be raw and from mostly grass-fed cows, since both the Alpine grasses and the bacteria naturally present in unpasteurized milk infuse the cheese with flavor. From there, the milk is mixed with cultures and rennet, which introduce more flavorful bacteria and cause the milk to coagulate into curds, respectively. Then it's heated in giant copper vats. That particular vessel is important not just because copper heats evenly and responds quickly to changes in temperature but also because copper ions from the surface of

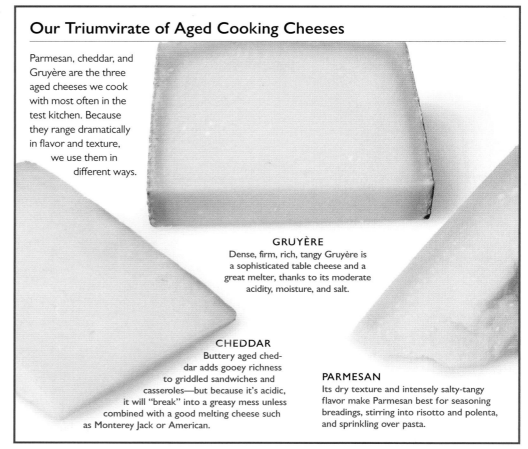

Our Triumvirate of Aged Cooking Cheeses

Parmesan, cheddar, and Gruyère are the three aged cheeses we cook with most often in the test kitchen. Because they range dramatically in flavor and texture, we use them in different ways.

GRUYÈRE
Dense, firm, rich, tangy Gruyère is a sophisticated table cheese and a great melter, thanks to its moderate acidity, moisture, and salt.

CHEDDAR
Buttery aged cheddar adds gooey richness to griddled sandwiches and casseroles—but because it's acidic, it will "break" into a greasy mess unless combined with a good melting cheese such as Monterey Jack or American.

PARMESAN
Its dry texture and intensely salty-tangy flavor make Parmesan best for seasoning breadings, stirring into risotto and polenta, and sprinkling over pasta.

the vat leach into the milk and curds and react with compounds in the milk to form desirable and distinct flavor compounds.

Once the curds have formed, they're transferred to large wheel-shaped molds to be pressed for the better part of a day; turned out and either salted or brined for another day or two; and, finally, aged for a minimum of five months before being sold. The wheels are regularly turned and rubbed with salt during the aging process, which ensures that the rind forms properly and that the butterfat is evenly distributed. They're also rubbed with a "smear" of cultures, which Dean Sommer, cheese and food technologist at the University of Wisconsin–Madison's Center for Dairy Research, explains is the most important factor in creating the flavor of each maker's Gruyère. "The surface 'smear' cultures are absolutely unique to each cheese plant," he said, "which means that no two plants making a

Gruyère-style cheese will have the exact same cheese flavor, even if the composition of the cheeses is nearly identical in the two plants."

With Age Comes Flavor

We weren't surprised to find that the Swiss-made cheeses, all of which we recommend, generally did taste noticeably "more intense," "complex," and "caramel-like" than the American-made ones. Two of the three domestic cheeses "lacked the characteristic notes" and "sparkle" of authentic Gruyère, and we can recommend them only with reservations. In fact, several tasters likened them to "bland" "deli Swiss" even in the cooked applications.

Those differences might be linked to the fact that domestic producers use pasteurized milk, which loses much of its flavorful bacteria in pasteurization's intense heat, or that the Alpine grasses or specific cocktails of cultures used by Swiss cheesemakers yield

High Alpine Standards

Creating Gruyère's distinctively nutty, tangy, rich flavor starts with the milk itself. According to strict Swiss standards, the milk must come from cows that grazed on Alpine grasses and be left raw to capitalize on all the subtle flavors and natural bacteria. Heating the milk in copper vats is also crucial, as the copper ions leach into and combine with the milk to form distinct flavor compounds. Finally, all Swiss-made Gruyères must be brined or salted, smeared with cultures that develop their unique flavors, and aged for at least five months, allowing ample time for the cultures to break down and develop more-complex flavors and for moisture to evaporate and concentrate flavorful fat and salt.

better flavor. But the most likely reason the imported cheeses taste deeper and more complex than most domestic versions is that they're aged longer. AOP standards dictate that Gruyère must be aged for at least five months. Our top four cheeses were aged for even longer—nine to 14 months. Among these was one of the domestic Gruyère-style cheeses, Emmi Roth Grand Cru Surchoix, whose relatively lengthy nine-month aging helped give it complex flavor despite the use of pasteurized milk. Of the other two domestic cheeses, one had no standards for aging and the other was aged for just four months.

Sommer confirmed that the longer a cheese is aged, the more intense and complex its flavor is going to be. That's partly because enzymes from the starter cultures have more time to break down at a molecular level, creating more robust, unique flavor. Plus, as cheeses like Gruyère age, they lose moisture, which concentrates the protein, milk fat, flavor compounds, and sodium as well as calcium lactate and tyrosine—those crunchy crystals that our tasters loved. We confirmed via lab analysis that the older, top-rated cheeses contain less moisture and more fat than the younger, blander samples.

Sophisticated enough for a cheese plate and equally great for melting, Gruyère might be one of the most versatile supermarket cheeses for eating and cooking. It doesn't come cheap—our favorite, 1655 Le Gruyère AOP, costs about $20 per pound—but we think it's worth the splurge.

TASTING GRUYÈRE

We sampled each cheese plain (at room temperature), baked in spinach-and-cheese squares, and melted onto crostini. Scores were averaged, and cheeses appear below in order of preference. Information on age, origin, ingredients, and pasteurization was obtained from manufacturers and product packaging, and an independent laboratory analyzed the cheeses for moisture, fat, and sodium; nutritional data is reported per 100 grams of cheese. Prices were paid in Boston-area supermarkets.

RECOMMENDED

1655 Le Gruyère AOP
PRICE: $19.99 per lb ($1.25 per oz)
INGREDIENTS: Raw cow's milk, salt, cultures, rennet
MILK: Raw
AGE: 12 to 14 months
ORIGIN: Switzerland
AOP: Yes
MOISTURE: 32.79%
FAT: 35.63%
SODIUM: 583.1 mg

COMMENTS

Our winner had the highest fat content and one of the lowest moisture contents, and it was aged the longest: 12 to 14 months. Those factors added up to a cheese that tasters raved about—specifically its "excellent crystalline structure"; "dense," "fudgy" texture; and "deeply aged, caramel-like," "grassy" flavor that came through even when baked with spinach and onions.

MIFROMA Le Gruyère Cavern AOP
PRICE: $19.99 per lb ($1.25 per oz)
INGREDIENTS: Fresh part-skim cow's milk, cheese cultures, salt and enzymes
MILK: Raw
AGE: 9 to 11 months
ORIGIN: Switzerland
AOP: Yes
MOISTURE: 33.17%
FAT: 34.46%
SODIUM: 585.5 mg

With low moisture, plenty of fat, and a judicious amount of salt, this long-aged Swiss import tasted "nutty" and complex—tasters picked up on fruity "pineapple" tang and a "savory onion quality." Its "creamy" texture was strewn with pleasantly crystalline bites. In fact, one taster found "five visible tyrosine crystals in a single piece!"

EMMI ROTH Grand Cru Surchoix
PRICE: $18.99 per lb ($1.19 per oz)
INGREDIENTS: Pasteurized cultured milk, salt, enzymes
MILK: Pasteurized
AGE: At least 9 months
ORIGIN: USA
AOP: No
MOISTURE: 31.27%
FAT: 34.94%
SODIUM: 534.6 mg

Despite being made with pasteurized milk, this domestic cheese (made by a subsidiary of the Switzerland-based Emmi Group) boasted "caramelized" sweetness; notes of mushroom, onion, and "fruity red wine"; and a "buttery" texture that was loaded with crunchy tyrosine crystals.

EMMI Le Gruyère AOP Kaltbach
PRICE: $23.99 per lb ($1.50 per oz)
INGREDIENTS: Milk, culture, salt, enzymes
MILK: Raw
AGE: More than 12 months
ORIGIN: Switzerland
AOP: Yes
MOISTURE: 31.95%
FAT: 34.41%
SODIUM: 526.6 mg

"Would be a showstopper on a cheese plate," one taster remarked about this particularly "funky," "fruity," and "nutty" sample. Several others noted a pleasant fermented quality—like "sour apple juice"—or a "deep, lingering muskiness."

GRAND SUISSE Le Gruyère
PRICE: $19.00 per lb ($1.19 per oz)
INGREDIENTS: Fresh part-skim cow's milk, cheese culture, salt, enzymes
MILK: Raw
AGE: 5 months
ORIGIN: Switzerland
AOP: Yes
MOISTURE: 34.46%
FAT: 32.76%
SODIUM: 463.1 mg

Aged for just five months, this "waxy" Swiss Gruyère tasted noticeably leaner and "milder" than the older samples. It was "tangy but flat," "semisharp," and tasted "young." That said, it still delivered "pleasant nuttiness" and "mellow tang."

EMMI Le Gruyère AOP
PRICE: $15.44 per lb ($0.97 per oz)
INGREDIENTS: Cultured milk, salt, enzymes
MILK: Raw
AGE: 5 to 6 months
ORIGIN: Switzerland
AOP: Yes
MOISTURE: 33.17%
FAT: 33.93%
SODIUM: 659.2 mg

"Gruyère for beginners" is how one taster described this young, "buttery," "nutty" import. Compared with the denser, more crystalline structure of our favorites, it was "smooth, soft, and creamy," though texture wasn't an issue in cooked applications.

RECOMMENDED WITH RESERVATIONS

BOAR'S HEAD Blanc Grue Gruyère Cheese
PRICE: $16.58 per lb ($1.04 per oz)
INGREDIENTS: Pasteurized milk, cheese cultures, salt, enzymes
MILK: Pasteurized
AGE: No standard time frame
ORIGIN: USA
AOP: No
MOISTURE: 34.38%
FAT: 32.90%
SODIUM: 461.6 mg

"Not offensive but no sparkle." "Waxy" and "bendy." "Innocuous." These comments indicate that this domestic facsimile was aged for far less time than other cheeses. However, it melted evenly on crostini, and its flavor was "mild but pleasant," with subtle nutty, sweet notes.

EMMI ROTH Grand Cru Original
PRICE: $14.99 per lb ($0.94 per oz)
INGREDIENTS: Pasteurized cultured milk, salt, enzymes
MILK: Pasteurized
AGE: 4 months
ORIGIN: USA
AOP: No
MOISTURE: 34.76%
FAT: 31.69%
SODIUM: 532.5 mg

Several tasters compared this young cheese with deli Swiss—even calling it a "faker"—citing its "mild" (albeit "pleasant") flavor and "rubbery" texture.

Tasting Coconut Milk

Coconut milk is made by shredding fresh coconut meat and pressing it to extract liquid, sometimes adding a little water to help the process. We tasted seven products plain (to get a sense of their differences) and then in coconut rice pudding and Thai-style chicken soup.

Coconut milk is an emulsion of coconut oil, coconut protein, and water. Because coconut oil solidifies into coconut cream at room temperature, canned coconut milk generally separates into two layers: liquid water at the bottom, cream at the top. The cream in some cans was as dense as Crisco, while others had a loose consistency. The liquid in some cans was opaque and smooth; in others, it was cloudy, with little specks of cream. And the ratio of cream to liquid ranged from about 50:50 to almost no liquid.

Why were they so different? Industry experts told us that the age and variety of coconut can have a large impact on the texture and flavor of the milk, as can processing methods. Perhaps most important, fluctuations in temperature can cause the natural emulsion of water, protein, and oil to break, thus impacting texture. Our tasters preferred creamy, full-bodied products that didn't register as greasy and had fresh, vibrant coconut flavor. One key: Our three highest-rated products had relatively high levels of naturally occurring sugar, likely due to the variety and age of the coconuts (manufacturers, however, wouldn't disclose specifics). Tasters praised our winner, Aroy-D Coconut Milk, for its velvety consistency and "clean," "balanced" coconut flavor. For the complete tasting results, go to CooksIllustrated.com/june17. –Kate Shannon

Some milks had the consistency of shortening (left), while others were like cream (right).

RECOMMENDED

AROY-D Coconut Milk

PRICE: $0.99 for 14-oz can ($0.07 per oz)

SUGAR: 1.8 g per ⅓-cup serving

COMMENTS: Our new winner impressed tasters with a texture that was "velvety" and "luxurious" but not too thick. It boasted "balanced," "clean" flavor that tasted strongly of coconut. It's also sold in cartons, but we don't recommend buying them because they are a nonstandard size for recipes at 16.9 fluid ounces.

ROLAND COCONUT MILK

PRICE: $2.79 for 14-oz can ($0.20 per oz)

SUGAR: 2.7 g per ⅓-cup serving

COMMENTS: With high levels of fat and several stabilizers, this sample was "thick," "rich," and "well emulsified." It was also described as "very sweet," especially in the rice pudding—no surprise, given that it has one of the highest sugar levels in our lineup.

NOT RECOMMENDED

A TASTE OF THAI Coconut Milk

PRICE: $2.99 for 13.5-oz can ($0.22 per oz)

SUGAR: 2 g per ⅓-cup serving

COMMENTS: This product's flavor was "weak," and its texture was "watery" and "greasy," landing it in last place.

What to Do with Pea Greens

Pea greens, also known as pea shoots or pea tendrils, are the tender tips of pea plants. You'll find them during spring and early summer at farmers' markets and some supermarkets. Both the rounded, bright green leaves and the thin, hollow stems topped with tendrils are edible, although the stems from older plants can be tough. We recommend discarding stems that are wider than ¼ inch in diameter (you can still eat the leaves).

Our tasters described the plain leaves and stems as grassy and faintly bitter—"like peas but not sweet." When using them in a salad, we found it best to pair them with delicate vinaigrettes instead of rich and creamy dressings, which muted their flavor and weighed them down. They can also be substituted for basil to make a more delicate pesto. To highlight their savory flavor, you can sauté pea greens with minced garlic; cook them quickly (for about 2 minutes) to retain their bright color, and avoid overcooking them, which will cause the leaves to disintegrate. –L.L.

RAW
Both the leaves and the stems of pea greens are edible. We recommend pairing the uncooked greens with a light vinaigrette so their delicate grassy flavor comes through.

COOKED
Lightly sauté the greens to highlight their savory flavor. They will wilt to about one-third of their uncooked volume.

The Best Way to Store Rhubarb

These days, rhubarb is available in many supermarkets from spring through summer. To determine the best way to store it, we trimmed and washed a few bunches and experimented with different methods. Leaving the rhubarb completely unprotected in the refrigerator caused the exposed ends to dry out, and the stalks turned limp within just a few days due to water loss. Sealing the stalks tightly in a zipper-lock bag or in plastic wrap caused them to soften in a few days as well. This is because airtight storage traps the ripening hormone ethylene, which activates enzymes that break down and soften the cell walls in many fruits and vegetables.

Though rhubarb and celery are unrelated, it turns out that the best method we've found for celery also works best for rhubarb: simply wrapping the stalks loosely in foil. The key is to wrap the stalks snugly enough to prevent the rhubarb from drying out—but not airtight (no need to tightly crimp) so ethylene can escape. Stored this way, our rhubarb maintained its juicy, ruby perfection for longer than two weeks. –A.G.

THAT'S A WRAP
Wrap the rhubarb tightly enough to make a tidy bundle, but don't tightly crimp the edges or the ethylene gas can't escape.

ILLUSTRATION: JOHN BURGOYNE

Pricing Chicken Parts

Chicken breasts have the highest yield of meat per pound of all chicken parts, but they're not the most economical cut.

When we cooked bone-in chicken breasts, thighs, drumsticks, and wings and then stripped the meat from the bones to determine the price per edible ounce, we found that drumsticks were easily the cheapest.

Part	Price per pound	Price per edible ounce
Drumsticks	$1.69	$0.23
Thighs	$2.19	$0.29
Breasts	$3.29	$0.36
Wings	$2.69	$0.40

(Surprisingly, wings were the most expensive.) They're also easy to cook, flavorful, and moist, so this finding is just one more reason to make our Grilled Spice-Rubbed Chicken Drumsticks (page 11). –A.G.

How to Cook with Chayote

Chayote—a fruit native to Mexico but now popular throughout Latin America and Asia—is a pale green, bumpy-skinned, pear-shaped member of the gourd family (*Cucurbitaceae*), which makes it a relative of melons, pumpkins, cucumbers, zucchini, and summer squash.

This fruit can be eaten both raw and cooked. We like it cut thin and cooked lightly—sautéed, stir-fried, or even stewed. When we swapped it for some of the squash in our recipe for Sautéed Summer Squash with Parsley and Garlic (September/October 2015), it shed a bit of moisture, as did the summer squash. But it retained a pleasant underlying crispness that the summer squash lost. We also like chayote raw in salads and salsas, where its jícama-like crunch really shines. It can be pickled (using vinegar or a brine) or simply tossed with sugar and salt (use 2 teaspoons of sugar and 1 teaspoon of salt for one 12-ounce chayote) and left to sit for about 10 minutes before eating.

To prep chayote for cooking, peel and discard the leathery rind and then cut it lengthwise into quarters. Use a paring knife to remove the hard central seed before slicing or cubing. –A.J.

Spotty Cabbage Leaves

When shopping for napa cabbage, we've noticed that some heads have tiny black spots, about the size of ground pepper, on both the leaves and ribs. The cause of these dots, known as "pepper spot" or "black spec," is unknown, but low light levels, high soil pH, harvesting and storage conditions, and excessive use of fertilizers high in nitrogen and phosphorus are all possibilities. Regardless of the cause, our science editor confirmed that cabbage leaves with these spots are perfectly safe to eat. But to find out if they affect flavor or texture, we set up a blind tasting. Tasters couldn't tell the difference between unblemished leaves and those with pepper spot. And unless we're using whole cabbage leaves, the dots are so small that they aren't even noticeable. From now on, we'll go ahead and buy heads of napa cabbage with the black dots without concern. –K.D.

DIY RECIPE Tortilla Chips

Even the best store-bought tortilla chips can't compare with the fresh corn flavor and ultracrispy texture of homemade. Starting with good-quality corn tortillas was key; thinner, fresh, locally made tortillas made the best chips. A frying temperature of 350 degrees browned the chips quickly without burning them, and frying in two batches ensured that the oil's temperature didn't drop too much when we added the tortilla wedges. As soon as they came out of the oil, we sprinkled them with kosher salt, which was easier to distribute evenly than table salt. –L.L.

HOMEMADE TORTILLA CHIPS
SERVES 4

For the best results, use fresh, locally made tortillas (the thinnest available). We prefer peanut oil for deep frying because of its high smoke point, but vegetable or corn oil will also work.

- 8 (6-inch) corn tortillas
- 5 cups peanut oil
  Kosher salt

1. Cut each tortilla into 6 wedges. Line 2 baking sheets with several layers of paper towels. Heat oil in Dutch oven over medium-high heat to 350 degrees.

2. Add half of tortillas and fry until golden and crispy around edges, 2 to 4 minutes. Transfer chips to prepared sheets, sprinkle lightly with salt, and let cool. Repeat with remaining tortillas. Serve. (Cooled chips can be stored in zipper-lock bag at room temperature for up to 4 days.)

Pancetta versus Prosciutto

Pancetta and prosciutto are often confused, since both are traditional Italian cured pork products that taste deeply savory and salty. That said, they come from different parts of the pig, the processes to make them are different, and we use them in different ways. Here's how to keep them straight. –S.D.

PANCETTA

What it is: Pancetta is seasoned salt-cured pork belly (just like bacon but not smoked) that's rolled and often put in a casing before being hung to dry to develop firm texture and deep flavor. It must be cooked before eating.
Forms: It can be sliced to order behind the deli counter or bought presliced in packages. (It also comes prediced, which we don't recommend—we've found that the cubes often taste sour.)
How we use it: We like to cut it into small chunks and sauté it to add savory depth as well as intensely flavorful, meaty bites to dishes from soups and stews to pastas.

PROSCIUTTO

What it is: Prosciutto is the salt-cured hind leg of the pig (i.e., ham) that's air-dried for months or even years, giving it a markedly dense, silky texture and a delicate, nutty flavor. Prosciutto is safe to eat without cooking.
Forms: It can be sliced to order at the deli counter or bought presliced in packages.
How we use it: We like raw slices as part of an antipasto platter or wrapped around fruit or vegetables. We also use it in cooked applications, such as saltimbocca, and we crisp it for a salad topping.

KITCHEN NOTES

⇒ BY STEVE DUNN, ANDREW JANJIGIAN, LAN LAM, ANNIE PETITO & DAN SOUZA ⇐

Troubleshooting a Weak Flame on a Gas Grill

We've occasionally fired up our gas grills only to have the burners emit a tepid flame no matter how high we set the knobs. This does not mean it's time to get a new tank of gas. Instead, we learned that a weak flame can be a signal that the safety regulator on the propane line—that aluminum device that sits near the end of the hose that attaches to the tank—has been tripped, slowing the flow of gas to a trickle.

This regulator is designed to respond to low gas pressure inside the hose, a sign that there's a leak, but it can also be tripped accidently if you turn on the grill burners before you open the valve on the tank. With the burner valves open, pressure never builds up inside the hose, and the regulator thinks it has detected a leak.

TO AVOID THE PROBLEM

Always make sure to open the valve on the tank before turning on the grill's burners. And when you have finished grilling, be sure to turn off the burners before shutting off the gas flow from the tank.

TO FIX THE PROBLEM

If you forget the order of operations above, the steps at the right will show you how to reset the regulator and get your grill back up and running. –A.J.

1. Turn off all burners.

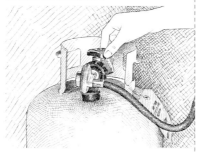

2. Turn off valve on tank.

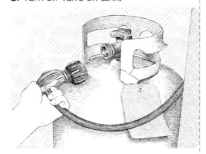

3. Detach regulator and hose from tank's nozzle; wait at least 30 seconds before reattaching it.

Seasonings Beyond Salt and Pepper

Toward the end of developing a recipe in the test kitchen, tasters often make comments such as "it tastes just a bit flat" or "a smidge lean" or "too rich." While salt and pepper are always a consideration for final tweaks, our test cooks also look to a range of other pantry ingredients that can help bring a dish into just the right balance. Such ingredients encompass sweet, bitter, sour, and umami (or savory) flavors; we also may adjust with ingredients that add richness. Just a small quantity of one of these finishing touches (from a pinch to ½ teaspoon) is a good starting place. Here are a few of our favorites. –A.P.

	Ingredient	What It Does	Suggested Uses
Sweet	Granulated or brown sugar, honey, maple syrup, mirin, sweet wines or liqueurs, jams or jellies	Rounds out sharp, bitter, or salty flavors	Salsas, relishes, sauces, vinaigrettes, bitter greens
Sour	Vinegars, citrus juice, pickled vegetables (such as jalapeños)	Adds brightness to flat-tasting dishes, cuts through richness or sweetness	Meaty stews or soups, creamy sauces and condiments, braised or roasted meats
Bitter	Dry or prepared mustard, fresh ginger, chili powder, unsweetened cocoa powder, dark chocolate, horseradish, cayenne pepper, coffee, citrus zest, beer	Cuts sweetness	Barbecue meats, slaws, chopped salads, chili
Umami	Worcestershire sauce, soy sauce, Parmesan cheese, fish sauce, anchovy, mushrooms, tomato paste, miso, sherry	Adds meatiness, depth, or earthiness; boosts dishes that taste a bit flat	Bolognese and other meaty sauces, hearty vegetarian sauces, soups, deli sandwich fillings such as tuna salad
Rich	Heavy cream, butter, olive oil	Rounds out flavors, adds viscosity	Vegetable-based soups, sauces

For the Best Pizza Crust, Easy Does It

Good, chewy texture in pizza requires strong gluten development in the dough. But too much handling can cause the gluten to tighten up like a rubber band, making stretching the dough a real challenge and leading to tough, rather than chewy, results. The key is to give the dough plenty of time to relax and to handle it as gently—and as little—as possible. –A.J.

1. Shape cold-fermented (refrigerator-proofed) pizza dough into balls 24 hours before stretching to give gluten ample time to relax.

2. Proof each ball in separate lightly oiled bowl; transfer to counter by inverting bowl. Flour top of dough.

3. Gently press down on dough with your fingertips. Lightly compress dough halfway toward counter, then lift your fingertips. Repeat across dough.

4. Once disk measures 6 to 8 inches across, gently lift it with both your hands, drape it over your closed fists, and use gravity and your knuckles to stretch it.

5. If dough tightens up at any point, lay it on floured counter and let it rest for 1 to 2 minutes to allow gluten to relax.

Boil versus Simmer

Whether we call for boiling or simmering in a recipe depends on the situation. We boil foods less often, but it can be beneficial in some situations, such as flash-cooking (or blanching) vegetables so that they lose their raw edge while retaining their flavor and bright color; speeding up the cooking of grains such as brown rice or wheat berries, since surrounding the grains with boiling water transfers heat more quickly than the absorption method; and cooking pasta, where the agitation helps keep the pieces from sticking to each other. More often, we turn to simmering. Less agitation means delicate foods won't break apart and fats and soluble proteins in stock won't coagulate and turn the liquid cloudy. Because lower burner temperatures allow time for heat to transfer evenly from the bottom of a pan to the top, there's also less risk of scorching. –L.L.

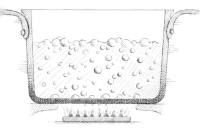

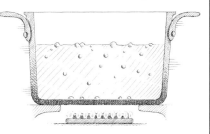

BOIL: Liquid reaches **212 degrees**; large bubbles vigorously rise from bottom of pot and continually break surface.

SIMMER: Liquid reaches **180 to 190 degrees**; small bubbles rise from bottom of pot and occasionally break surface.

Lazy Cook's Frosting

Need a simple frosting that takes barely a minute to make? Whip some cream and sugar in a food processor. Whereas whipping cream in a stand mixer produces light, billowy peaks, the sharp, fast-moving blades of a food processor can't add as much air. Instead, they produce a dense, creamy consistency that works well as a quick, spreadable topping for snack cakes, angel food and chiffon cakes, and cupcakes; it was also very effective when piped through a pastry bag to make decorative edging. Even better, because the smaller air bubbles created by the food processor are more stable than the bigger bubbles created by a stand mixer, we found that the processed cream kept its thick, dense texture for two full weeks.
➤**Method:** Process 2 cups heavy cream, 2 teaspoons sugar, and ½ teaspoon vanilla extract in food processor for 45 seconds. Pulse in 5-second intervals for another 15 to 20 seconds, until cream has reached consistency of buttercream frosting. –S.D.

Is Tofu Worth Marinating?

We know that, contrary to popular belief, marinades do most of their work on the surface of meat and poultry. That's because very few flavor compounds can make it deep into the meat, no matter how long it soaks in the marinade. Tofu is often substituted for meat and poultry in recipes, but it doesn't behave in exactly the same way. How would it respond to marinating? We set up an experiment to find out.

EXPERIMENT

We marinated blocks of firm tofu in four different marinades—using soy sauce, red wine, yogurt, and lemon and garlic as the various bases—for 15 minutes, 30 minutes, 1 hour, and 2 hours. We then wiped off the excess marinade and baked the tofu in a 300-degree oven until hot throughout. We also baked a control block of tofu that we hadn't marinated. We trimmed the outer 3 millimeters off each block and had 10 tasters sample the remaining tofus blind, asking them to identify the marinade for each.

RESULTS

Tasters were relatively unsuccessful at matching the sample to the marinade at the 15-minute mark, but their results improved dramatically for the 30-minute set. All 10 tasters correctly identified the sample soaked in the soy-based marinade, and eight of the tasters did the same for tofu from the lemon-garlic marinade, while six were accurate for the red wine and yogurt marinades. Interestingly, the accuracy increased only slightly for the 1- and 2-hour batches.

TAKEAWAY

Unlike meat and poultry, firm (and extra-firm) tofu can be thoroughly seasoned by marinades of all types due to its relatively loose structure. Meat is made up of individual muscle fibers bundled together in tight packages by connective tissue, which translates to a dense, resilient texture. The flavors in most marinades don't get much farther than skin-deep, with a few exceptions—alliums such as garlic and glutamate-rich foods such as soy sauce, both of which have small, water-soluble molecules. By comparison, firm tofu is made of coagulated curds of soy protein pressed into block form. Marinades are able to seep between curd clumps and migrate toward the center.

That said, some marinades are more effective than others. It was easier for tasters to identify the soy and lemon-garlic marinades because the water-soluble flavor compounds in soy sauce and garlic are better at moving through high-moisture tofu than are the compounds found in red wine or yogurt. Considering that we often cut tofu into bite-size pieces with greater surface area (thus creating more points of entry for marinade), marinating can have a profound impact, seasoning the tofu not only at the surface but also deep inside. –D.S.

CHICKEN
Marinade doesn't go past the edge.

TOFU
Marinade reaches deeper.

Recrisping Stale Crackers and Cookies

The staling of dry, crisp foods such as crackers, tortilla chips, and crunchy cookies occurs because moisture from the atmosphere gets absorbed by the item's starches, which soften and rob it of its crisp texture. Luckily, this process is reversible. And as long as you keep the recrisped items dry by storing them in an airtight container or zipper-lock bag, they will stay crisp.
➤**Method:** Spread foods such as soda crackers and tortilla chips in an even layer on a rimmed baking sheet (avoiding overlap) and place larger items such as cookies and graham crackers on a wire rack set in a baking sheet. Place the sheet on the middle rack of a 225-degree oven for 15 to 25 minutes (the timing will vary, depending on the item), until the food is crisp again, stirring (or flipping, in the case of cookies) halfway through baking. –A.J.

HIGHLY RECOMMENDED

ELITE CUISINE 1.5 Quart Mini Slow Cooker
MODEL: MST250XW
PRICE: $24.02

HIGHLY RECOMMENDED

ALL-CLAD 12-Inch Stainless Steel Fry Pan with Lid
MODEL: 41126
PRICE: $119.00

RECOMMENDED

THERMOWORKS Fridge/Freezer Alarm
MODEL: RT8100
PRICE: $22.00

RECOMMENDED

YAMAZAKI Home Ladle and Lid Stand
MODEL: 2249
PRICE: $18.00

RECOMMENDED

BLUEAVOCADO (re)Zip Stand-Up 4 Cup/32 oz
MODEL: BA339-4C
PRICE: $8.99

Mini Slow Cookers

Small slow cookers are convenient for keeping dips warm at parties, they easily stow away in small kitchens, and they're useful for making scaled-down versions of slow-cooker recipes. They are also inexpensive. To find the best one, we gathered four models priced from $13.79 to $24.02—all with 1½-quart capacities—and used them to make slow-cooker recipes for cheese fondue and chicken soup, as well as to keep hot spinach and artichoke dip and *queso fundido* warm (tracking the temperature of each for 3 hours).

All the models were pretty rudimentary, with no digital temperature settings or timers like our winning full-size slow cooker from KitchenAid has. Each model consists of a removable ceramic crock outfitted with a glass lid and set in a metal-lined shell that houses the heating elements. We quickly noted that all the crocks and lids were very similar in size, shape, material, and thickness (in fact, we had to label them to keep from getting them mixed up). It's no surprise, then, that they were all equally durable, roomy (all comfortably held an entire bone-in chicken breast), and easy to clean.

The shells looked pretty similar, too—except for one key difference: their temperature controls. While two models had dials for three temperature settings (warm, low, and high), one product had options for only low and high. Another didn't have a temperature dial at all; it was either on or off, with no variable settings.

All handled the fondue, soup, and spinach dip well, but two—those without "warm" settings—had problems with the more finicky *queso* dip, which can separate if it gets too hot. Our favorite, the Elite Cuisine 1.5 Quart Mini Slow Cooker ($24.02), aced every test. –L.S.

UPDATE Traditional Skillets

Recently, All-Clad introduced a lidded version of our favorite traditional skillet, the All-Clad 12-Inch Stainless Steel Fry Pan, so we compared the new model, the All-Clad 12-Inch Stainless Steel Fry Pan with Lid ($119.00), with the original. Lid aside, the two pans are identical, and All-Clad plans to offer both models indefinitely. We used the new lidded model to cook a chicken-and-rice casserole and to contain simmering tomato sauce, pitting it against our favorite universal lid, the RSVP Endurance Stainless Steel Universal Lid with Glass Insert ($19.99). The new All-Clad lid has a small but easy-to-grip handle and fits securely on top of the skillet, helping cook the rice evenly and keeping spatters to a minimum. The lid works very well and adds value to an already excellent pan.

If you don't yet own a traditional skillet, we recommend buying the new lidded model. As a bonus, the All-Clad lid also fits our winning nonstick skillet, the OXO Good Grips Non-Stick 12-Inch Open Fry Pan ($39.99). Unfortunately, it is not currently possible to buy the All-Clad skillet lid separately. –M.B.

Refrigerator/Freezer Thermometers

Digital refrigerator/freezer thermometers provide concrete data to those who are concerned that their refrigerators and freezers run too warm or too cold. The most useful models have audio and/or visual indicators to tell you if the temperature goes off course; we gathered four of these, priced from $17.99 to $41.99, and put them to the test. Our winner, the ThermoWorks Fridge/Freezer Alarm ($22.00), was the most accurate thermometer in our testing. Its display was easy to read, but the interface was a little tricky to navigate. However, an extra feature more than made up for this minor flaw: This unit alerts you when temperatures go above or below the temperatures you designate and also tracks when temperatures remain outside those points for longer than a half-hour. –M.B.

Lid Holders

Many cooks swear by lid holders, claiming that they contain mess and save counter space. To put those assertions to the test, we bought four models priced from $11.99 to $80.00: three heat-resistant stands with troughs that cradle the lids (some also hold utensils) and contain any drips and a fourth model that holds lids faceup so they can't drip in the first place. In general, we preferred models that sat securely on the counter without taking up too much room and that could handle all sizes of lids with aplomb. But one lid holder's versatility really won us over. The Yamazaki Home Ladle and Lid Stand ($18.00) held every lid and utensil we set inside it, and it was the only model that could also hold tablets and even magazines—doing so just as securely as our favorite tablet stand. –M.B.

Reusable Storage Bags

Are reusable sandwich-size storage bags viable replacements for disposable zipper-lock bags? To find out, we bought five 3- to 4-cup bags, priced from $2.32 to $11.99 each and made of either silicone or vinyl, and used them to store a variety of foods in the freezer, in the refrigerator, and in a backpack. We filled them with water, sealed them, inverted them, and shook them; we also dropped the sealed water-filled bags from counter height. All the bags proved easy to clean, but the vinyl bags were superior to their silicone counterparts, because they sealed more securely, allowing them to better contain foods and protect against freezer burn. Vinyl bags also proved easier to fill than the small, thick silicone bags. Our winner, the BlueAvocado (re)Zip Stand-Up 4 Cup/32 oz, stored all food well, had gussets that made it especially easy to fill, and was very leak-resistant. It performs comparably to a disposable bag, but without the waste. –M.B.

For complete testing results, go to CooksIllustrated.com/june17.

INDEX

May & June 2017

BONUS ONLINE CONTENT

*More recipes, reviews, and videos are available
at* **CooksIllustrated.com/june17**

RECIPES

Brown Sugar–Banana Topping
German Pancake for Two
Grilled Pork Tenderloin with Grilled
Tomatillo Salsa
Grilled Pork Tenderloin with Grilled
Tomato–Ginger Salsa
Napa Cabbage Slaw with Snow Peas
and Mint
Ras el Hanout Spice Rub
Spicy Napa Cabbage Slaw with Red
Bell Pepper

EXPANDED REVIEWS

Tasting Coconut Milk
Testing Lid Holders
Testing Mini Slow Cookers
Testing Refrigerator/Freezer Thermometers
Testing Reusable Storage Bags
Testing Syrup Dispensers

▶ **RECIPE VIDEOS**

Want to see how to make any of the recipes
in this issue? There's a free video for that.

FOLLOW US ON SOCIAL MEDIA

facebook.com/CooksIllustrated
twitter.com/TestKitchen
pinterest.com/TestKitchen
google.com/+AmericasTestKitchen
instagram.com/CooksIllustrated
youtube.com/AmericasTestKitchen

German Pancake, 15

Panang Beef Curry, 7

Risi e Bisi, 19

Grilled Pork Tenderloin, 18

Grilled Spice-Rubbed Chicken Drumsticks, 11

Classic Guacamole, 5

Napa Cabbage Slaw with Carrots and Sesame, 22

Olive Oil Cake, 21

Stir-Fried Shrimp and Asparagus, 13

Meatless "Meat" Sauce, 9

PHOTOGRAPHY: CARL TREMBLAY; STYLING: MARIE PIRAINO

Chinese Chives

Kaffir Lime Leaves

Cilantro

Culantro

Shiso

Cilantro Roots

Thai Basil

Yellow Chinese Chives

Lemon Grass

Mitsuba

ASIAN HERBS

NUMBER 147

JULY & AUGUST 2017

COOK'S
ILLUSTRATED

Thai Grilled Chicken
Easy Method, Bold Taste

Crispy Corn Fritters
Southern Classic Perfected

Smoky Grilled Steak
Plus: Best Grill Tongs

Midpriced Blenders
One Stands Above the Pack

Italian Seafood Pasta
Translating the Flavors of Liguria

Turkey Meatloaf
Don't Treat It Like Beef

Modern Fruit Tart
Not Just a Pretty Face

Chinese Smashed Cucumbers
Summer Tomato Gratin
Home-Roasted Bell Peppers

CooksIllustrated.com
$6.95 U.S.

Display until August 7, 2017

COOK'S
ILLUSTRATED ®

JULY & AUGUST 2017

PAGE 4

CHERRY TOMATOES

BACK COVER ILLUSTRATED BY JOHN BURGOYNE
Cherry Tomatoes
The origin of the cherry tomato is unclear—Greece, Peru, Mexico, and Israel all lay claim to it—but its worldwide popularity is undisputed, as more than 100 varieties are now grown. Among them, the **SUN GOLD** tastes as vibrant as its color suggests, and its juice is syrupy and tangy. Pea-size and perfectly spherical, the **CURRANT** pops with sweetness that's bright, nutty, and a touch smoky. The skin of the lush, soft **INDIGO CHERRY DROP** fades from dark red to purplish black, while the crisp, oblong **INDIGO KUMQUAT** is golden with a purplish blush at the stem end. Streaky-looking and pointy at the tip, the **PINK TIGER** resembles a small shallot and is loaded with tart juice. Given the floral, lilac-like aroma of a **PINK COCKTAIL**, its flavor is surprisingly watery. Streaked with peach-pink tones, the **SUNRISE BUMBLE BEE** is plump, with supersweet juice and hints of raspberry. The **YELLOW PEAR** teardrop is meaty-textured and has tropical, low-acid juice.

AMERICA'S TEST KITCHEN ®
RECIPES THAT WORK ®

America's Test Kitchen, a 2,500-square-foot kitchen located just outside Boston, is the home of more than 60 test cooks, editors, and cookware specialists. Our mission is to test recipes until we understand exactly how and why they work and eventually arrive at the very best version. We also test kitchen equipment and supermarket ingredients in search of products that offer the best value and performance. You can watch us work by tuning in to *America's Test Kitchen* (AmericasTestKitchen.com) and *Cook's Country from America's Test Kitchen* (CooksCountry.com) on public television and listen to our weekly segments on *The Splendid Table* on public radio. You can also follow us on Facebook, Twitter, Pinterest, and Instagram.

EDITORIAL STAFF

Chief Executive Officer David Nussbaum
Chief Creative Officer Jack Bishop
Editorial Director John Willoughby
Executive Editor Amanda Agee
Deputy Editor Rebecca Hays
Executive Managing Editor Todd Meier
Executive Food Editor Keith Dresser
Senior Editors Andrea Geary, Andrew Janjigian, Lan Lam,
Senior Editors, Features Elizabeth Bomze, Louise Emerick
Associate Editor Annie Petito
Lead Cook, Photo Team Daniel Cellucci
Test Cook Steve Dunn
Assistant Test Cooks Mady Nichas, Jessica Rudolph
Senior Copy Editor Krista Magnuson
Copy Editor Jillian Campbell
Executive Editor, Cook's Science Dan Souza
Science Editor Guy Crosby, PhD, CFS
Director, Creative Operations Alice Carpenter

Executive Editor, Tastings & Testings Lisa McManus
Deputy Editor Hannah Crowley
Associate Editors Miye Bromberg, Lauren Savoie,
    Kate Shannon
Assistant Editor Emily Phares
Editorial Assistant Carolyn Grillo

Test Kitchen Director Erin McMurrer
Assistant Test Kitchen Director Alexxa Benson
Test Kitchen Manager Meridith Lippard
Senior Kitchen Assistant Sophie Clingan-Darack
Lead Kitchen Assistant Ena Gudiel
Kitchen Assistants Gladis Campos, Blanca Castanza

Creative Director John Torres
Design Director Greg Galvan
Photography Director Julie Cote
Designer Maggie Edgar
Art Director, Marketing Melanie Gryboski
Deputy Art Director, Marketing Janet Taylor
Associate Art Director, Marketing Stephanie Cook
Senior Staff Photographer Daniel J. van Ackere
Staff Photographers Steve Klise, Kevin White
Photography Producer Mary Ball
Styling Catrine Kelty, Marie Piraino

Executive Editor, Web Christine Liu
Managing Editor, Web Mari Levine
Senior Editors, Web Roger Metcalf, Briana Palma
Associate Editors, Web Terrence Doyle
Senior Video Editor Nick Dakoulas

BUSINESS STAFF

Chief Financial Officer Jackie McCauley Ford
Production Director Guy Rochford
Imaging Manager Lauren Robbins
Production & Imaging Specialists Heather Dube,
    Dennis Noble, Jessica Voas
Senior Controller Theresa Peterson
Director, Business Partnerships Meghan Conciatori

Chief Digital Officer Fran Middleton
Director, Sponsorship Marketing & Client
    Services Christine Anagnostis
Client Services Manager Kate Zebrowski
Client Service & Marketing Representative Claire Gambee
Partnership Marketing Manager Pamela Putprush
Marketing Director, Social Media & Content
    Strategy Claire Oliverson
Senior Social Media Coordinators Kelsey Hopper,
    Morgan Mannino
Director, Customer Support Amy Bootier
Senior Customer Loyalty & Support Specialists
    Rebecca Kowalski, Andrew Straaberg Finfrock

Senior VP, Human Resources & Organizational
    Development Colleen Zelina
Human Resources Director Adele Shapiro
Director, Retail Book Program Beth Ineson
Retail Sales Manager Derek Meehan

Director, Public Relations & Communications
    Rebecca Wisdom

Circulation Services ProCirc

Cover Illustration Robert Papp

PRINTED IN THE USA

WHY WE COOK

At the most basic level, we cook to provide nourishment. But that's only the very beginning. We also cook to express our love, our desire to care for others. Some of us cook as an outlet for creative instincts, to fashion out of a set of ingredients something new that is much more than the sum of its parts. Or we may cook to explore different cultures, to better understand the way others experience the world. Many of us cook for solace and a sense of familiar comfort, instinctively turning to the kitchen in difficult times. And, of course, we cook because it gives a satisfying sense of accomplishment; you can actually achieve something worthwhile in a short period of time.

But even that list is just a start. Each of you could probably add several more personal reasons that you head to the kitchen. And truthfully, we cook for different reasons on different days and in different parts of our lives.

Here at *Cook's Illustrated* we understand this, and we try to provide cooking experiences to satisfy every mood. Take this issue, for example. If you are in the mood to explore other cuisines, take a look at

our version of Thai grilled chicken, in which Cornish hens stand in for the very small chickens grilled on the streets of Bangkok. Or try Chinese Smashed Cucumbers, an astonishingly easy and refreshing summer side dish that originated in Sichuan. (And if you're wondering whether "smashed" really works better than "sliced," the answer is a very clear yes.) For a brush with coastal Italian flavors, check out Linguine with Seafood, our rendition of the classic *linguine allo scoglio*.

If it's a particularly keen sense of accomplishment you're after, try our Modern Fresh Fruit Tart. It not only looks spectacular as a whole but also slices into gorgeous portions without mashing or crumbling, unlike most other versions we tried.

You'll also find the comfort of familiarity in many of the dishes in this issue, from Southern Corn Fritters to Smoked Steak, Turkey Meatloaf, and an old-timey Summer Tomato Gratin.

So go on—take a look. Whatever your reason for wanting to cook today, it's very likely that we've got you covered.

–The Editors

FOR INQUIRIES, ORDERS, OR MORE INFORMATION

COOK'S ILLUSTRATED MAGAZINE

Cook's Illustrated magazine (ISSN 1068-2821), number 147, is published bimonthly by America's Test Kitchen Limited Partnership, 17 Station St., Brookline, MA 02445. Copyright 2017 America's Test Kitchen Limited Partnership. Periodicals postage paid at Boston, MA, and additional mailing offices, USPS #012487. Publications Mail Agreement No. 40020778. Return undeliverable Canadian addresses to P.O. Box 875, Station A, Windsor, ON N9A 6P2. POSTMASTER: Send address changes to *Cook's Illustrated*, P.O. Box 6018, Harlan, IA 51593-1518. For subscription and gift subscription orders, subscription inquiries, or change of address notices, visit AmericasTestKitchen.com/support, call 800-526-8442 in the U.S. or 515-248-7684 from outside the U.S., or write to us at *Cook's Illustrated*, P.O. Box 6018, Harlan, IA 51593-1518.

CooksIllustrated.com

At the all new CooksIllustrated.com, you can order books and subscriptions, sign up for our free e-newsletter, or renew your magazine subscription. Join the website and gain access to 24 years of *Cook's Illustrated* recipes, equipment tests, and ingredient tastings, as well as companion videos for every recipe in this issue.

COOKBOOKS

We sell more than 50 cookbooks by the editors of *Cook's Illustrated*, including *The Cook's Illustrated Cookbook* and *Paleo Perfected*. To order, visit our bookstore at CooksIllustrated.com/bookstore.

EDITORIAL OFFICE 17 Station St., Brookline, MA 02445; 617-232-1000; fax: 617-232-1572.
For subscription inquiries, visit AmericasTestKitchen.com/support or call 800-526-8442.

QUICK TIPS

⋟ COMPILED BY ANNIE PETITO ⋞

Cleaning Narrow Vessels with Rice

Whenever a carafe, cruet, or syrup dispenser that is too narrow to clean with a sponge becomes cloudy, Roma Heerhartz of Sacramento, Calif., cleans it with cool water, a little dish soap, and a small amount of dry rice. After adding these ingredients to the vessel, she covers the top and rapidly swishes the rice kernels around, which loosens any residue so that it washes away.

Fitting Bread to a Toaster

To fit oblong artisan-style breads into her pop-up toaster, Diane Delu of Pleasant Hill, Calif., cuts the bread against a homemade cardboard pattern that mirrors the dimensions of her toaster's slot.

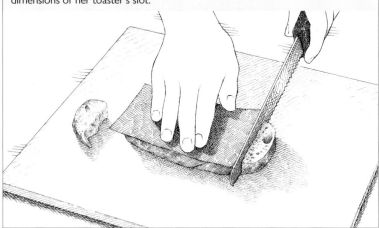

An Ice Bath That Doesn't Need a Refill

When blanching and shocking large batches of vegetables, George Stone of Colfax, Wis., finds that his ice maker can't keep up with the demand for ice baths. His solution: freezing water in pint-size plastic storage containers, which produces larger ice cubes that melt more gradually than those his ice maker cranks out.

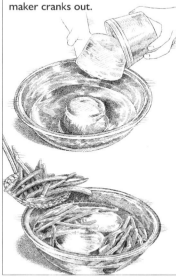

Shower-Capping a Sifter

Ellen Fuss of Woodbury, N.Y., wraps an unused hotel shower cap around the bottom of her flour sifter when she's storing it or needs to put it down between tasks. The elastic holds the cap in place around the base, so no flour falls into the bottom of her kitchen drawers or onto the counter.

Nonstick Cookie Portioning

When scooping cookie dough, Sharon Ito of Sunnyvale, Calif., lightly sprays her portion scoop with vegetable oil spray. This makes the scooping process faster and the cookies tidier. She reapplies the spray as necessary and sprays the scoop over the sink to avoid dirtying her counter.

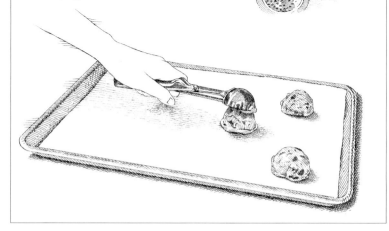

Stacking Bowls of Soft Food

Creamy desserts, such as pudding or crème brûlée, are often portioned into small dishes and covered with plastic wrap to chill before serving, but they take up a lot of refrigerator space. Mary Veazey Clark of Greensburg, Pa., makes them stackable by covering the dishes with stiff plastic lids she saves from yogurt containers. (This also works for portioned sauces, dips, and condiments.)

SEND US YOUR TIPS We will provide a complimentary one-year subscription for each tip we print. Send your tip, name, address, and daytime telephone number to Quick Tips, *Cook's Illustrated*, P.O. Box 470589, Brookline, MA 02447, or to QuickTips@AmericasTestKitchen.com.

Easily Removing Lids from Cans

When you are using an old-fashioned can opener, the lid sometimes drops into the can and needs to be fished out. Donnah Brnger of Buxton, Maine, makes a "handle" with masking tape: Take a 4-inch strip of masking tape and fold one end over on itself about halfway to form a handle. Press the other end onto the lid before opening the can and then pull the handle to lift the lid from the can.

Storing Fragile Figs

Figs bruise and spoil quickly if kept in a bowl or dish where they are all touching each other, so Emma Brinkmeyer of San Luis Obispo, Calif., keeps them in an empty egg carton. Each fig gets its own space, and the spaces are just big enough to allow the figs to sit upright.

Minimizing the Mess of Stovetop Splatter

To keep stovetop grease from splattering onto unused burners, Drew Goodwin of Maynard, Mass., puts a new 12 by 12-inch floor tile over each one. The tiles are easy to clean, and they act as added counter space.

Bag up Wood Chunks for Soaking

To keep wood chunks submerged while they soak, Donnie Young of Vero Beach, Fla., places them in a zipper-lock bag and fills it with water. The water surrounds the chunks, and it's easy to transport the bag out to the grill.

Trim Lemons to Get the Most Juice

While juicing lemons, Barbara Belknap of Oneonta, N.Y., found that the hard, pointy end of the fruit kept her from squeezing out the maximum amount of juice. By trimming off the end and creating a flat edge, she discovered she could press out more juice.

Chill Sangria with Frozen Fruit

When serving sangria, Stephanie La Porta of West Vancouver, British Columbia, freezes the fruit she would use as a garnish (such as grapes, melon, apples, and citrus) or opens a bag of frozen berries and uses the frozen pieces as ice cubes. They look pretty in the glass and chill the wine without diluting it.

Thai Grilled Chicken

You don't need a well-stocked Asian pantry or specialty equipment to make this street-food classic. Just a low fire, a bold marinade, and Cornish hens.

⇒ BY ANNIE PETITO ⇐

I can't think of a cuisine that doesn't lay claim to a grilled chicken dish, but the Thai version might be my favorite. Called *gai yang*, it's street food that originated in Thailand's northeastern Isan region but has become ubiquitous throughout the country. Countless variations exist, but the most popular features small whole chickens that are butterflied, flattened, and marinated in a garlic-herb paste. To keep the hens flat, cooks position them between bamboo clips that look like giant clothespins; they then grill the hens over a low charcoal fire so that their fat renders and their skin crisps. What you get is the best version of grilled chicken—juicy meat, bronzed skin, and smoky char—made extraordinary by the flavor-packed marinade. The chicken is cut into pieces and served with a tangy-sweet-spicy dipping sauce and sticky rice, which soaks up the assertive flavors.

As a bonus, this dish can be prepared using mostly pantry staples. The only ingredient I'd have to work around was the bird itself. Thai chickens typically weigh between 1 and 3 pounds, so I'd have to find an alternative. After that, it would be a matter of ironing out the marinade and the fire setup, as many recipes are vague on the grill instructions.

Flat Out

I discovered that the Thai chickens are often replaced with whole conventional chickens, while other recipes call for parts or Cornish hens. Cornish hens offer a few unique benefits that make them ideal for this recipe: They have a high ratio of skin to meat, so both the dark and white portions cook up juicy; they weigh 1¼ pounds or so (about the same size as the Thai chickens) and cook in about 30 minutes when butterflied; and they're convenient and elegant for portioning—one bird per person.

Gai yang vendors typically butterfly chickens along the breastbone, but I found that this method

▶ **Annie Grills the Birds**
A step-by-step video is available at CooksIllustrated.com/aug17

Cornish hens are a good substitute for small Thai chickens. Plus, they're easy to portion when entertaining—one bird per person.

caused the skin to pull away from the breast, leaving the lean white meat exposed and at greater risk of drying out. Butterflying by cutting out the backbones with kitchen shears and flattening the birds was the better approach. The skin stayed intact on one side, so it browned evenly, and the hens were uniformly flat, so they cooked at the same rate. As for the bamboo "clothespins," they flatten the birds and function as handles that make them easier to flip. But as long as I handled the hens carefully with tongs, I could move them on the grill without skewering.

Cut and Paste

I marinated the hens overnight in a paste made from garlic, cilantro stems (a substitute for the traditional cilantro root), white pepper, and fish sauce—the four marinade components I found in every recipe. Then I grilled the hens skin side up over the cooler side of a half-grill fire. Just before the meat was done, I placed them over the coals to crisp the skin.

They cooked up juicy and savory, thanks in large part to the salty fish sauce, which essentially brined the meat, seasoning it and helping it retain moisture during cooking. To bolster that effect, I added a couple of teaspoons of salt. But many recipes further season the marinade with soy sauce, ginger, lemon grass, ground coriander, or sugar (usually Thai palm sugar or brown sugar). When I added some of these to the base ingredients for evaluation, I liked the nutty, citrusy flavor of ground coriander (made from the seeds of the cilantro plant) and the malty sweetness of brown sugar, so these were in. I also thickened the marinade, which tended to slide off the meat, to a clingy, pesto-like consistency by adding cilantro leaves along with the stems.

Sweet and Hot

On to fixing the flavor and consistency of the dipping sauces, which ranged from sticky and cloyingly sweet to thin and fiery. I wanted a balance of sweetness and tang, so I simmered white vinegar and sugar until the mixture thickened to a light syrup. Minced raw garlic and Thai chiles gave the sauce a fruity burn that red pepper flakes just couldn't match.

I set out the hens and sauce along with sticky rice, which I made by mimicking the equipment used in Thailand (see "The Traditional Sticky Rice Setup"). As my colleagues tore into the burnished hens, sweet-tangy sauce dripping from their fingers, they joked (sort of) that I should set up a gai yang stand of my own.

Stick 'em Up

Street vendors all over Thailand hawk grilled chicken (called *gai yang*) from setups like this, with the bird pinned between bamboo holders positioned over a low fire. That way, the meat stays moist as the skin renders and browns.

Grill—and Serve—Chicken the Thai Way

Gai yang isn't your garden-variety grilled chicken. These Cornish hens are flavor-packed and portion nicely, and the sticky rice and chili dipping sauce served alongside complete the package.

USE CORNISH HENS
➤ Like the smaller chickens grilled in Thailand, Cornish hens have a high ratio of flavorful skin to meat.
➤ Butterflying the hens keeps the skin intact and helps them cook evenly.

MARINATE IN FLAVORFUL PASTE
➤ Cilantro leaves and stems, garlic, fish sauce, brown sugar, salt, and spices create a thick, superflavorful marinade that seasons the birds.

MAKE A QUICK DIPPING SAUCE
➤ This sweet-spicy-tangy dipping sauce is viscous enough that the garlic and chiles it contains stay suspended rather than sink to the bottom.

STEAM SOME STICKY RICE
➤ Densely packed sticky rice is ideal for soaking up the bold flavors (steamed regular white rice is a fine substitute).

THE TRADITIONAL STICKY RICE SETUP

The traditional vessel for steaming Thai sticky rice is a bamboo basket set over an hourglass-shaped aluminum pot, which allows the rice to steam on all sides. We mimicked that setup with a saucepan and a fine-mesh strainer.

THAI-STYLE STICKY RICE (KHAO NIAW)
SERVES 4

This recipe requires letting the rice soak in water for at least 4 hours before cooking. When shopping, look for rice labeled "Thai glutinous rice" or "Thai sweet rice"; do not substitute other varieties. Thai glutinous rice can be found in Asian markets and some supermarkets or online.

> 2 cups Thai glutinous rice

1. Place rice in medium bowl and pour enough water over rice to cover by 2 inches. Let stand at room temperature for at least 4 hours or up to 8 hours.

2. Cut 18-inch square of double-thickness cheesecloth. Line large fine-mesh strainer with cheesecloth, letting excess hang over sides. Drain rice in prepared strainer, then rinse under running water until water runs clear. Fold edges of cheesecloth over rice and pat surface of rice smooth.

3. Bring 1½ inches water to boil in large saucepan. Set strainer in saucepan (water should not touch bottom of strainer), cover with lid (it will not form tight seal), reduce heat to medium-high, and steam rice for 15 minutes. Uncover and, using tongs, flip cheesecloth bundle (rice should form sticky mass) so side that was closer to bottom of saucepan is now on top. Cover and continue to steam until rice is just translucent and texture is tender but with a little chew, 15 to 20 minutes longer, checking water level occasionally and adding more if necessary.

4. Remove saucepan from heat, drain excess water from saucepan and return strainer to saucepan. Cover and let rice stand for 10 to 15 minutes before serving.

THAI GRILLED CORNISH HENS WITH CHILI DIPPING SAUCE (GAI YANG)
SERVES 4

The hens need to marinate for at least 6 hours before cooking (a longer marinating time is preferable). If your hens weigh 1½ to 2 pounds, grill three hens instead of four and extend the initial cooking time in step 6 by 5 minutes. If you can't find Thai chiles, substitute Fresno or red jalapeño chiles. Serve with Thai-Style Sticky Rice or steamed white rice.

Hens
4	Cornish game hens (1¼ to 1½ pounds each), giblets discarded
1	cup fresh cilantro leaves and stems, chopped coarse
12	garlic cloves, peeled
¼	cup packed light brown sugar
2	teaspoons ground white pepper
2	teaspoons ground coriander
2	teaspoons salt
¼	cup fish sauce

Dipping Sauce
½	cup distilled white vinegar
½	cup granulated sugar
1	tablespoon minced Thai chiles
3	garlic cloves, minced
¼	teaspoon salt

1. **FOR THE HENS:** Working with 1 hen at a time, place hens breast side down on cutting board and use kitchen shears to cut through bones on either side of backbones; discard backbones. Flip hens and press on breastbones to flatten. Trim any excess fat and skin.

2. Pulse cilantro leaves and stems, garlic, sugar, pepper, coriander, and salt in food processor until finely chopped, 10 to 15 pulses; transfer to small bowl. Add fish sauce and stir until marinade has consistency of loose paste.

3. Rub hens all over with marinade. Transfer hens and any excess marinade to 1-gallon zipper-lock bag and refrigerate for at least 6 hours or up to 24 hours, flipping bag halfway through marinating.

4. **FOR THE DIPPING SAUCE:** Bring vinegar to boil in small saucepan. Add sugar and stir to dissolve. Reduce heat to medium-low and simmer until vinegar mixture is slightly thickened, 5 minutes. Remove from heat and let vinegar mixture cool completely. Add chiles, garlic, and salt and stir until combined. Transfer sauce to airtight container and refrigerate until ready to use. (Sauce can be refrigerated for up to 2 weeks. Bring to room temperature before serving.)

5A. **FOR A CHARCOAL GRILL:** Open bottom vent completely. Light large chimney starter filled with charcoal briquettes (6 quarts). When top coals are partially covered with ash, pour evenly over half of grill. Set cooking grate in place, cover, and open lid vent completely. Heat grill until hot, about 5 minutes.

5B. **FOR A GAS GRILL:** Turn all burners to high, cover, and heat grill until hot, about 15 minutes. Leave primary burner on high and turn off other burner(s). Adjust primary burner (or, if using three-burner grill, primary burner and second burner) as needed to maintain grill temperature between 400 and 450 degrees.

6. Clean and oil cooking grate. Remove hens from bag, leaving any marinade that sticks to hens in place. Tuck wingtips behind backs and turn legs so drumsticks face inward toward breasts. Place hens, skin side up, on cooler side of grill (if using charcoal, arrange hens so that legs and thighs are facing coals). Cover and cook until skin is browned and breasts register 145 to 150 degrees, 30 to 35 minutes, rotating hens halfway through cooking.

7. Using tongs, carefully flip hens skin side down and move to hotter side of grill. Cover and cook until skin is crisp, deeply browned, and charred in spots and breasts register 160 degrees, 3 to 5 minutes, being careful to avoid burning.

8. Transfer hens, skin side up, to cutting board; tent with aluminum foil and let rest for 10 minutes. Slice each hen in half or into 4 pieces and serve, passing dipping sauce separately.

Really Good Turkey Meatloaf

For a lighter, summery take on this comfort-food favorite, our goal was to enhance the ground turkey's clean, mild flavor without obscuring it.

⇾ BY LAN LAM ⇽

Swapping ground turkey for the usual ground beef and pork mixture can give meatloaf a lighter flavor profile that makes it more summertime-friendly. But simply substituting turkey for the beef and pork in the typical recipe, which calls for little more than the ground meat, an egg binder, and a tenderizer in the form of a panade (a mixture of bread crumbs and milk), results in a loaf that cooks up pasty and bland. Rather than solve these issues, most recipes try to merely distract from the problems by adding a thick glaze or folding in lots of vegetables or spices. Surely I could do better. I hoped to turn out a juicy, tender turkey meatloaf with complementary additions that highlighted the turkey's mild, meaty flavor instead of overshadowing it.

Time to Open Up

Here's the main problem: Compared with beef or pork, turkey becomes very soft, with a slightly pasty consistency, when ground (see "Firming up Ground Turkey"). This translates to a meatloaf that can't hold its shape and has a compact, mushy texture. Grinding the turkey myself would help since I could grind it more coarsely, but this was more trouble than I wanted. I'd need to find a way to improve the preground stuff. I knew that 99 percent lean ground turkey was a nonstarter; the greater amount of fat in 85 percent lean turkey would provide more flavor and help keep the meatloaf from being too dry.

My first move was to drop the panade. It might often be the key to a moist and tender traditional meatloaf, but in this case the wet bits of bread throughout were exacerbating the pasty, dense consistency. Instead, I needed to add a more resilient ingredient, something that would lend some texture and break up the finely ground meat to make the loaf less dense. I baked up an assortment of meatloaves that contained just turkey, egg, salt, and pepper, along with one of several possible texturizers.

▶ **See the Loaf Happen**
A step-by-step video is available at CooksIllustrated.com/aug17

Quick oats help loosen the dense texture of the ground turkey while Worcestershire sauce and Dijon mustard add dimension.

Tasters rejected ground nuts (too crunchy), bulgur and couscous (too wheaty), and pieces of turkey sausage (too springy). There was just one ingredient that they liked: quick oats. The flakes were the perfect size to break up the meat without calling too much attention to themselves, and they retained just the right amount of bite (sturdier rolled oats also worked if I chopped them finely).

Oats were in, but now I had a new problem: The loaf seemed wet; some tasters described it as almost watery. I realized I had stumbled upon another difference between turkey and beef/pork meatloaf: the meat's juices. While the juices in a traditional meatloaf have richness and viscosity from the fat and gelatin naturally found in ground beef and pork, turkey has less of both of these, and so its juices are thin in flavor and consistency. This was not as noticeable in a loaf made with a panade, as the bread soaked up almost all the juices. But the oats didn't soak up the juices as thoroughly; plus, they created a more open texture, with gaps where the juices could pool. The result: The shortcomings in the turkey's

juices were now much more noticeable. I'd have to figure out a way to give them more flavor and body.

The surest way to add more flavor would be to add fat. But I wouldn't want to add much since I was aiming for a lighter dish. Happily, just 3 tablespoons of melted butter mixed into the ground turkey made a big difference. As a bonus, the melted butter firmed up when mixed into the cold ground turkey, giving the mixture some structure that made it easier to shape. I also added grated Parmesan, and instead of using whole eggs as a binder, I used just the less watery yolks. These changes made the whole loaf taste richer, juices included.

Now what about bumping up the turkey juices' viscosity? I considered adding gelatin but instead turned to cornstarch, an ingredient home cooks are more likely to keep on hand. I settled on 2 teaspoons, which I added to the oats, salt, and pepper in a small bowl before combining the mixture with the turkey.

I set my loaf on an aluminum foil–lined wire cooling rack set in a rimmed baking sheet, our go-to setup for meatloaf (see "A Setup for Better Meatloaf"), and popped it into the oven. I now had an impressively tender, juicy turkey meatloaf with a texture that rivaled that of the classic beef and pork version.

Glazed Over

Next, I focused on adding some complementary supporting flavors. To start, I sautéed onions gently in the melted butter until soft. To save time, I turned to a test kitchen trick to speed up their breakdown: adding a pinch of baking soda. Onion cell walls will break down more readily in an alkaline environment, so rather than the onion taking 15 minutes to soften, it took just 5 minutes. To further round out the flavor, I added garlic, thyme, and some tangy-savory Worcestershire sauce. Dijon mustard lent additional punch, and parsley contributed freshness. After letting this mixture cool slightly, I added the oat mixture, Parmesan, egg yolks, and ground turkey; shaped the loaf; and baked as before.

The flavor was leagues better than any turkey meatloaf I'd ever had. My only complaint was that it seemed a bit too plain. Though not always a must for traditional meatloaf, a glaze seemed in order here—not only to bump up its looks but also to add another layer of flavor. I whisked together ketchup, brown sugar, cider vinegar, and hot sauce. Cooking the mixture for 5 minutes reduced it to the right consistency. To ensure that the glaze stayed put, I turned to a two-step technique we've used in the past. I applied half the glaze to the loaf before popping it into the oven. After 40 minutes, at which point the glaze had become firm and tacky, I brushed on another coat.

By the time the meatloaf reached 160 degrees, the glaze was starting to brown in spots and the meatloaf looked and smelled great. In fact, my tasters' only request was that I come up with another glaze option to give the dish some variety. For a lighter, brighter flavor, I warmed some apricot preserves until fluid, strained them, and combined them with ketchup and Dijon mustard. The preserves helped thicken the glaze, so I didn't even have to reduce it before applying it to the meatloaf. My turkey meatloaf might be perfect warmer-weather fare, but it's so good that I'll be making it year-round.

TURKEY MEATLOAF WITH KETCHUP–BROWN SUGAR GLAZE
SERVES 4 TO 6

Do not use 99 percent lean ground turkey in this recipe; it will make a dry meatloaf. Three tablespoons of rolled oats, chopped fine, can be substituted for the quick oats; do not use steel-cut oats.

Meatloaf
- 3 tablespoons unsalted butter
-   Pinch baking soda
- ½ onion, chopped fine
-   Salt and pepper
- 1 garlic clove, minced
- 1 teaspoon minced fresh thyme
- 2 tablespoons Worcestershire sauce
- 3 tablespoons quick oats
- 2 teaspoons cornstarch
- 2 large egg yolks
- 2 tablespoons Dijon mustard
- 2 pounds 85 or 93 percent lean ground turkey
- 1 ounce Parmesan cheese, grated (½ cup)
- ⅓ cup chopped fresh parsley

Glaze
- 1 cup ketchup
- ¼ cup packed brown sugar
- 2½ teaspoons cider vinegar
- ½ teaspoon hot sauce

1. FOR THE MEATLOAF: Adjust oven rack to upper-middle position and heat oven to 350 degrees. Line wire rack with aluminum foil and set in rimmed baking sheet. Melt butter in 10-inch skillet over low heat. Stir baking soda into melted butter. Add onion and ¼ teaspoon salt, increase heat to medium, and

Glaze: Twice Is Nicer

We brush our meatloaf with glaze twice to get a thick, uniform application. The first coat needs to dry slightly before the second coat is applied so that the second coat has something to stick to.

cook, stirring frequently, until onion is softened and beginning to brown, 3 to 4 minutes. Add garlic and thyme and cook until fragrant, about 1 minute. Stir in Worcestershire and continue to cook until slightly reduced, about 1 minute longer. Transfer onion mixture to large bowl and set aside. Combine oats, cornstarch, ¾ teaspoon salt, and ½ teaspoon pepper in second bowl.

2. FOR THE GLAZE: Whisk all ingredients in saucepan until sugar dissolves. Bring mixture to simmer over medium heat and cook until slightly thickened, about 5 minutes; set aside.

3. Stir egg yolks and mustard into cooled onion mixture until well combined. Add turkey, Parmesan, parsley, and oat mixture; using your hands, mix until well combined. Transfer turkey mixture to center of prepared rack. Using your wet hands, shape into 9 by 5-inch loaf. Using pastry brush, spread half of glaze evenly over top and sides of meatloaf. Bake meatloaf for 40 minutes.

4. Brush remaining glaze onto top and sides of meatloaf and continue to bake until meatloaf registers 160 degrees, 35 to 40 minutes longer. Let meatloaf cool for 20 minutes before slicing and serving.

Firming up Ground Turkey

Compared with ground beef and pork, ground turkey can cook up pasty, even mushy, and its juices are more watery and thin. Why the difference? Poultry has less fat than most ground red meat, of course, but it also has less connective tissue. Connective tissue provides support and texture to meat, so with less of it, meat becomes mushy and compact when cooked. Also, less-fatty poultry juices lack the unctuous viscosity of red meat juices.

To address these issues, we turned to three pantry ingredients: oats, which we mixed into the turkey to help give the loaf more structure and make it less dense, and cornstarch and butter, which added appealing body to the juices.

TURKEY MEATLOAF WITH APRICOT-MUSTARD GLAZE

Microwave ¼ cup apricot preserves until hot and fluid, about 30 seconds. Strain preserves through fine-mesh strainer into bowl; discard solids. Stir in 2 tablespoons Dijon mustard, 2 tablespoons ketchup, and pinch salt. Proceed with recipe, substituting apricot mixture for glaze.

A Setup for Better Meatloaf

Many recipes call for cooking meatloaf in a loaf pan, but we found that this method causes the meat to steam and stew in its own juices. We take a different approach.

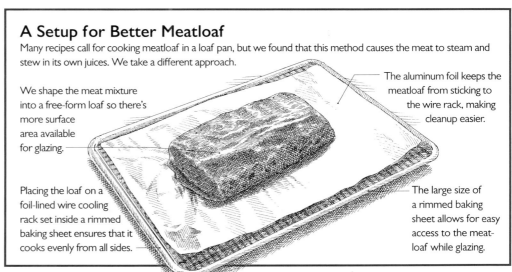

We shape the meat mixture into a free-form loaf so there's more surface area available for glazing.

The aluminum foil keeps the meatloaf from sticking to the wire rack, making cleanup easier.

Placing the loaf on a foil-lined wire cooling rack set inside a rimmed baking sheet ensures that it cooks evenly from all sides.

The large size of a rimmed baking sheet allows for easy access to the meatloaf while glazing.

Smoked Steak

Adding a packet of wood chips to the grill can take an inexpensive steak to the next level. But there's a fine line between perfection and going up in smoke.

> ⫸ BY ANDREW JANJIGIAN ⫷

I've always wondered why there isn't a tradition of smoking more cuts of beef. We smoke chicken, turkey, pork, and many kinds of fish, but when it comes to beef, not so much. Sure, there are some notable exceptions, such as Texas-style barbecued ribs and brisket. But why don't we smoke quicker-cooking cuts; for example, steak?

It turns out I'm not the only one to have this thought, as I was able to rustle up a few recipes for smoked steaks. While most called for rib eye or porterhouse, I was more intrigued by those calling for flat-iron steak, a cut we haven't used much in the test kitchen. It's a beefy-tasting steak from the shoulder that's decently marbled and tender and also has the advantage of being relatively inexpensive. Its only drawback is that it can have a slightly mineral flavor. To my mind, that made it a perfect candidate for smoking, as the smoke would camouflage any overly metallic notes and give the steak even more dimension. Since blade steaks are cut from the same part of the cow (see "Two Great—and Inexpensive—Steaks to Try"), I'd make sure my recipe also worked with them for those who can't find flat iron.

Most recipes I found for smoked steak, no matter the cut, took a similar approach, essentially treating the steaks like slow-cooked barbecue. They called for setting up the grill with a hotter and a cooler side by arranging the coals over half the grill and putting an aluminum foil packet of soaked wood chips on the coals. They cooked the steak covered (to trap smoke and direct its flow over the meat) on the cooler side of the grill until it neared its target temperature and then moved it to the hotter side, directly over the coals, to give it a good char on the exterior.

I gave this approach a try and immediately hit two snags: First, cooked to the typical medium-rare, the steak was still chewy. It turns out that flat-iron steak needs to be cooked to medium for the muscle fibers to shrink and loosen enough to be tender. Second, tasters were unanimous that the smoke flavor was overwhelming. I realized that while collagen-rich barbecue cuts (such as brisket) that are cooked far beyond well-done benefit from lots of smoke flavor to give them more complexity, steaks cooked to medium-rare or even medium have a more nuanced flavor that is easily lost with too much smoke.

Over the next few tests, I dialed back the smoke, eventually cutting the amount of wood chips to just 1 cup. Since we've found that wood chips can pack very differently depending on their shape and size, I switched to using a set weight (2½ ounces) to better control the amount of smoke. I also raised the grill's temperature by adding more coals so that the steaks would cook through more quickly, thus lessening their exposure to the smoke; they cooked in about 12 minutes per side. And yet, even with these changes, they were too smoky.

Suddenly, the answer seemed obvious. I shouldn't be following the lead of all those recipes by cooking the steaks over indirect heat like barbecue. I should be cooking them how we normally cook steaks—quickly, over direct heat—but with smoke.

With that in mind, I dusted another batch of steaks with salt and let them sit for an hour to ensure that the seasoning penetrated below the surface. In the meantime, I set up the grill. I used a full chimney of charcoal, spreading the coals evenly across half the grill as before. But this time, I topped them off with a packet of wood chips I hadn't soaked. Soaking the chips serves only to delay the onset of

A little smoke, an herb-spice rub, and lemons grilled and served alongside add impressive flavor to these inexpensive steaks.

▶ **See Andrew Smoke**
A step-by-step video is available at CooksIllustrated.com/aug17

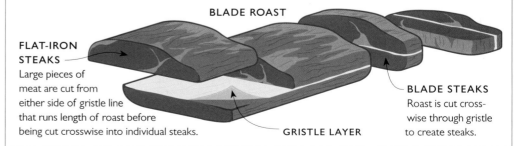

Two Great—and Inexpensive—Steaks to Try

Named for their anvil-like shape, flat-iron steaks are cut from the blade roast at the top of the cow's shoulder. Once available mainly in restaurants, they have become more popular and thus more widely available in supermarkets. Flat iron is an affordable cut with a beefy flavor and tenderness comparable to that of steaks cut from the prime rib roast. If you can't find flat iron, blade steak is a great alternative. It comes from the same larger cut, the blade roast. Its only downside is a line of gristle down the middle, which flat iron is cut to avoid.

BLADE ROAST

FLAT-IRON STEAKS
Large pieces of meat are cut from either side of gristle line that runs length of roast before being cut crosswise into individual steaks.

GRISTLE LAYER

BLADE STEAKS
Roast is cut crosswise through gristle to create steaks.

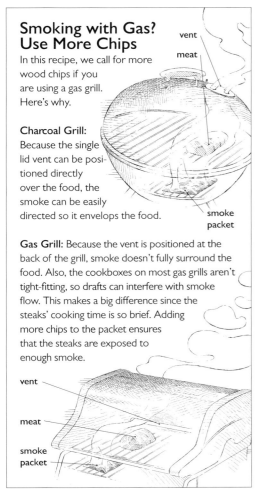

Smoking with Gas? Use More Chips

In this recipe, we call for more wood chips if you are using a gas grill. Here's why.

Charcoal Grill: Because the single lid vent can be positioned directly over the food, the smoke can be easily directed so it envelops the food.

Gas Grill: Because the vent is positioned at the back of the grill, smoke doesn't fully surround the food. Also, the cookboxes on most gas grills aren't tight-fitting, so drafts can interfere with smoke flow. This makes a big difference since the steaks' cooking time is so brief. Adding more chips to the packet ensures that the steaks are exposed to enough smoke.

smoking; now that I would be grilling for such a short period, I needed the chips to begin smoking right away. I dropped the steaks onto the grate and cooked them directly over the coals, covered, until they reached the 130-degree target for medium (our preferred doneness for flat-iron steaks), which took just 5 minutes per side.

These steaks were just what I wanted: juicy and kissed with a hint of smoke that enhanced rather than overwhelmed. To complement the smoke flavor, I put together a dry rub featuring thyme, rosemary, fennel seeds, black peppercorns, and red pepper flakes to apply to the steaks just before grilling. For some tempered brightness, I grilled lemon wedges alongside the steaks to serve with them. When I tried swapping in blade steaks, they worked perfectly (folks just had to cut around the line of gristle that runs down the middle).

Now my recipe was perfect on a charcoal grill, but what about gas? Gas grills are less efficient at smoking foods than charcoal grills since they aren't as tightly sealed and don't have vents that can be positioned and adjusted to help draw smoke over the meat. In order to give the steaks comparable exposure to smoke in such a short amount of time, I found that it was necessary to increase the amount of chips to 1½ cups.

Whether I used flat-iron or blade steak, I knew I'd deliver an impressive steak dinner.

GRILL-SMOKED HERB-RUBBED FLAT-IRON STEAKS
SERVES 4 TO 6

This recipe requires rubbing the steaks with salt and letting them sit at room temperature for 1 hour before cooking. You can substitute blade steaks for the flat-iron steaks, if desired. We like both cuts cooked to medium (130 to 135 degrees). We like hickory chips in this recipe, but other kinds of wood chips will work. Gas grills are not as efficient at smoking meat as charcoal grills, so we recommend using 1½ cups of wood chips if using a gas grill.

- 2 teaspoons dried thyme
- 1 teaspoon dried rosemary
- ¾ teaspoon fennel seeds
- ½ teaspoon black peppercorns
- ¼ teaspoon red pepper flakes
- 4 (6- to 8-ounce) flat-iron steaks, ¾ to 1 inch thick, trimmed
- 1 tablespoon kosher salt
- 1–1½ cups (2½–3¾ ounces) wood chips
  Vegetable oil spray
- 2 lemons, quartered lengthwise

1. Grind thyme, rosemary, fennel seeds, peppercorns, and pepper flakes in spice grinder or with mortar and pestle until coarsely ground. Transfer to small bowl. Pat steaks dry with paper towels. Rub steaks evenly on both sides with salt and place on wire rack set in rimmed baking sheet. Let stand at room temperature for 1 hour. (After 30 minutes, prepare grill.)

2. Using large piece of heavy-duty aluminum foil, wrap wood chips (1 cup if using charcoal; 1½ cups if using gas) in 8 by 4½-inch foil packet. (Make sure chips do not poke holes in sides or bottom of packet.) Cut 2 evenly spaced 2-inch slits in top of packet.

3A. FOR A CHARCOAL GRILL: Open bottom vent completely. Light large chimney starter filled with charcoal briquettes (6 quarts). When top coals are partially covered with ash, pour evenly over half of grill. Place wood chip packet on coals. Set cooking grate in place, cover, and open lid vent completely. Heat grill until hot and wood chips are smoking, about 5 minutes.

3B. FOR A GAS GRILL: Remove cooking grate and place wood chip packet directly on primary burner. Set grate in place, turn all burners to high, cover, and heat grill until hot and wood chips are smoking, about 15 minutes. Leave primary burner on high and turn other burner(s) to medium.

4. Clean and oil cooking grate. Sprinkle half of herb rub evenly over 1 side of steaks and press to adhere. Lightly spray herb-rubbed side of steaks with oil spray, about 3 seconds. Flip steaks and repeat process of sprinkling and pressing steaks with remaining herb rub and coating with oil spray on second side.

5. Place lemons and steaks on hotter side of grill, cover (position lid vent over steaks if using charcoal), and cook until lemons and steaks are well browned on both sides and meat registers 130 to 135 degrees (for medium), 4 to 6 minutes per side. (If steaks are fully charred before reaching desired temperature, move to cooler side of grill, cover, and continue to cook.) Transfer lemons and steaks to clean wire rack set in rimmed baking sheet, tent with foil, and let rest for 10 minutes. Slice steaks thin against grain and serve, passing lemons separately.

Linguine with Seafood

No matter how much shellfish you pack into the pot, the pasta in dishes such as *linguine allo scoglio* often doesn't taste at all like the sea. We wanted to change that.

⇒ BY STEVE DUNN ⇐

Italian seafood pastas such as *frutti di mare* and *pescatore* promise noodles teeming with shellfish and saturated with clean, briny-sweet flavor. And while many versions are chock-full of shrimp, clams, mussels, lobster, scallops, squid, or any combination thereof, I've yet to eat one in which the pasta actually tastes much like the sea. The shellfish flavor tends to be locked up in the pieces of seafood themselves rather than awash throughout the dish. Together with the typical tomato-based sauce, these dishes resemble nothing more than pasta drenched in marinara and punctuated by the occasional bite of seafood.

Most recently I came across this problem in a bowl of *linguine allo scoglio*, another mixed shellfish–and–pasta classic that's named for the rocky Italian seashores where seafood is abundant (*scoglio* means "rock"). Tangled in the noodles were shell-on mussels and clams, shrimp, and squid, as well as cherry tomatoes, garlic, and fresh herbs. The sauce was white wine–based, which gave me hope that the seafood flavor might come through more clearly here than it does in tomato-based preparations. But instead the pasta barely tasted like seafood and was relatively dry, as the thin sauce had slipped right off the linguine and puddled at the bottom of the bowl. Worse, the mussels, shrimp, and squid were dense and rubbery, obviously having toughened while waiting for the longer-cooking clams to pop open.

Overcooked seafood would be easy enough to fix with a strategic cooking method. But for this dish, I also had my sights set on a light-bodied sauce that clung nicely to the noodles and infused them with the flavor of the sea.

Shellfish Sequence

I ignored recipes that suggested sautéing or simmering the shrimp, clams, mussels, and squid together in a pot until every piece was cooked through, since that would surely lead to the rubbery results I'd had before. But I didn't want to tediously cook one type of shellfish at a time, transferring each to a bowl as it finished cooking. I had to figure out how long it would take each type of seafood to cook, add the longest-cooking item first, and stagger the additions of the others.

Fresh tomatoes, loads of garlic, and parsley keep the flavors in this classic pasta dish clean and bright.

First I sautéed minced garlic and red pepper flakes in a Dutch oven over moderately high heat, which would get the sauce base going. In went the clams, which popped open after about 8 minutes, followed midway through cooking by the mussels. With no hard, protective shells, shrimp and squid cook very quickly, so I lowered the flame and added them to the pot. They plumped nicely in about 4 minutes and 2 minutes, respectively—but would have toughened if I hadn't kept a close watch on them. Down the road, I'd see if there was an even gentler way to cook them, but for now, I had at least established a sequence.

Clamming Up

Left behind in the pot were the aromatics and the liquor shed by the cooked shellfish, which would fortify my sauce. It wasn't much, though, so I borrowed a technique we've used in other shrimp preparations and made a quick stock with the shells by browning them in a skillet and simmering them with wine. In this case, I finished building the sauce by adding lots of chopped parsley, a dash of fresh thyme, and about ¾ pound of whole cherry tomatoes; as the sauce simmered, the tomatoes collapsed into a pulp that added body to the sauce. Meanwhile, I boiled the linguine in a separate pot. I then tossed the cooked seafood into the sauce and poured it over the drained pasta.

The seafood was well cooked, but the sauce was still thin in both body and seafood flavor. To kick it up another notch, I skipped the shrimp broth and instead added a bottle of clam juice and four minced anchovies. If that sounds like it would be unpleasantly fishy, trust me that it's not; we often use an anchovy or two to add rich, savory flavor in both seafood and nonseafood preparations, and mincing them to a fine paste ensures that they meld seamlessly.

Adding a spoonful of tomato paste along with the anchovies and simmering the liquid until it had reduced by about one-third yielded much richer, rounder flavor—but only marginally better body. When I poured the sauce over the linguine, it still slipped right through to the bottom of the bowl.

Marrying Early

That's when I realized I hadn't implemented one of the oldest Italian pasta-cooking tricks in the book: parboiling the pasta until it's just shy of al dente, draining it, and simmering it directly in the sauce to finish cooking. Doing so not only allows the pasta to soak up the flavor of the sauce but the starches it sheds during cooking also thicken the liquid. (I made sure to reserve some of the starchy pasta cooking water in case I needed to adjust the consistency of the sauce before serving.) At last, the sauce was viscous enough to cling to the strands.

I was about to declare my recipe finished when I got a forkful of squid that was a tad rubbery. So were

No More Spotty Seafood Flavor

Even when a bowl of pasta is teeming with shellfish, the seafood flavor is typically isolated rather than infused throughout the dish. To change that, we made a clam juice–based sauce and added four minced anchovies with the aromatics. We also finished cooking the pasta in the sauce to let it soak up the seafood flavor.

PRECOOK THE CLAMS AND MUSSELS

Cook clams   Add mussels   Set clams and mussels aside

We give the clams and the mussels a head start by cooking them first over medium-high heat. Their liquor is the base for the sauce.

PARBOIL THE PASTA

Boil water for pasta   Cook pasta for 7 minutes

We parboil the linguine and add it to the sauce when it's just shy of al dente. That way, it soaks up flavor while giving up starch that lends body to the sauce.

Perfectly cooking pasta, sauce, and four kinds of shellfish at the same time was complicated—and often ended badly. We got around this by precooking some of the components and adding other components near the end of cooking. With the right order of operations, our version of *linguine allo scoglio* is much easier to prepare.

Continue to build sauce in pot used to cook clams and mussels   Add parboiled pasta to pot   Add shrimp to pot   Add squid to pot   Return clams and mussels to pot   Warm through and serve

Adding the shrimp and squid to the pot just before the pasta turns al dente keeps them from overcooking.

After returning the clams and mussels to the pot, we let the dish stand, covered, for a couple of minutes to warm through before serving.

the shrimp, I realized with another bite. Both had overcooked as they'd sat in the warm bowl, which got me thinking that I could add them to the sauce along with the pasta rather than precook them with the clams and mussels. After I'd let the pasta simmer in the sauce for about 2 minutes, I lowered the heat and added the shrimp and a lid. About 4 minutes later, I followed with the squid.

Now plump and tender, the shrimp and squid were perfect. To freshen up the flavors before serving, I tried one more batch in which I added lemon zest, halved cherry tomatoes, and more parsley along with the squid, plus a drizzle of olive oil and a squeeze of lemon juice. Every bite was bright, fresh, perfectly cooked, and—most important—packed with seafood flavor from top to bottom.

LINGUINE WITH SEAFOOD (LINGUINE ALLO SCOGLIO)
SERVES 6

For a simpler version of this dish, you can omit the clams and squid and increase the amounts of mussels and shrimp to 1½ pounds each; you'll also need to increase the amount of salt in step 2 to ¾ teaspoon. If you can't find fresh squid, it's available frozen (thaw it before cutting and cooking) at many supermarkets and typically has the benefit of being precleaned. Bar Harbor makes our favorite clam juice.

6	tablespoons extra-virgin olive oil
12	garlic cloves, minced
¼	teaspoon red pepper flakes
1	pound littleneck clams, scrubbed
1	pound mussels, scrubbed and debearded
1¼	pounds cherry tomatoes, half of tomatoes halved, remaining tomatoes left whole
1	(8-ounce) bottle clam juice
1	cup dry white wine
1	cup minced fresh parsley
1	tablespoon tomato paste
4	anchovy fillets, rinsed, patted dry, and minced
1	teaspoon minced fresh thyme
	Salt and pepper
1	pound linguine
1	pound extra-large shrimp (21 to 25 per pound), peeled and deveined
8	ounces squid, sliced crosswise into ½-inch-thick rings
2	teaspoons grated lemon zest, plus lemon wedges for serving

1. Heat ¼ cup oil in large Dutch oven over medium-high heat until shimmering. Add garlic and pepper flakes and cook until fragrant, about 1 minute. Add clams, cover, and cook, shaking pan occasionally, for 4 minutes. Add mussels, cover, and continue to cook, shaking pan occasionally, until clams and mussels have opened, 3 to 4 minutes longer. Transfer clams and mussels to bowl, discarding any that haven't opened, and cover to keep warm; leave any broth in pot.

2. Add whole tomatoes, clam juice, wine, ½ cup parsley, tomato paste, anchovies, thyme, and ½ teaspoon salt to pot and bring to simmer over medium-high heat. Reduce heat to medium and cook, stirring occasionally, until tomatoes have started to break down and sauce is reduced by one-third, about 10 minutes.

3. Meanwhile, bring 4 quarts water to boil in large pot. Add pasta and 1 tablespoon salt and cook, stirring often, for 7 minutes. Reserve ½ cup cooking water, then drain pasta.

4. Add pasta to sauce in Dutch oven and cook over medium heat, stirring gently, for 2 minutes. Reduce heat to medium-low, stir in shrimp, cover, and cook for 4 minutes. Stir in squid, lemon zest, halved tomatoes, and remaining ½ cup parsley; cover and continue to cook until shrimp and squid are just cooked through, about 2 minutes longer. Gently stir in clams and mussels. Remove pot from heat, cover, and let stand until clams and mussels are warmed through, about 2 minutes. Season with salt and pepper to taste and adjust consistency with reserved cooking water as needed. Transfer to large serving dish, drizzle with remaining 2 tablespoons oil, and serve, passing lemon wedges separately.

Simplest Shellfish in the Pot

If you've never cooked with squid, you should try it. It's inexpensive, cooks in minutes, and is typically sold precleaned. If you want rings, simply slice the bodies crosswise. If tentacles are available, buy some and add them to your dish.

If you can't find fresh squid, many supermarkets carry frozen squid packaged in a block of whole bodies. To use part of a frozen block, wrap the block in a kitchen towel and press it against the edge of a counter or table to break it.

FROZEN SQUID

▶ **See the Sequence**
A step-by-step video is available at CooksIllustrated.com/aug17

TESTING LARGE SAUCEPANS

HIGHLY RECOMMENDED

ALL-CLAD Stainless 4-Qt Sauce Pan

MODEL: 4204

PRICE: $179.13

FULLY CLAD: Yes

FEATURES: Helper handle, dishwasher-safe, oven- and broiler-safe to 600 degrees (without lid)

WEIGHT WITH LID: 4 lb, 2⅜ oz

COOKING SURFACE DIAMETER: 7½ in

PERFORMANCE	★★★
EASE OF USE	★★★
CLEANUP	★★★
DURABILITY	★★★

COMMENTS: Our longtime winner excelled, with steady heating and good visibility to monitor browning. Its stay-cool handle was easy to grip, and a helper handle provided another grabbing point. After being whacked on concrete, it emerged with only tiny dents.

RECOMMENDED

ZWILLING J.A. HENCKELS Aurora 5-ply 4-qt Stainless Steel Saucepan

MODEL: 66085-220

PRICE: $214.99

FULLY CLAD: Yes

FEATURES: Oven- and broiler-safe to 500 degrees, dishwasher-safe

WEIGHT WITH LID: 5 lb, 5⅝ oz

COOKING SURFACE DIAMETER: 8¼ in

PERFORMANCE	★★★
EASE OF USE	★★½
CLEANUP	★★★
DURABILITY	★★½

COMMENTS: Onions cooked evenly and rice came out fluffy in this wide, sturdy saucepan. The round handle stayed cool but sometimes slipped in our hands because the saucepan is heavy. It cleaned up well and emerged from abuse testing with only small dents.

CUISINART MultiClad Unlimited 4 Quart Saucepan with Cover

BEST BUY

MODEL: MCU194-20N

PRICE: $65.12

FULLY CLAD: Yes

FEATURES: Oven- and broiler-safe, dishwasher-safe

WEIGHT WITH LID: 3 lb, 5 oz

COOKING SURFACE DIAMETER: 7½ in

PERFORMANCE	★★★
EASE OF USE	★★½
CLEANUP	★★
DURABILITY	★★

COMMENTS: This lightweight pan had a few drawbacks: It cooked fast, leading to minor browning when we softened onions; the handle got hot, so a potholder was needed; and it lacked a helper handle. In abuse tests, it warped slightly and suffered minor dents and surface cracks at the points of impact. But given its bargain price, its performance was impressive.

TRAMONTINA Gourmet Tri-Ply Clad 4 Qt. Covered Sauce Pan

MODEL: 80116/024DS

PRICE: $89.95

FULLY CLAD: Yes

FEATURE: Helper handle

WEIGHT WITH LID: 3 lb, 14⅞ oz

COOKING SURFACE DIAMETER: 7 in

PERFORMANCE	★★½
EASE OF USE	★★½
CLEANUP	★★½
DURABILITY	★★

COMMENTS: This pan's narrow surface ran a bit hot, so onions at the perimeter browned slightly. Its moderately heavy frame was easy to lift, but the handle got hot during extended cooking. It suffered more damage in our abuse testing than higher-ranked models.

RECOMMENDED WITH RESERVATIONS

OXO Stainless Steel Pro 3.5 qt. Sauce Pan + Cover

MODEL: CW000975-003

PRICE: $79.99

FULLY CLAD: Yes

FEATURE: Helper handle

WEIGHT WITH LID: 4 lb, 6 oz

COOKING SURFACE DIAMETER: 7½ in

PERFORMANCE	★★½
EASE OF USE	★★
CLEANUP	★★
DURABILITY	★★½

SCANPAN CTX 4 qt Covered Saucepan

MODEL: 65232000

PRICE: $159.99

FULLY CLAD: Yes

FEATURES: Ceramic nonstick coating, ovensafe to 500 degrees, dishwasher-safe (but hand-washing recommended)

WEIGHT WITH LID: 4 lb, 11⅝ oz

COOKING SURFACE DIAMETER: 7½ in

PERFORMANCE	★★
EASE OF USE	★½
CLEANUP	★★½
DURABILITY	★★

LE CREUSET Tri-Ply Stainless Steel Saucepan with Lid and Helper Handle, 4-Quart

MODEL: SSP1100-20

PRICE: $159.95

FULLY CLAD: Yes

FEATURES: Oven- and broiler-safe to 500 degrees, dishwasher-safe

WEIGHT WITH LID: 3 lb, 8¾ oz

COOKING SURFACE DIAMETER: 7 in

PERFORMANCE	★★
EASE OF USE	★★
CLEANUP	★★½
DURABILITY	★½

SIMPLY CALPHALON Nonstick 4-Quart Saucepan

MODEL: 1770502

PRICE: $40.84

FULLY CLAD: No

FEATURES: Nonstick interior, built-in strainer

WEIGHT WITH LID: 3 lb, 8 oz

COOKING SURFACE DIAMETER: 7 in

PERFORMANCE	★½
EASE OF USE	★½
CLEANUP	★★½
DURABILITY	★★

NOT RECOMMENDED

T-FAL Initiatives Nonstick Saucepan with Glass Lid, 3-Quart, Gray

MODEL: A85724

PRICE: $18.99

FULLY CLAD: No

FEATURES: Nonstick interior, dishwasher-safe, ovensafe to 350 degrees

WEIGHT WITH LID: 2 lb, ⅜ oz

COOKING SURFACE DIAMETER: 6½ in

PERFORMANCE	★★
EASE OF USE	★½
CLEANUP	★½
DURABILITY	★

TRAMONTINA Gourmet Domus Tri-Ply Base 4 Qt Covered Sauce Pan

MODEL: 80102/006DS

PRICE: $79.95

FULLY CLAD: No

FEATURES: Ovensafe to 450 degrees

WEIGHT WITH LID: 3 lb, 15 oz

COOKING SURFACE DIAMETER: 7¼ in

PERFORMANCE	★½
EASE OF USE	★
CLEANUP	★½
DURABILITY	★

Figuring Out Feta

After sorting through three different milks, three countries, and eight products, we found what makes the finest feta.

≥ BY HANNAH CROWLEY ≤

Versatility is important in feta. To see how the cheeses performed when heated, we tasted them baked into the classic Greek spinach and feta pie, spanakopita.

The Greeks have been perfecting feta cheese since Homer's time—the early process for making it is mentioned in *The Odyssey*. Thousands of years later, Greek immigrants brought feta to the United States in a wave of migration that started in the 1880s. It remained a specialty item for most of the last century, but in recent years it has become as common in American refrigerators as cheddar. In the test kitchen, we add it to salads, pastas, dips, pizza, and more.

This rise in feta's popularity has meant more options to choose from—and, as we discovered, those options can vary wildly. First, there was the source to consider: We found top-selling cheeses that were made in Greece, France, and the United States. We also learned that in the European Union, only cheeses made in Greece according to specific Protected Designation of Origin (PDO) requirements, including being composed of at least 70 percent sheep's milk with any remainder made up of goat's milk, may be labeled "feta." In the United States, there are no labeling requirements for feta, so any cheese—whether it's made with sheep's, goat's, or cow's milk or any combination thereof, and no matter where it's manufactured—can be labeled "feta."

Of the eight cheeses we tasted, priced from $0.41 to $1.19 per ounce, three were authentic Greek fetas bearing the PDO stamp, including our former winner from Mt. Vikos. Four other products were domestic cheeses made from cow's milk. And the eighth was a sheep's-milk cheese from France. Our question: How would the imitations compare with the real deal from Greece? To find out, we sampled the cheeses plain, crumbled into couscous salad, and—to see how they behaved when heated—baked in Greek spinach and feta pie, spanakopita.

A Bettah Feta

Differences among the cheeses were apparent from the first bite, particularly when it came to saltiness. Sampled plain, all four of the American cow's-milk cheeses were markedly saltier than the Greek and French cheeses, eliciting comments such as "salt bomb!" or "[tastes] like I took a swig of ocean water." Sure enough, these cheeses had some of the highest sodium contents in the lineup (ranging from 320 to 430 milligrams per 1-ounce serving), though that overt salinity mellowed once the cheeses were baked with spinach and phyllo.

But beyond saltiness is where the differences got interesting. Richness was one factor; not surprisingly, we liked decadent-tasting fetas with relatively high fat contents. Our first- and second-place cheeses boasted 7 and 6 grams of fat per ounce, respectively, compared with just 4 grams in some others. In addition, whereas many of the cheeses exhibited simple "milky" flavors, the two front-runners were remarkably complex, with "savory" "barnyard" notes as well as "lemony," toasty," "nutty," and "grassy" nuances.

Texture also influenced our preferences. The French cheese was so soft that it was "spreadable." Not bad—but not what we want in feta. The American cheeses tended to be dry and "pebbly," which we found acceptable but nothing to get too excited about. But once again, we found a feature to love in the two high-fat cheeses: a lush, moist texture that retained its shape in salad and spanakopita.

It turns out that the Greeks really have perfected the crafting of feta. The manufacturers of our two favorites, Real Greek and Dodoni, nailed it: Their cheeses offer the right balance of salt, a luxurious yet firm texture, and an impressive range of bold, gamy, complex flavors. So what are these Greek producers doing differently?

Greek Formula for Great Feta

It's not just folklore that Greeks make great feta cheese. Tradition—and Protected Designation of Origin requirements—ensure cheese that is rich and uniquely flavorful.

MOSTLY SHEEP'S MILK

Greek feta must be at least 70 percent sheep's milk (which has twice as much fat as cow's milk), with any remainder made up of goat's milk. Both sheep's and goat's milks contain fatty acids that give them slightly gamy, savory flavors not found in cow's milk.

FLAVORED BY GREEK FLORA

Greek sheep (and goats) eat a uniquely diverse diet—at least 6,000 different types of plants, including many that grow only in Greece. Since flavor compounds in feed make it into milk, that translates into milk with uniquely complex flavor.

DRY-SALTED

Unlike commercial producers of feta in the United States, Greek manufacturers dry-salt their cheese (cut first into blocks) before brining it, a step that allows flavorful bacteria to grow on its surface, which the cheese readily absorbs.

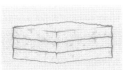

RIPENED IN BRINE

After salting, the feta is brined for at least two months, which allows time for enzymes from the bacteria, the rennet, and the milk itself to create additional flavor molecules. U.S.-made feta is typically brined in its packaging and for only as long as it takes to arrive at stores and be sold.

All feta begins with the same basic process: Rennet (a natural enzyme) is added to the milk, causing it to separate into curds and whey. The curds are placed in a mold or cloth bag to freely drain. The drained curds are then cut into large pieces (*féta* means "a slice" in Greek). Here's where the process diverges. In Greece, these blocks of cheese are salted and left to sit for a day or two, after which they are placed in brine and left to ripen for a period of at least two months; Greek producers believe that these steps create more complex flavor in the cheese. In contrast, according to Dean Sommer, cheese and food technologist at the University of Wisconsin–Madison's Center for Dairy Research, commercial feta producers in the United States skip the dry-salting step and place the drained curds directly in the brine, sometimes in the very containers in which the feta will be sold so that salt uptake (the main flavor boost in the cow's-milk cheeses) happens on the way to the consumer.

Our science editor confirmed that these different methods will affect the final flavor of the cheese. The Greek producers' dry-salting step allows time for the cheese to absorb the salt and for flavorful bacteria and aromatic compounds to grow on the surface of the cheese and be readily absorbed, while the aging period in the brine allows for enzymes from the bacteria, the rennet, and the milk itself to create and contribute additional flavor molecules.

And then, of course, there's the milk used by the Greek producers in our lineup—100 percent sheep's milk for Real Greek and a combination of sheep's and goat's milks for Dodoni. Sheep's milk has twice as much fat as cow's milk (6 to 8 percent by weight compared with 3 to 4 percent). Moreover, both sheep's and goat's milks contain three fatty acids with names that sound like Greek islands (caprioc, caprylic, and capric), which lend them gamy, savory flavors not found in cow's milk.

But there's also a *terroir* factor that makes Greek fetas stand out. According to a report by the World Intellectual Property Organization, sheep and goats in Greece consume a more diverse diet than other animals around the Mediterranean; the hillsides where they graze are covered in at least 6,000 different types of plant life, including numerous species that don't grow anywhere else, and that translates to milk with uniquely complex flavor.

Champion Cheeses

Both of our top fetas are so good that we would be happy eating them simply topped with a drizzle of olive oil and a sprinkling of black pepper. Made from sheep's and goat's milk, our runner-up from Dodoni had the boldest flavor profile in the lineup. Our winner, Real Greek Feta ($13.99 per pound), was marvelously complex when baked, in salad, and on its own but was a little less funky and gamy. Surprisingly, our former winner, Mt. Vikos, also produced in Greece, finished near the bottom of the rankings. When compared with the new Greek cheeses, it simply wasn't as rich, tangy, or boldly flavored.

TASTING FETA

We tasted eight widely available feta cheeses (priced from $0.41 to $1.19 per ounce) plain, in couscous salad, and in spanakopita. Scores were averaged, and products appear below in order of preference. Sodium, milk type, and fat content were taken from product labels and are per 1 ounce of cheese.

RECOMMENDED

REAL GREEK FETA Feta Cheese
PRICE: $13.99 per lb ($0.87 per oz)
ORIGIN: Greece
SODIUM: 260 mg
MILK: Sheep
FAT: 7 g

TESTERS' COMMENTS

This superb sheep's-milk feta was complex yet balanced. It was "buttery" and "savory" with a "milky," "clean dairy flavor" but also "tart" and "lemony," with a gutsy funk and a "perfect" salt level. Texture-wise, it was "silky," "luxurious," and "tender" but "firm" enough to maintain its presence when stirred into salads or baked.

DODONI Feta Cheese
PRICE: $9.49 per lb ($0.59 per oz)
ORIGIN: Greece
SODIUM: 310 mg
MILK: Sheep and goat
FAT: 6 g

This Greek feta was sharper than our winner: "bracingly tangy" and "pungent," with "lots of personality." Tasters also called it "grassy," "intense," and "gamy." A few found it too strong, but most raved, especially when it was baked into pastry, which muted its bold flavor a bit. It was "moist" and "dense," with tender yet distinct crumbles.

BOAR'S HEAD Feta Cheese
PRICE: $4.99 for 8 oz ($0.62 per oz)
ORIGIN: USA
SODIUM: 370 mg
MILK: Cow
FAT: 4 g

This American-made feta was "quite salty," with a "subtle milky" flavor and a "vinegary tang." Made from cow's milk, it was "fairly mild," but if you're looking for a simple feta with clean dairy flavor, this one might be for you. Though its texture was drier and a few tasters found it "tough" in couscous salad and "pebbly" in spanakopita, most didn't mind.

NIKOS Feta Cheese
PRICE: $8.99 per lb ($0.56 per oz)
ORIGIN: USA
SODIUM: 320 mg
MILK: Cow
FAT: 6 g

"Inoffensive but undistinguished" is how one taster described this American feta. When we tried it plain, it had a "rubbery," "squeaky" texture, but once we'd mixed it into couscous or baked it in phyllo with spinach and ricotta, most tasters found it perfectly acceptable.

RECOMMENDED WITH RESERVATIONS

EUPHRATES Feta Cheese
PRICE: $6.49 per lb ($0.41 per oz)
ORIGIN: USA
SODIUM: 360 mg
MILK: Cow
FAT: 4 g

When eaten plain and in couscous salad, this American feta was too salty for most tasters: "Like I took a swig of ocean water," said one. But it was good baked in phyllo. Its texture was pleasing throughout: "discrete without being dry" and "creamy."

VALBRESO Feta Cheese
PRICE: $12.99 per lb ($0.81 per oz)
ORIGIN: France
SODIUM: 270 mg
MILK: Sheep
FAT: 6 g

Made in France from excess milk from Roquefort cheese production, this feta was "very soft" and "almost spreadable," which was "pleasant but not feta-like." It "melted" into the salad and disappeared in the spanakopita. It was "creamy" and "rich," with "full milk flavor" and a mild funk, "like a sheepy ricotta." We liked it, but it's not what we want in a feta cheese.

MT. VIKOS Feta Cheese
PRICE: $9.50 for 8 oz ($1.19 per oz)
ORIGIN: Greece
SODIUM: 350 mg
MILK: Sheep and goat
FAT: 7 g

Our old winner couldn't compete with bolder new products. It was "fine, nice even," with a "pleasant sheepy-goaty" flavor, but it wasn't as strong or rich-tasting as we wanted. It was dense but crumbled well.

NOT RECOMMENDED

ORGANIC VALLEY Feta Cheese
PRICE: $7.99 for 8 oz ($1.00 per oz)
ORIGIN: USA
SODIUM: 430 mg
MILK: Cow
FAT: 4 g

When eaten plain, tasters described this feta as having a "sour" tang that was "superassertive" and "more like a blue cheese than a feta." Its high sodium content didn't cover up its funk in a salad where it was described as "citrusy" and "bitter." Once it was baked into spanakopita, it was simply "milky" and "bland." Texture-wise, it was "firm," and "on the drier side."

Tasting Tahini

Tahini is a potent paste made from toasted sesame seeds. Apart from being a core ingredient in hummus, tahini is often thinned with water or lemon juice and drizzled over falafel, kebabs, pilaf, and roasted or raw vegetables. Sesame seeds are generally the sole ingredient, so how different could competing tahinis be? To find out, we tasted seven products, priced from $6.44 to $11.99 and sold in 15- to 16-ounce containers, plain and in hummus.

Our tasters noticed big flavor differences in the plain tasting, calling our preferred tahinis "toasty" and "nutty" and lower-scoring tahinis "bitter" and "sour." Although tahini can be made with sesame seeds that have their seed coats (hulls) intact, most manufacturers remove the hulls before grinding because they contain compounds that can cause unpleasant bitter flavors. Overroasting the seeds is another factor that can lead to bitterness. Off-flavors can also be the result of rancidity from poor handling or storage. That said, flavor discrepancies were less evident in hummus.

As for texture, some tahinis were smooth, others gritty, some light and loose, others thick. Our favorite, Ziyad Tahini Sesame Paste, is made with hulled sesame seeds and is fairly pale in color, indicating gentle roasting. It's also very smooth, making "silky" hummus that tasters loved. To see the full tasting results, go to CooksIllustrated.com/oct17. –Kate Shannon

RECOMMENDED

ZIYAD Tahini Sesame Paste
PRICE: $7.59 for 16-oz jar ($0.47 per oz)
SESAME SEEDS HULLED: Yes
COMMENTS: Both plain and in hummus, our new favorite had "distinct," "intense sesame flavor" that was neither bitter nor harsh. Its "smooth" and fluid consistency made for exceptionally "creamy," "buttery" hummus.

ROLAND Tahini Pure Sesame Paste
PRICE: $6.44 for 16-oz jar ($0.40 per oz)
SESAME SEEDS HULLED: Yes
COMMENTS: Sampled plain, the only Israeli import in our lineup tasted "very roasty" and had "deep sesame flavor." In hummus, that flavor translated to "subtle nutty background notes." Tasters also approved of its "very smooth," "almost whipped" consistency.

KEVALA Organic Sesame Tahini
PRICE: $7.81 per 16-oz jar ($0.49 per oz)
SESAME SEEDS HULLED: Yes
COMMENTS: Tasters liked this tahini's "bold sesame flavor" and thought that its hummus tasted "authentic." Even though it had a slightly "grainy" quality that was absent in our top two choices, it was still pleasantly "creamy" and earned high marks for texture.

RECOMMENDED WITH RESERVATIONS

KRINOS Tahini
PRICE: $6.99 for 16-oz jar ($0.44 per oz)
SESAME SEEDS HULLED: Not disclosed
COMMENTS: Tasters loved the "smooth, rich consistency" of hummus made with this tahini; it was the flavor that drew criticism. Tasters noticed "sour," "musty" notes that stood out both in the plain tasting and in hummus.

Why You Should Weigh Confectioners' Sugar

Our Cider-Glazed Apple Bundt Cake (page 21) is finished with an icing that drizzles smoothly in thin, delicate lines and turns matte but not brittle when it dries. But when some of our recipe testers made it, they found the icing thick and gloppy and reported that it fell off in chunks when the cake was sliced. What gives?

The recipe calls for ¾ cup (3 ounces) of confectioners' sugar, but if you measure by volume rather than weight, you could end up with an icing that's too thick. Because powdered sugar is so fine and fluffy, the amount you can fit into a ¾-cup measuring cup can vary considerably depending on how compactly you fill the cup.

When we tested various volume measuring methods—sifting the sugar before spooning it into the measuring cups, a more conventional dip-and-sweep approach, and digging into the sugar container and pressing the cup against the side to level the top—we found that the weight varied by as much as 35 percent. That variation has a significant impact on the icing's consistency.

So if your goal is an icing with a graceful drizzling consistency, we strongly recommend that you weigh your confectioners' sugar. –A.G.

MEASURED BY VOLUME
When tightly packed, ¾ cup of confectioners' sugar can weigh more than 4 ounces, producing a too-thick glaze.

WEIGHED
Three ounces of confectioners' sugar produced a thinner glaze that we could easily drizzle over the cake.

Choosing the Sweetest Sweet Potato

For our Best Baked Sweet Potatoes (page 19), we recommend passing on tan- or purple-skinned sweet potatoes (so-called dry varieties) and sticking with red or orange, which are known as "moist" varieties. These contain more of the enzyme amylase, which breaks down starches into sugars. This not only makes them taste sweeter but also means that, with less starch to absorb moisture, these sweet potatoes have a moister, creamier texture than the dry varieties. –A.P.

SWEET PICK

ON THE DRY SIDE

Sweet potato varieties with orange or red skin and deep orange flesh, including Red Garnet (our favorite) and Jewel, cook up sweet and moist.

Sweet potato varieties with tan or purple skin, such as Sweet Hannah, Japanese, and Purple, bake up dry and starchy, more like russet potatoes.

➤ SIDE NOTE Red and orange sweet potatoes are often labeled "yams." This is a misnomer. True yams are unrelated tubers that are starchier and drier than even purple- and white-fleshed sweet potatoes, with a thick, fibrous skin; they're generally hard to find in American supermarkets.

What to Do with Shiso

Shiso, the aromatic heart-shaped leaf with a saw-toothed edge, is probably most familiar to Americans as a sushi garnish. But this relative of mint and basil, available at farmers' markets and Asian groceries, is employed in a number of Asian cuisines for more than its attractive appearance. Botanically known as *Perilla frutescens* var. *crispa*, it is often tucked into Vietnamese summer rolls or shredded and added to cold noodle salads.

ASIAN STAPLE
Shiso is minty, with a bitter finish.

The two common varieties of shiso are green and reddish-purple in color. We found the former to have a minty, bitter, lemony flavor with a faintly sweet finish. The latter variety is milder in flavor, though some tasters found it extremely bitter (the purple color is due to a compound called anthocyanin to which some people are more sensitive than others; it is thought to be the cause of the leaf's bitter taste). Both the red and green leaves are slightly astringent.

In addition to its traditional uses, we liked shiso tossed into salads as we would herbs such as mint or basil. However, larger leaves can be tough, so make sure to tear or shred them first. Shiso can also be used in cooked applications, such as fried rice or ramen, or fried whole and used as a garnish. Even a small amount of heat will cause the leaves to brown slightly, but their flavor will be preserved as long as you add them toward the end of cooking. –L.L.

Baby Kale: Not Just for Salads

Since it came onto the scene, baby kale has been billed as a salad green. But, we wondered, why not cook it? A quick test showed us that it behaves like baby spinach when exposed to heat: It wilts rapidly and releases copious amounts of water. We often gently parcook and drain baby spinach before combining it with other ingredients. We tried this approach with baby kale, subbing it for the baby spinach in our recipe for Fusilli with Ricotta and Spinach (May/June 2014). Though the baby kale's stems were more noticeable than those of the baby spinach and it imparted a mildly pungent flavor instead of spinach's more mineral notes, on the whole it worked well as a substitute.

So if you want to move beyond salad and cook with baby kale, feel free to use it as you would baby spinach. But don't try to use it as a straight substitute for regular kale, which typically needs much longer cooking times and doesn't shrink down as much or require draining. –S.D.

How to Gauge Tofu Texture

Tofu, which is made by coagulating soy milk and then pressing the curds to various degrees to drain the liquid whey, is typically classified according to its texture: Silken, soft, firm, and extra-firm are the most common. But because these categories are not industry-regulated, we've found that one manufacturer's "soft" tofu can be pudding-like, while another's is dense enough to cut into pieces. That's a problem when you need firm curds that will hold up to breading and frying or plush-but-set curds for our Sichuan Braised Tofu with Beef (page 13).

The best way to eliminate ambiguity is to use the names as a general guideline and then inspect the protein content per serving listed on the package—a tip we picked up from cookbook author Andrea Nguyen. In general, the more protein each 3-ounce serving contains, the firmer the tofu will be. For shopping purposes, we evaluated the firmness of several tofus that ranged from 4 to 14 grams of protein per serving. We coated and fried them, braised them, and simmered them in miso soup before settling on the following preferred protein content ranges for each category. –A.J.

DETERMINING TOFU TYPE BY PROTEIN CONTENT

SILKEN	SOFT	FIRM	EXTRA-FIRM
4 to 5 grams	5 to 7 grams	7 to 8 grams	8+ grams

Pickled Jalapeños

Most store-bought pickled jalapeños are preserved in a vinegar brine and seasoned with bay leaf and onion. Their flavor is not complex. To add deeper flavors, we ferment our jalapeños and add shallot and garlic. Cumin seeds lend earthiness while lime zest adds brightness. Over time, we found that the jalapeños took on complex floral notes and also increased in spiciness since the cell walls of the chiles continued to break down, releasing more of the spicy capsaicinoid compounds. –Anne Wolf

PICKLED JALAPEÑOS
MAKES 10 JALAPEÑOS

For spicier results, don't remove the jalapeño seeds. For a balanced flavor, we prefer fermenting at a cool room temperature of 65 degrees (consider locations such as a basement, a den, or a cabinet in an air-conditioned room). We don't recommend fermenting above 70 degrees, as the flavor suffers; above 75 degrees food safety becomes a concern. The fermentation temperature will affect the timing and flavor of the jalapeños; warmer temperatures will result in faster fermentation and sharper, more pungent flavors.

3	cups water
7	teaspoons canning and pickling salt
1½	tablespoons sugar
1	tablespoon cumin seeds
10	small jalapeño chiles (2 to 3 inches long), halved lengthwise and seeded
1	shallot, peeled and halved through root end
6	(2-inch) strips lime zest
4	garlic cloves, smashed and peeled

1. Bring water, salt, sugar, and cumin seeds to boil in small saucepan over high heat. Remove from heat and let cool completely. Cut out parchment paper round to match diameter of 1-quart wide-mouth jar.

2. Tightly pack jalapeños, shallot, lime zest, and garlic into jar, leaving 1½ inches headspace. Pour cooled brine over jalapeños to cover and leave 1 inch headspace; vegetables should be so tightly packed that jalapeños don't float. Press parchment round flush to surface of brine and press gently to submerge. Cover jar with triple layer of cheesecloth and secure with rubber band.

3. Place jar in 50- to 70-degree location away from direct sunlight and let ferment for 10 days; check jar daily, skimming residue from surface. After 10 days, taste jalapeños daily until they have reached desired flavor (this may take up to 4 days longer; jalapeños should be softened, with tangy, floral flavor).

4. When jalapeños have reached desired flavor, remove cheesecloth and parchment and skim off any residue. Serve. (Pickled jalapeños and brine can be transferred to clean jar, covered, and refrigerated for up to 5 months; once refrigerated, flavor of jalapeños will continue to mature and they will darken in color.)

Grip the apple by the top and the bottom of the core and grate it on the large holes of a paddle or box grater. When you reach the core, turn the apple 90 degrees. Repeat until only the core remains.

Easiest Way to Grate Apples

When prepping apples for our Cider-Glazed Apple Bundt Cake (page 21), we occasionally pulled out the food processor to do the job, but more often we opted to simply use the large holes of a paddle or box grater. When grating, we found it easiest (and least wasteful) to leave the core intact and use it as a handle. –A.G.

KITCHEN NOTES

≥ BY STEVE DUNN, ANDREA GEARY, ANDREW JANJIGIAN, LAN LAM & ANNIE PETITO ≤

WHAT IS IT?

The industrial-looking tool below is a Danish bread slicer. The manufacturer, Raadvad, a company known for its high-end kitchen equipment, introduced this guillotine-style slicer in 1939. Weighing in at just under 8 pounds, it was designed to efficiently cut the dense rye breads that Danes use in their famed *smørrebrød* sandwiches (buttered rye bread with meat, fish, or cheese arranged on top). It could also be used to slice hard meats and cheeses. To use it, you raise the blade handle, set the loaf on the wooden tray, slide the tray to position the loaf beneath the blade, and pull down the handle to cut a slice from the loaf. The slicers were made in a wide range of colors, with rare ones now fetching hundreds of dollars on auction sites. (We acquired ours on eBay for $85.00.)

How did it work? Dense, firm German rye breads from a bakery sliced beautifully to a thickness of less than ¼ inch. Softer breads, including a wheat loaf and a white *pan de mie*, were too fragile and were crushed by the weight of the heavy blade's downward motion. But knowing that this tool wasn't intended for use on such breads in the first place, we'd give the Raadvad bread slicer high marks for performing its intended task quite well. –S.D.

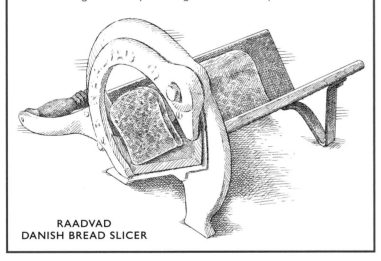

**RAADVAD
DANISH BREAD SLICER**

Flipping the Microwaving Setup

We often rely on the microwave to parcook vegetables before using them in a recipe, as we do in our recipe for Grilled Cauliflower (page 10). It's a common practice to place cut-up vegetables in a bowl and cover the bowl with a plate so

that the pieces steam while they cook. But in the case of our cauliflower recipe, we flip the script by evenly arranging the wedges of cauliflower on a plate and covering them with a bowl. Arranging the cauliflower in a single layer allows for more-even cooking and prevents us from having to stop the microwave to rearrange the hot wedges. –A.P.

How to Divvy Up the Frosting for Layer Cakes

One key to a great layer cake is balancing the amounts of frosting and cake in each bite, but it's not that easy. We put too little frosting on one layer and too much on another and then don't have the right amount to evenly cover the exterior. All that's needed is a little planning. In general, we recommend a total of 5 cups of frosting for three 8- or 9-inch round layers and 4 cups for two layers. Here's how to divvy it up. –L.L.

Use ¾ cup of frosting between each layer.

Put 1½ cups on top of the cake.

Use the remainder around the sides.

TIP: Spread the frosting between the cake layers to just past the edges of each layer. This will make coating the sides faster and easier.

A Simpler Julienne

The classic julienne or "matchstick" cut looks impressive (think carrot, summer squash, potato, or even ginger) but can be a bit tricky to execute correctly. You traditionally start by squaring off a 2-inch length of a vegetable; you then cut the block lengthwise into rectangular slices, gather those into a stack, and slice lengthwise to produce 2-inch by ⅛-inch by ⅛-inch sticks. But squaring off vegetables is a bit wasteful, and the resulting rectangles are prone to slipping and sliding under the knife. This simpler, more casual technique will yield sticks that vary a bit in length, but we think it's fine for most applications. –A.G.

➤ Method: Slice vegetable on bias to create approximately 2-inch-long slices. Shingle slices in line parallel to edge of cutting board and cut vegetable into thin sticks, using knuckles of your nonknife hand as guide.

Butchering with a Paring Knife

We love using our paring knife for tasks such as coring fruit, hulling strawberries, scraping the seeds from a vanilla bean, and deveining shrimp. But we also call upon it for detail work including trimming, boning, and cutting up meat. Its small size makes it much more maneuverable than a larger chef's knife and thus better at executing these tasks.

We also don't rely on the main cutting edge alone. While that edge is suited to cubing or slicing meat, when separating meat from bones or from seams of fat, we typically use the tip of the paring knife, almost like a scalpel, because it allows us to slice more precisely. –A.J.

To remove bones from meat, use the tip of a paring knife, drawing it slowly along the line between meat and bone while pulling the bone away with your other hand. The same technique can be used to remove seams of fat.

Chocolate in the Microwave: Less Fussy and Faster

Our preferred method for melting chocolate is to use the microwave, whether it's to simply liquefy it (for a frosting or a cake) or to temper it (so it hardens into a shiny, snappy glaze). The microwave is far less fussy than the old-fashioned method of warming chopped chocolate in a bowl set over a saucepan of simmering water, and it's also a lot quicker: 3.5 minutes versus 6.5 minutes to melt 4 ounces of chocolate, and about 5 minutes versus 10 minutes to temper the same amount of chocolate. The microwave method is more efficient because heat surrounds the chocolate completely, while in the stovetop method the heat is concentrated at the bottom of the bowl.

We recently found another application where the microwave bested the traditional method: reheating ganache. This simple emulsion, made by heating chocolate and cream together, makes a decadent glaze when warm and a beautifully spreadable frosting when slightly cooled. But if it gets too cool (or if you chill it), you'll need to reheat it. When we compared microwaving 1¼ cups of ganache to warming it gently in a double boiler, it took just 55 seconds versus 8 minutes. That's one more chocolate-warming technique we'll now always assign to the microwave. –S.D.

➤ **To melt 4 ounces chocolate:** Microwave finely chopped chocolate in bowl at 50 percent power, stirring occasionally, until melted, 2 to 4 minutes.

➤ **To temper 4 ounces chocolate:** Microwave 3 ounces finely chopped chocolate in bowl at 50 percent power, stirring every 15 seconds, until melted but not much warmer than body temperature (check by holding in palm of your hand), 1 to 2 minutes. Add 1 ounce grated chocolate and stir until smooth, returning chocolate to microwave for no more than 5 seconds at a time to finish melting if necessary.

➤ **To reheat 1¼ cups ganache:** Microwave on high power in 10-second bursts until warm; stir gently for about 10 seconds until smooth.

	Melting	Tempering	Reheating Ganache
Stovetop	6.5 minutes	10 minutes	8 minutes
Microwave	3.5 minutes	5 minutes	<1 minute

Quickest Way to Cool Hot Liquids

It's important that liquids are cool before you put them in the refrigerator; if the liquid is too hot, it will increase the temperature inside the refrigerator and potentially cause food to rise to unsafe temperatures. To rapidly chill soups and stocks, our usual approach is to transfer the liquid to a bowl set in larger bowl of ice and whisk until cool. Since different materials transfer heat at different rates, we wondered if we could get faster results by using a certain type of bowl. We cooled 2½-quart batches of hot soup in stainless-steel, glass, and heatproof plastic bowls, all with similar diameters, and timed how long it took the liquid to drop from 174 degrees to 80 degrees while stirring constantly. The differences were dramatic: Soup took more than twice as long to cool in glass as in metal and more than three times as long to cool in plastic. To encourage the quickest cooling, we'll always be sure to transfer our hot liquids to a metal bowl since it transfers heat the fastest. –S.D.

THE COOLEST SETUP
Transfer hot liquid to a metal bowl, set the bowl in a larger bowl filled with ice, and whisk or stir constantly.

COOLING TIME

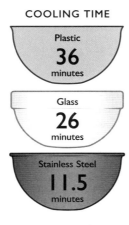

Plastic
36 minutes

Glass
26 minutes

Stainless Steel
11.5 minutes

Baking with Raw Sugars

Shoppers often buy "raw" sugars such as Demerara and turbinado because they are less processed and offer a more complex, molasses-like flavor than granulated sugar. We wondered if they could be swapped into baked good recipes that call for granulated sugar.

EXPERIMENT

We baked muffins, sugar cookies, layer cakes, and shortbread with granulated sugar and Demerara and turbinado sugars and compared the texture, flavor, and appearance of each.

RESULTS

Across the board the raw sugars added a slight molasses-like flavor that most tasters preferred to the cleaner flavor of granulated sugar. But texture was another matter. Both raw-sugar layer cakes had a moist and uniform crumb and were fluffier than the cakes made with granulated sugar. But the other baked goods didn't fare as well. The raw-sugar muffins were denser and slightly squatter and tougher than those made with granulated sugar. The raw-sugar cookies were slightly mounded rather than flat and were a touch dry. The shortbread made with raw sugar was a total failure; it was speckled with sugar crystals and had a brittle, grainy texture.

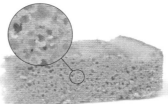

FINE FOR BATTERS
Pourable cake batter contains enough moisture to dissolve the large crystals of raw sugar.

NO-GO FOR DOUGH
The large grains of raw sugar won't dissolve in low-moisture doughs, so the results are grainy.

EXPLANATION

Demerara and turbinado sugar crystals are larger than granulated sugar crystals and therefore don't dissolve as quickly in dry batters. The moist cake batters made with the raw sugars were the most similar to the versions made with granulated sugar. The muffin batters and cookie doughs contained enough moisture to dissolve most of the raw sugar granules but not all. Shortbread dough contains little moisture, so the raw sugar crystals remained whole and adversely affected the texture of the shortbread.

TAKEAWAY

Raw sugars should be fine in moist, pourable batters but won't work in drier doughs. To ensure success across the board, we recommend simply measuring and then grinding raw sugars in a spice grinder until fine and powdery before using them in baking recipes that call for granulated sugar. –L.L.

Cooking Pasta for a Crowd

You can cook 2 pounds of pasta in a 6-quart Dutch oven in the same 4 quarts of boiling water and 1 tablespoon of salt you'd use for 1 pound of pasta. The salt amount doesn't change since the ratio of salt to water (not salt to pasta) is the key. Be sure to constantly stir the water after adding the pasta to keep it from sticking to itself (once the water is boiling, the bubbles will do the job). Also, this cooking water will be starchy, so add it in only small increments when using it to adjust the consistency of a sauce, and switch to hot water if you find that the sauce isn't thinning properly. –L.L.

EQUIPMENT CORNER

≥ BY MIYE BROMBERG, LISA McMANUS & EMILY PHARES ≤

RECOMMENDED	HIGHLY RECOMMENDED	HIGHLY RECOMMENDED	RECOMMENDED WITH RESERVATIONS	RECOMMENDED
OXO Good Grips Classic Tea Kettle in Brushed Stainless Steel MODEL: 1479500V1 PRICE: $39.95	STRETCH-TITE Wrap'n Snap 7500 Dispenser MODEL: WNS7500 PRICE: $22.00	WÜSTHOF Gourmet 4¾-inch Cheese Plane MODEL: 2483832 PRICE: $19.95	OXO Good Grips 3-Blade Handheld Spiralizer MODEL: 11194200 PRICE: $24.99	EXO Polymer Sealed Super Peel MODEL: 2414-AP PRICE: S54.95

Stovetop Kettles

Using a kettle is simple: Fill it with water, place it on a stovetop burner, and wait for the whistle. But the sad truth is that many models are poorly designed—they're too small or too heavy, their handles get too hot to comfortably touch, or they pour awkwardly (just some of the many potential faults). We set out to find the best stovetop kettle, testing six models priced from $9.99 to $74.95. We put every kettle through a gamut of tests, including evaluating how easy it was to fill and lift, as well as how long it took to reach a boil.

In the end we found three kettles we fully recommend, with one standout. The OXO Good Grips Classic Tea Kettle in Brushed Stainless Steel ($39.95) had a lot going for it: This kettle is sturdy but lightweight for its size and has a generous but not overwhelming capacity, a pleasantly grippy silicone handle, a curving spout that pours "remarkably smoothly," a wide opening, a handle that folds down for easy filling and cleaning, a light-colored interior that is readily visible, and a brushed exterior finish that resists fingerprints. As a bonus, it has a clear, loud whistle that you can disable by leaving the spout open during boiling. –L.M.

Plastic-Wrap Dispensers

Store-bought boxes of plastic wrap feature metal teeth or slide cutters that require the user to keep one hand on the box while attempting to pull and cut clean sheets with their other hand; this leads to ragged cuts and tangles. Plastic-wrap dispensers promise to remedy these issues. These products have built-in cutters—with either a slide cutter or a push-down blade—and are designed to remain stationary on the counter, freeing up both of the user's hands to evenly pull and cut a tangle-free sheet.

To find out if these dispensers were worth using, we purchased three models priced from $11.95 to $23.38 and put them to the test. Two models crept toward us as we tried to pull out plastic wrap—not ideal. But one model, the Stretch-Tite Wrap'n Snap ($22.00), was fantastic, acing every test we threw at it and working better and faster than the box you buy at the supermarket. One quibble: Its nearly 5-inch height means it doesn't fit in most kitchen drawers. –E.P.

Cheese Planes

A cheese plane makes it easy and safe to cut consistently thin, even slices of semi-hard cheeses. This tool resembles a small trowel with a horizontal blade embedded in the flat head. To find the best one, we bought nine models priced from $6.75 to $28.00 and put them to work slicing blocks of sharp cheddar and Manchego cheeses. We discovered that we preferred models with straight (not serrated) blades, thin and flexible heads, and relatively large, cushioned handles that made it easy and comfortable to pull consistent slices. One last thing: We found that we preferred models that cut slices measuring between 0.08 and 0.09 inches thick (slightly thicker than a nickel). Our winner, the Wüsthof Gourmet 4¾-inch Cheese Plane ($19.95), produced perfect 0.08-inch-thick slices every time. It had a comfortable handle, a relatively long and sharp blade, and one of the thinnest and most flexible heads in the lineup, making for effortless, responsive slicing. –M.B.

Handheld Spiralizers

Handheld spiralizers promise to cut ribbons and "noodles" from a variety of produce without taking up as much room as tabletop models. They operate like pepper mills or pencil sharpeners: Holding the canister-like base with one hand, you use your other hand (or a pronged holder) to twist a piece of produce over blades set into the spiralizer's top, and noodles or ribbons come out the other side. To see if any handheld model could compete with our favorite tabletop spiralizer, the Paderno World Cuisine Tri-Blade Plastic Spiral Vegetable Slicer ($33.24), we tested four models, priced from $14.95 to $24.99, along with the Tri-Blade, using each to spiralize zucchini, beets, apples, carrots, and butternut squashes.

At the end of testing, we found only two models that were decent. Tabletop models are simply faster, less wasteful, and easier to use. Still, if you have limited storage and strong wrists and plan to use your spiralizer only occasionally, look for a wider handheld model (less trimming required) that comes with three different blades, which make it more versatile. Our winner, the OXO Good Grips 3-Blade Handheld Spiralizer ($24.99), was the easiest and most comfortable model to use. –M.B.

Baking Peels

If you bake a lot of pizza or free-form loaves of bread, a peel will make these tasks easier. To find the best peel for the home baker, we tested five models (including a redesigned version of our former winner from EXO) priced from $9.79 to $57.95, using them to make our recipes for Thin-Crust Pizza and Rustic Italian Bread. We used the peels to unload the raw pizza and bread doughs onto a preheated baking stone, to rotate the items halfway through baking, and to remove the finished products. Which peel should you buy? While it has a bit of a learning curve (it has an innovative cloth conveyer-belt design on the paddle), we still think our former champ, the EXO Polymer Sealed Super Peel ($54.95), is the best peel for most home bakers. It excels at the riskiest task a peel performs—unloading delicate doughs without deforming them—and does a decent job of removing the finished baked goods, too. –M.B.

For complete testing results, go to CooksIllustrated.com/oct17.

INDEX

September & October 2017

MAIN DISHES

SIDE DISHES

STARTERS

DESSERT

ACCOMPANIMENTS

BONUS ONLINE CONTENT

More recipes, reviews, and videos are available at **CooksIllustrated.com/oct17**

RECIPES

Almond, Raisin, and Caper Relish
Dried Cherry Mostarda
Kalamata Olive Relish
Sichuan Braised Tofu with Shiitakes (Mapo Tofu)
Za'atar

EXPANDED REVIEWS

Tasting Tahini
Testing Baking Peels
Testing Cheese Planes
Testing Handheld Spiralizers
Testing Large Saucepans
Testing Plastic-Wrap Dispensers
Testing Splatter Screens
Testing Stovetop Kettles

RECIPE VIDEOS

Want to see how to make any of the recipes in this issue? There's a free video for that.

BONUS VIDEO

Breading Chicken Cutlets

FOLLOW US ON SOCIAL MEDIA

facebook.com/CooksIllustrated
twitter.com/TestKitchen
pinterest.com/CooksIllustrated
instagram.com/CooksIllustrated
youtube.com/AmericasTestKitchen

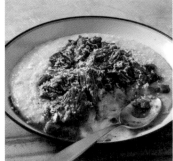

Best Baked Sweet Potatoes, 19

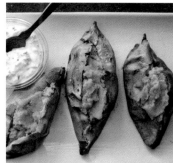

Beef Short Rib Ragu on Parmesan Polenta, 7

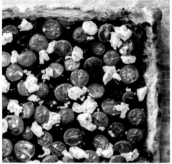

Onion, Tomato, and Goat Cheese Tart, 15

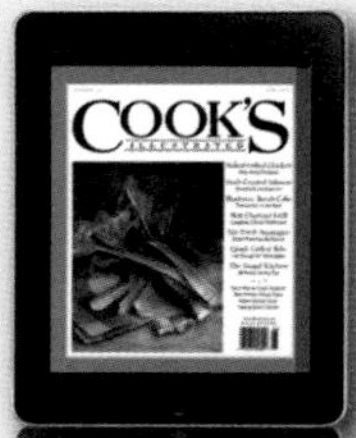

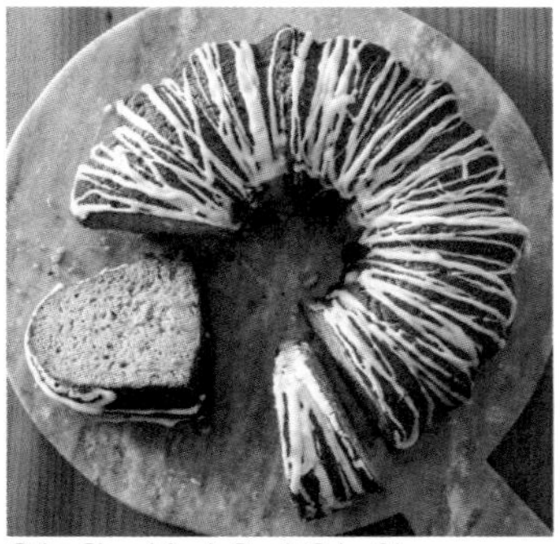

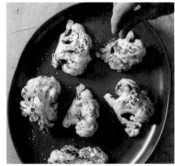

Cider-Glazed Apple Bundt Cake, 21

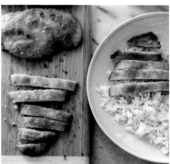

Crispy Pan-Fried Chicken Cutlets, 5

Grilled Cauliflower, 10

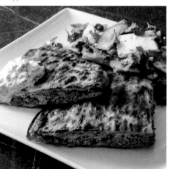

Grilled Lamb-Stuffed Pitas with Yogurt Sauce, 9

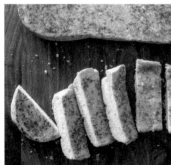

Really Good Garlic Bread, 22

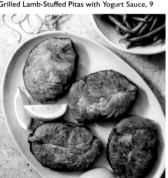

Pan-Seared Salmon Steaks, 11

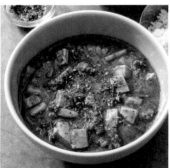

Sichuan Braised Tofu with Beef (Mapo Tofu), 13

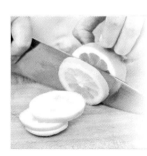

PHOTOGRAPHY: CARL TREMBLAY; STYLING: MARIE PIRAINO

Watermelon Rind

Bread and Butter

Beet-Pickled Eggs

Cocktail Onions

Relish

Green Tomatoes

Dilly Beans

Kosher Dill

Beet

Okra

AMERICAN
PICKLES

NUMBER 149

NOVEMBER & DECEMBER 2017

COOK'S
ILLUSTRATED

Roast Turkey Breast
Juicy Meat and Rich, Crispy Skin

Tuscan Bean Soup
Hearty One-Pot Meal

Best-Ever Skillet Brussels Sprouts

Braised Beef Brisket
We Broke the Collagen Code

Which Supermarket Turkey Is Best?

Gingerbread Layer Cake
Sophisticated Showstopper

Guide to Prime Rib
Reaching Roast Beef Perfection

Best Turkey Soup
Duchess Potatoes
Chinese Dumplings

CooksIllustrated.com
$6.95 U.S.

0 71486 02744 7

1 2>

Display until December 11, 2017

NOVEMBER & DECEMBER 2017

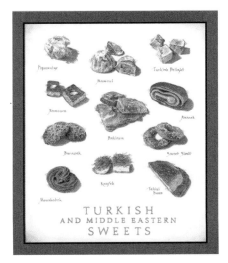

TURKISH
AND MIDDLE EASTERN
SWEETS

BACK COVER ILLUSTRATED BY JOHN BURGOYNE

Turkish and Middle Eastern Sweets

Flaky, syrup-soaked **BAKLAVA** might be the most familiar of the region's sweets. **PIŞMANIYE** is the Turkish equivalent of cotton candy, with a hint of nuts. Sugar-dusted **MAMOUL** cookies, which crumble like shortbread, house ground nuts at their centers. Cubes of **TURKISH DELIGHT** are flavored with fruits, nuts, herbs, or spices and are springy like gumdrops. The nubbly crumb of semolina-based **NAMOURA** cake is drenched in syrup or honey, each piece crowned with an almond. Yeasted **NAZOOK** pastries are similar to Danish, with nuts or fruit peeking out. The sesame seeds that cover crisp **BARAZEK** cookies are glued in place with a gloss of honey. **SWEET SIMIT** is a cross between a cookie and a pretzel and is scented with warm spices. **MOUSHABEK** dough is piped into ridged coils, fried, and glazed with floral syrup. Crispy noodle threads soaked in aromatic syrup atop a layer of gooey cheese defines **KNAFEH**. Beneath the nutty-sweet surface of **TAHINI BUNS** lie pleasant hints of bitterness and cinnamon.

AMERICA'S TEST KITCHEN ®
RECIPES THAT WORK

America's Test Kitchen is a real test kitchen located in Boston. It is the home of more than 60 test cooks, editors, and cookware specialists. Our mission is to test recipes until we understand exactly how and why they work and eventually arrive at the very best version. We also test kitchen equipment and supermarket ingredients in search of products that offer the best value and performance. You can watch us work by tuning in to *America's Test Kitchen* (AmericasTestKitchen.com) and *Cook's Country from America's Test Kitchen* (CooksCountry.com) on public television and listen to our weekly segments on *The Splendid Table* on public radio. You can also follow us on Facebook, Twitter, Pinterest, and Instagram.

PRODIGAL VEGETABLE

Consider the Brussels sprout. Not so long ago it was a vegetable pariah in this country, something that parents threatened their children with if they didn't behave. Usually prepared by being boiled to near-death, these bitter miniature cabbages—as most people seemed to think of them—were a prime example of healthy food that no one actually wanted to eat.

Nowadays, though, these little green bundles have become culinary stars. You can't avoid them on the menus of trendy restaurants, often combined with bacon to tempt young pork-obsessed diners. In farmers' markets, you can find them still on the stalk, a kind of vegetable modernist sculpture. Home cooks have come to love them, too. No Thanksgiving dinner, for example, would seem complete these days without Brussels sprouts.

We think this is a very positive development, a good example of how the palate in this country has expanded in recent years. Plus, we have to admit that we love the sprouts. We've prepared them every which way—we've braised them, steamed them, used them both raw and wilted in salads, and roasted them (yes, sometimes with bacon).

In this issue, you'll find our new favorite, a quick and easy skillet-roasted approach. Unlike any other stovetop versions that we've found, these sprouts end up with brilliant green rounded sides and crisp-tender interiors contrasted by nutty-sweet, crusty façades. They're not only delicious but also beautiful. It's hard to imagine that a vegetable like this was once scorned.

Welcome home, sprouts.

–The Editors

FOR INQUIRIES, ORDERS, OR MORE INFORMATION

COOK'S ILLUSTRATED MAGAZINE

Cook's Illustrated magazine (ISSN 1068-2821), number 149, is published bimonthly by America's Test Kitchen Limited Partnership, 21 Drydock Avenue, Suite 210E, Boston, MA 02210. Copyright 2017 America's Test Kitchen Limited Partnership. Periodicals postage paid at Boston, MA, and additional mailing offices, USPS #012487. Publications Mail Agreement No. 40020778. Return undeliverable Canadian addresses to P.O. Box 875, Station A, Windsor, ON N9A 6P2. POSTMASTER: Send address changes to *Cook's Illustrated*, P.O. Box 6018, Harlan, IA 51593-1518. For subscription and gift subscription orders, subscription inquiries, or change of address notices, visit AmericasTestKitchen.com/support, call 800-526-8442 in the U.S. or 515-237-3663 from outside the U.S., or write to us at *Cook's Illustrated*, P.O. Box 6018, Harlan, IA 51593-1518.

CooksIllustrated.com

At the all new CooksIllustrated.com, you can order books and subscriptions, sign up for our free e-newsletter, or renew your magazine subscription. Join the website and gain access to 24 years of *Cook's Illustrated* recipes, equipment tests, and ingredient tastings, as well as companion videos for every recipe in this issue.

COOKBOOKS

We sell more than 50 cookbooks by the editors of *Cook's Illustrated*, including *The Complete Mediterranean Cookbook* and *Vegan for Everybody*. To order, visit our bookstore at CooksIllustrated.com/bookstore.

EDITORIAL OFFICE 21 Drydock Avenue, Suite 210E, Boston, MA 02210; 617-232-1000; fax: 617-232-1572. For subscription inquiries, visit AmericasTestKitchen.com/support or call 800-526-8442.

A Fast, Tidy Way to Chop Carrots

To speed the process of cutting carrots and keep the cut pieces from rolling around on the cutting board, Brett Beauregard of Arlington, Mass., makes two lengthwise slices through the carrot, one on each side, leaving the top inch intact. He then slices the cut portion crosswise to produce uniform pieces.

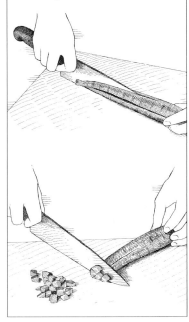

A Tight Foil Cover

When covering a roasting pan of braising meat with aluminum foil, Richard Le of Cambridge, Mass., uses metal binder clips to hold the foil in place.

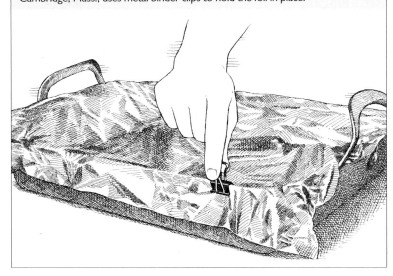

Strain Broken Wine Corks

To strain broken cork bits out of a bottle of wine, John Barcus of Fort Worth, Texas, pours the wine into glasses through a small fine-mesh strainer.

Cheesecloth Sugar Shaker

Lorna Freed of Grand Rapids, Mich., doesn't own a dedicated sugar shaker, so when she needs to dust confectioners' sugar or cocoa powder over desserts or sprinkle flour on a counter, she fashions a shaker from cheesecloth. She cuts a small square, heaps the powder in the center, and knots the top of the cheesecloth.

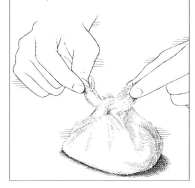

Cut-Your-Own Leveling Tab for Spices

Karen Cofino of Bridgeville, Del., doesn't completely remove the seal on new jars of spices. She cuts half away with a paring knife and then uses the straight edge of the remaining seal to level off measuring spoons.

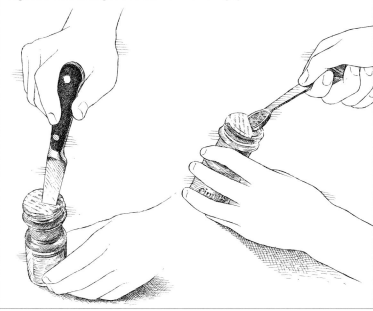

Keeping Food Processor Lids Clean

To avoid gunking up her hard-to-clean food processor lid, Teresa Teague of Springfield, Va., covers the workbowl with plastic wrap before processing any food. It protects the lid so effectively, there's no need to clean it at all.

Homemade Hand Towels

To avoid wasting paper towels, Cathy Smith of Swansboro, N.C., cuts up old bath towels to use as small kitchen rags, which she then washes and reuses.

Recycle Soda Cans as Grease Receptacles

Jeff Bartlett of Hopedale, Mass., uses empty soda cans as receptacles for hot cooking fats, such as bacon grease or frying oil. He removes the top of the can completely with a can opener, making it easy to pour the fat into the wide opening.

Large Bowl Substitute

When Dianna Marshall of Monroe Township, N.J., runs out of large mixing bowls when baking, she borrows her slow cooker's ceramic insert. The wide, deep basin offers plenty of space for mixing batters.

Pinch-Crimp Pie Pastry

Claire Schaffer of Denver, Colo., crimps the edges of pie dough with a pair of tongs. Gently pressing the pincers into the pastry leaves identical impressions for a neat-looking finish.

A Tip for Cleaning Stovetops

The nooks and crannies of stovetop burners can be difficult to clean with a wide sponge. Sara Hasenstab of Memphis, Tenn., uses cotton swabs to swipe in tight spaces.

Disposable Mess Rest

Susan Gardner of Kew Gardens, N.Y., saves butter wrappers to use as resting spots for messy items such as eggshells or dirty utensils. When she's done, she simply throws the wrappers away.

Helping Foil Grip a Baking Sheet

It can be tricky to spread aluminum foil smoothly in a rimmed baking sheet. Eric Gugger of Plymouth, Minn., uses his fingers to drip a little water on the surface of the sheet, which helps hold the foil firmly in place so that he can easily spread it into the corners.

Roast Turkey Breast with Gravy

A perfectly cooked, crispy-skinned turkey breast can be just the ticket
for a smaller holiday gathering—particularly if it comes with gravy.

≥ BY ANNIE PETITO ≤

Here's a Thanksgiving secret: You don't have to roast a whole turkey to get all the glory. A bone-in, skin-on turkey breast can be a great option when hosting a smaller crowd or if your guests simply prefer white meat. Other benefits: A breast requires less cooking time, which frees up your oven for other dishes, and it's much easier to carve than a whole bird. In fact, a whole turkey breast has so many advantages that you'll likely find yourself roasting one at other times of the year, too, whether for sandwiches or as a simple main course.

But I'm getting ahead of myself: To produce a true holiday centerpiece, I'd have to overcome a few turkey breast hurdles. White meat is notorious for emerging from the oven dry and chalky, and the skin is rarely adequately browned and crispy. What's more, since a breast doesn't offer much in the way of pan drippings, making gravy isn't always a given. I resolved to deliver an impressive roast turkey breast boasting juicy, well-seasoned meat; crispy, deeply browned skin; and a savory gravy to serve alongside.

Salt Treatment

First on my list: salt, which would keep the turkey juicy. When rubbed over the flesh, salt draws out moisture. The moisture then mixes with the salt and forms a concentrated solution, which, over time, migrates back into the meat, seasoning it and altering its proteins so that they retain moisture during cooking.

To carve, simply use a chef's knife to remove each breast half from the bone and then slice the meat crosswise.

Using my fingers, I carefully peeled back the turkey breast's skin and rubbed salt onto the flesh and then on the bone side. I then smoothed the skin back into place and refrigerated the turkey for 24 hours. The next day, I placed the turkey breast, skin side up, in a V-rack set inside a roasting pan,

brushed it with butter (its milk solids would encourage browning), sprinkled it with a bit more salt, and roasted it in a 450-degree oven. After about an hour, the breast reached the target temperature of 160 degrees. However, the meat was somewhat dry despite the salting, and browning was patchy. Plus, because the fat didn't have enough time to fully render, the skin wasn't particularly crispy. Finally, the breast itself was rather unwieldy—it tipped onto its side when I transferred it to the oven, and it was difficult to keep it upright during carving.

Removing the turkey's backbone would make it sit flat and be stable; this would also encourage even browning since the breast would be more level. Fortunately, this was easily accomplished with the help of kitchen shears. I set the backbone aside—I would use it later to make gravy.

As I prepared to arrange the now-backless breast in the roasting pan, it struck me that the pan was excessively large. Plus, the minimal drippings in the roasting pan tended to scorch in the oven. Instead, I switched to a 12-inch ovensafe skillet. Freed of its backbone, the breast rested securely on its flat underside and fit snugly in the skillet so juices could collect directly beneath it with no risk of scorching.

Turkey in the Pan

Now, about that dry meat and the skin that never fully rendered. Substantially lowering the oven temperature helped with the former problem: When

---

STEP BY STEP **Roast Turkey Breast with Gravy**

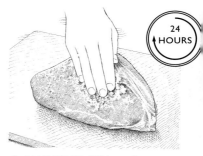

(24 HOURS)

I. BUY CORRECT BREAST
Look for a whole turkey breast with the backbone attached; we use it to flavor the gravy. If you can't find one with a backbone (the label usually indicates if the backbone is attached), use 1 pound of chicken wings for the gravy instead.

2. CUT RIBS Cut through the ribs following the line of fat where the breast meets the back, from the breast's tapered end to the wing joint.

3. REMOVE BACKBONE Bend the back away from the breast to pop the shoulder joints out of the sockets. Cut through the joints to remove the back.

4. SALT MEAT Without the backbone in the way, it's easy to pull back the skin so you can evenly season the breast meat.

roasted at 325 degrees, the meat stayed moist. Unfortunately, the skin was now pale, though much of its fat had rendered. I decided to try a reverse-sear technique, a method we sometimes use with smaller cuts such as steaks and chicken breasts, in which we cook the meat in a low oven until it reaches the desired temperature and then sear it on the stovetop. The interior stays incredibly juicy while the exterior browns quickly. In this case, I'd use a hot oven for the final "sear" rather than move the pan to the stovetop.

Eager to try this approach, I roasted the breast at 325 degrees until it reached an internal temperature of 145 degrees. Then I took it out of the oven and cranked the heat to 500 degrees. Once the oven was up to temperature, I returned the breast to the oven and roasted it until it hit 160 degrees, which happened faster than I expected. I hadn't accounted for carryover cooking while the breast sat in the hot skillet between oven stints, so it came to temperature before it could get much color. I tried again, removing the breast from the oven when the meat registered just 130 degrees, so it would have more time to brown in the hotter oven. This was my best turkey breast yet: The skin was a deep mahogany and beautifully crispy, and the well-seasoned meat was juicy.

Put Your Back Into It

While my final turkey breast was in the oven roasting, I used the reserved turkey back to make a simple broth that would be the gravy base. I browned the back; added onion, celery, carrot, fresh herbs, and water; and then simmered and strained the mixture. When I transferred the breast to a carving board to rest, I built the gravy right in the skillet, which was full of flavorful fat and drippings. I sprinkled flour into the fat to make a roux, added white wine followed by my quick turkey broth, and let the gravy simmer to reduce. After about 20 minutes, the gravy was nicely thickened and the breast was ready to carve.

I served up my impressive platter of turkey—burnished and crispy on the outside, moist and well seasoned within—and its flavorful gravy, without missing the dark meat at all.

ROAST WHOLE TURKEY BREAST WITH GRAVY
SERVES 6 TO 8

Note that this recipe requires refrigerating the seasoned breast for 24 hours. This recipe was developed using Diamond Crystal Kosher Salt. If you use Morton Kosher Salt, which is denser, reduce the salt in step 2 to 2½ teaspoons, rubbing 1 teaspoon of salt into each side of the breast and ½ teaspoon into the cavity. If you're using a self-basting (such as a frozen Butterball) or kosher turkey breast, do not salt in step 2. If your turkey breast comes with the back removed, you can skip making the gravy or substitute 1 pound of chicken wings for the turkey back.

1	(5- to 7- pound) bone-in turkey breast
	Kosher salt and pepper
2	tablespoons unsalted butter, melted
2	teaspoons extra-virgin olive oil, plus extra as needed
1	small onion, chopped
1	small carrot, chopped
1	small celery rib, chopped
5	cups water
2	sprigs fresh thyme
1	bay leaf
¼	cup all-purpose flour
¼	cup dry white wine

1. Place turkey breast on counter skin side down. Using kitchen shears, cut through ribs, following vertical line of fat where breast meets back, from tapered end of breast to wing joint. Using your hands, bend back away from breast to pop shoulder joints out of sockets. Using paring knife, cut through joints between bones to separate back from breast. Reserve back for gravy. Trim excess fat from breast.

2. Place turkey breast, skin side up, on counter. Using your fingers, carefully loosen and separate turkey skin from each side of breast. Peel back skin, leaving it attached at top and center of breast. Rub 1 teaspoon salt onto each side of breast, then place skin back over meat. Rub 1 teaspoon salt onto underside of breast cavity. Place turkey on large plate and refrigerate, uncovered, for 24 hours.

Get Sauced After the Holidays

For a nonholiday meal, pair the turkey with a quick, bright-tasting sauce. Our recipes for Salsa Verde, Quick Roasted Red Pepper Sauce, and Cilantro-Mint Chutney are available for free for four months at CooksIllustrated.com/salsaverde, CooksIllustrated.com/redpeppersauce, and CooksIllustrated.com/cilantromintchutney.

3. Adjust oven rack to middle position and heat oven to 325 degrees. Pat turkey dry with paper towels. Place turkey, skin side up, in 12-inch ovensafe skillet, arranging so narrow end of breast is not touching skillet. Brush melted butter evenly over turkey and sprinkle with 1 teaspoon salt. Roast until thickest part of breast registers 130 degrees, 1 to 1¼ hours.

4. Meanwhile, heat oil in large saucepan over medium-high heat. Add reserved back, skin side down, and cook until well browned, 6 to 8 minutes. Add onion, carrot, and celery and cook, stirring occasionally, until vegetables are softened and lightly browned, about 5 minutes. Add water, thyme sprigs, and bay leaf and bring to boil. Reduce heat to medium-low and simmer for 1 hour. Strain broth through fine-mesh strainer into container. Discard solids; set aside broth (you should have about 4 cups). (Broth can be refrigerated for up to 24 hours.)

5. Remove turkey from oven and increase oven temperature to 500 degrees. When oven reaches 500 degrees, return turkey to oven and roast until skin is deeply browned and thickest part of breast registers 160 degrees, 15 to 30 minutes. Using spatula, loosen turkey from skillet; transfer to carving board and let rest, uncovered, for 30 minutes.

6. While turkey rests, pour off fat from skillet. (You should have about ¼ cup; if not, add extra oil as needed to equal ¼ cup.) Return fat to skillet and heat over medium heat until shimmering. Sprinkle flour evenly over fat and cook, whisking constantly, until flour is coated with fat and browned, about 1 minute. Add wine, whisking to scrape up any browned bits, and cook until wine has evaporated, 1 to 2 minutes. Slowly whisk in reserved broth. Increase heat to medium-high and cook, whisking occasionally, until gravy is thickened and reduced to 2 cups, about 20 minutes. Season with salt and pepper to taste. Carve turkey and serve, passing gravy separately.

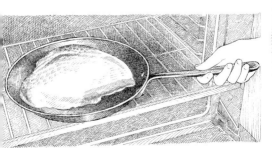

5. ROAST LOW; BROWN HIGH Arrange the breast in an ovensafe skillet so the drippings collect underneath without scorching. Roast at 325 degrees, and then crank the heat to 500 to brown the skin.

6. BUILD BROTH Use the reserved backbone, along with a few aromatics and herbs, to make 4 cups of broth.

7. MAKE GRAVY In the skillet used to roast the turkey, make a quick gravy with turkey fat, flour, wine, and broth.

▶ **See Every Step**
A step-by-step video is available at CooksIllustrated.com/dec17

How to Braise Brisket

Beefy in flavor and size, brisket has the potential to be the ultimate braised dish for company. The trick is turning this notoriously tough cut both moist and tender.

⇒ BY ANDREW JANJIGIAN ⇐

When brisket is done right, there is perhaps no better cut of beef to braise, especially when serving a crowd. It's beefy, velvety, and moist, and it slices beautifully. The braising liquid can be seasoned with any aromatic vegetable, herb, or spice, and during the long cooking time, it reduces to a rich-tasting jus or full-bodied gravy. The final product is ideal as a Sunday dinner for family or for company.

Most recipes follow more or less the same script. Brown the meat, usually in a Dutch oven; set it aside; and then cook aromatics (usually including loads of onions) until softened and browned. Return the brisket to the pot, add enough liquid (wine, beer, water, stock, tomatoes, etc.) to partially submerge it, and braise it, covered, in the oven until the meat is fork-tender and easily sliced. Many recipes, particularly classic Jewish versions, call for adding vegetables or fruits late in the process to be served alongside the meat.

Anyone who's made brisket knows that producing fork-tender meat takes a long time—upwards of 5 hours, according to the recipes I've tried. But more problematic is the fact that by the time the meat is tender, it's

Tangy pomegranate balances the meat's richness, and its bright color and sweetness make this dish more festive.

usually dry, too. That's because brisket is loaded with collagen, the main structural protein in meat that makes it tough. Collagen requires long, steady heat exposure to break down, but in that time the meat's muscle fibers are also contracting and squeezing out moisture. So in a sense, braising meat is a balancing act: using enough heat to break down collagen while still keeping the heat low enough to retain moisture.

I was determined to produce brisket that was both tender and moist. And while I was at it, I'd see how I could dress up the flavors so the dish would feel special enough to serve at the holidays.

High and Dry

Butchers typically divide whole briskets into two cuts, the point and the flat. I would go with the flat cut, which is available in most supermarkets and, as its name suggests, is flatter and more uniform and thus easier to slice (for more information, see "Buying Brisket").

When we want meat to retain moisture, our first move is almost always to apply salt, which not only seasons the meat but also, if left on long enough before cooking, changes the protein structure so that the meat better holds on to moisture. Brisket is particularly dense, so to help the salt penetrate, I halved the brisket lengthwise to create two slabs (doing so would also speed cooking and make for more-manageable slices) and poked each slab all over on both sides with a skewer. Even so, after a series of tests, I determined that the meat tasted juicier and better seasoned when the salt had at least 16—or up to 48—hours to work its magic.

On to the cooking. For the time being, I skipped searing the meat, which is messy and time-consuming, and focused on enlivening the braising liquid instead. I started by sautéing onions and garlic in a Dutch oven, and I made an unconventional choice for the braising liquid: pomegranate juice. Its acidity would balance the unctuous meat, and its fruity flavor would be a nod to traditional Jewish versions. I added some chicken stock and bay leaves along with the juice and brought the liquid to a simmer. I then added the brisket with the fat cap facing up so that the bulk of the meat would be submerged and the exposed part would be protected by the fat. I covered the pot and placed it in a 325-degree oven. After about 5 hours, it was tender but—despite having salted it for 48 hours—still too dry.

I reasoned that reducing the oven temperature would prevent the meat from drying out as much, even though I knew that it would add to the cooking time. I dropped the temperature from 325 degrees to 250 degrees—but now the brisket took far longer to cook than I would ever have expected. In fact, after 6 hours, the brisket still wasn't even remotely tender, and when I took its temperature, I was surprised to see that it never exceeded 165 degrees. That wasn't hot enough for significant collagen breakdown, which happens most rapidly above 180 degrees, so the meat never tenderized.

Puzzled as to why the meat's temperature had plateaued, I did some research and discovered that this issue is familiar to anyone who has barbecued large pieces of meat. As meat gets hot enough for moisture to be driven off, its surface cools, preventing the interior of the meat from getting any hotter. Known as evaporative cooling, it's the same process

Should You Buy a Santoku?

With its petite build and curved tip, this friendly-looking Japanese blade is giving Western-style chef's knives a run for their money. But does it offer something unique?

⇒ BY LISA McMANUS ⇐

Santoku knives became an overnight sensation in the United States in the early 2000s, when Rachael Ray declared on TV that she loved her Wüsthof model. Sales shot up, and several knife manufacturers, both Asian and Western, scrambled to create their own versions or promote their models to Americans. The appeal was the friendly shape of the blade: 5 to 7 inches long, with a rounded front edge and a boxier build than the typical chef's knife, which usually stretches between 8 and 10 inches long and has a sleeker profile and a sword-like point. The style was developed for postwar Japanese home cooks as a more versatile alternative to vegetable cleavers—*santoku* reportedly means "three virtues," which are described variously as "meat, fish, and vegetables," or "chopping, slicing, and dicing"—and quickly became the country's most popular kitchen knife.

We, too, were fans of the santoku style when we first tested them; many of us still swear by our 2004 winner, the MAC Superior Santoku 6½" ($74.95). But now that santoku sales in the United States are rivaling those of chef's knives and all major knifemakers are peddling versions, we wanted to recheck the competition. We bought 10 models, priced from $24.99 to $199.95, focusing on blades that were at least 6 inches long, the size we previously found most useful. Some knife experts claim that santokus are suited only for cutting softer vegetables and boneless meat, not for thornier kitchen tasks such as breaking down bone-in chicken and hard vegetables. So our question was: Are santoku knives a viable alternative to chef's knives, or are they in fact more specialized?

To answer this question, we put every model

Santoku's Ancestor

Santoku knives appeared in Japan after World War II as a home cook–friendly alternative to the traditional vegetable cleaver called a *nakiri*. Knifemakers retained the vegetable cleaver blade's height and straight edge but made the santoku less intimidating by rounding down its top front edge.

NAKIRI CLEAVER

We put each knife through a series of tests to evaluate precision cutting.

through our usual battery of chef's knife tests: mincing fresh herbs, dicing onions, butchering whole raw chickens, and quartering unpeeled butternut squashes. We also threw a ringer into the testing—our favorite chef's knife, the Victorinox Swiss Army Fibrox Pro 8" Chef's Knife ($39.95)—for comparison. Then, to see if santokus add unique value to a knife collection, we tacked on precision work: cutting carrot matchsticks and slicing semifrozen strip steaks across the grain into slivers. Finally six testers, including three self-described knife novices, chopped onions and rated the knives, including how well each model performed and if it was comfortable and easy to use.

How They Handled

A great kitchen knife almost leaps into your hand, feeling natural, ready to work, and effortless as it moves through food. Some of this is individual preference, but the knife's handle, weight, balance, and blade geometry all contribute to the user experience.

For example, we generally preferred handles that measured no more than 3 inches around at their widest point. Any skinnier or thicker and testers strained to keep a secure grip. Big bumps, curves,

and strongly tapered shapes also forced our hands into specific and uncomfortable positions, and handles made from all metal or smooth plastic slipped if our hands were wet or greasy. Then there was the portion of the blade's spine that meets the handle. If that top edge was sharp, cooks who use a pinch grip—meaning that they gain leverage by choking up over the front of the handle to pinch the blade between their thumb and forefinger—felt the metal digging into their fingers. The bottom line is that the qualities you want in a santoku handle are no different from what you'd want in any knife handle: something that feels substantial but not bulky, is neutrally shaped so that it affords a variety of comfortable grips, and is made from lightly textured materials that offer good purchase.

Cutting-Edge Features

A truly sharp blade is the key to any kitchen knife. And what helps determine the sharpness of that edge is the angle of the bevel—the slim strip on either side of the blade that narrows to form the cutting edge. Over the years, we've found that more-acute angles on the cutting edge make slicing easier, so we checked our blades: Nearly all were the expected 15 degrees, a standard angle for an Asian-style knife (and the angle increasingly found on Western knives such as our favorite chef's knife from Victorinox), but a couple were even narrower—just 10 degrees.

Surprisingly, not all these extra-thin edges felt extra-sharp when cutting. In a few cases, that was because the knives arrived moderately dull or dulled quickly during testing—big drawbacks in our book. But it wasn't until we measured the top edges of all the knives, pinching their spines with a caliper, that we understood why some of the seemingly thin blades also struggled: Our top-ranked knives were all thinner (2 millimeters or less) at the spine than lower-rated models that measured up to 2.6 millimeters. That might sound like a minuscule difference, but knives with narrower spines felt more like razors gliding through food and less like wedges prying it apart. This was especially true when cutting vegetables: Wedge-like blades crushed onions instead of slicing them, causing them to spray juices, and one model with a broader spine (and a duller blade) got stuck in a butternut squash—twice.

From there, we took a closer look at the core traits that distinguish a santoku blade from that of a conventional chef's knife, starting with its most recognizable feature, a turned-down "sheep's foot"

The Spine Matters, Too

We've long been fans of knives with ultrathin cutting edges, since the slimmer the edge is, the easier it will be for the blade to slip through food. But while testing santoku knives, we also came to appreciate slim blade spines—the top of the blade opposite the cutting edge. The reason is the same: There is less metal to push through the food, so the blade feels more like a razor gliding through food (dense vegetables in particular) than like a wedge pushing it apart.

THE KNIFE'S OTHER EDGE
The sharpest knives are slim from top to bottom.

tip. This design is simply meant to make the knife look less intimidating and minimize the risk of piercing something unintentionally, but frankly we found it more of a problem than a perk. It puts more metal behind the tip than there is on a typical chef's knife, which meant that we had to push harder when making delicate vertical cuts through onions

Santoku or Chef's: Which Knife Is for You?

In many applications, a santoku and a traditional chef's knife perform comparably. But there are design differences between the two styles that might make you prefer one to the other. Here's how our two favorites compare.

**MISONO UX10 SANTOKU 7.0"
($179.50)**
• Shorter blade with rounded tip feels less intimidating
• Lightweight and particularly agile in hand
• Thinner spine helps blade easily slip through food
• Rounded tip requires user to push harder when slicing vegetables or butchering meat

VICTORINOX SWISS ARMY FIBROX PRO 8" CHEF'S KNIFE ($39.95)
• Longer blade easily handles any task
• Sharp tip effortlessly slips into food and can nick open packaging
• Bigger blade with sharp tip can feel intimidating to novice cooks

or separating whole chickens into parts. In fact, one of the appealing features of our two favorite knives is that their tips curved less than those of other models, and thus they functioned more like chef's knives.

Next was the traditional straight bottom edge—or lack thereof. Originally, santoku blades were modeled after Japanese vegetable cleavers and as such were conducive to straight-down slicing, not a Western-style rocking motion. But newer models, including most of the ones we tested, feature gently curved bottom edges that allow for a subtle rocking motion, which we found effective and comfortable for mincing herbs. The lone exception was our runner-up, a "rocking santoku," which features a deeply curved bottom edge that permits a full rocking motion.

Finally, we considered Granton edges. These oval hollows (also called cullens) that run along the sides of the blade supposedly prevent food from sticking to the metal, but we didn't notice any less sticking to the seven Granton-edge blades in our lineup; in fact, two of our top three performers lacked this feature, so we consider it unnecessary.

How They (Com)pared

By the end of testing, we'd found multiple santokus that we'd happily take home, most notably the Misono UX10 Santoku 7.0" ($179.50). That price makes it an investment, but its lithe, agile frame and neutral handle feel great to hold, and its edge stayed bitingly sharp throughout testing, even after separating chicken joints and breaking down butternut squash. But for less than half the price, you can do very well with the MAC Superior Santoku 6½" ($74.95). Its wooden handle seemed slightly bulky to testers with smaller hands, but slicing and precision cutting with it felt truly effortless.

What was the answer, then, to our primary question: Is the santoku a viable alternative to a chef's knife? In the end, we decided that it's really a personal choice. A good santoku can certainly mince, slice, and chop as well as any good chef's knife (in fact, some testers even liked the Misono a tad more than our winning chef's knife from Victorinox), and if you prefer a smaller tool, one of our top-ranked santokus might suit you just fine. However, if you're comfortable with the extra length and heft of a chef's knife and would miss the pointed tip, you might want to consider a santoku only as an addition to your arsenal, not as a replacement.

PERFORMANCE

We minced fresh herbs, diced onions, broke down whole raw chickens into parts, and quartered unpeeled butternut squashes. To assess precision, we cut carrots into matchsticks and sliced slightly frozen boneless steak against the grain into uniform slivers (a technique used when preparing beef for Vietnamese *pho*). Knives that sliced smoothly and helped us complete the tasks with crisp cuts and neat results scored highest. We also assessed the sharpness of each knife before and after testing by slicing sheets of copy paper; blades that started sharp and stayed that way rated highest.

EASE OF USE

Throughout testing we rated the knives on how comfortable and easy they were to hold and use, evaluating the handle shape, spine sharpness (if we used a pinch grip), weight, and balance of the blade. Six testers of varying heights and handedness, including three proficient with knives and three self-described knife novices, chopped onions and rated the knives. Knives rated higher if most testers found them comfortable and easy to use.

How to Sharpen a Santoku

Since our three favorite santoku knives have a variety of blade angles on their cutting edges, we wondered whether our winning knife sharpener, the electric Chef'sChoice Trizor XV ($149.99), could sharpen them all. Happily, we discovered that it can; when we uniformly dulled and resharpened their edges, they were as good as new. Note that for knives with an asymmetrical edge, such as our winning santoku from Misono, the owner's manual directs you to use only one side of the machine's paired slots at each stage of honing, confining the sharpening action to that single side of the blade. In the final polishing slot, pass the other side of the blade through once, just to finish it off smoothly. To see step-by-step sharpening photos, go to CooksIllustrated.com/sharpeningsantokus.

⊙ **See Lisa Cut It Up**
A free video is available at CooksIllustrated.com/dec17

TESTING SANTOKU KNIVES

We tested 10 santoku knives and also compared their feel and performance to that of our favorite chef's knife, the Victorinox Swiss Army Fibrox Pro 8" Chef's Knife. We measured the knives' blade length, blade angle, and spine thickness. All knives were purchased online, and prices shown are what we paid. Test results were averaged, and the knives appear below in order of preference.

HIGHLY RECOMMENDED

	CRITERIA		TESTERS' COMMENTS

MISONO UX10 Santoku 7.0"
MODEL: HMI-UXSA-180 PRICE: $179.50
BLADE ANGLE: Approximately 21°/9° (asymmetrical)
BLADE LENGTH: 7 in
THICKNESS OF SPINE 1 INCH FROM HANDLE: 1.99 mm

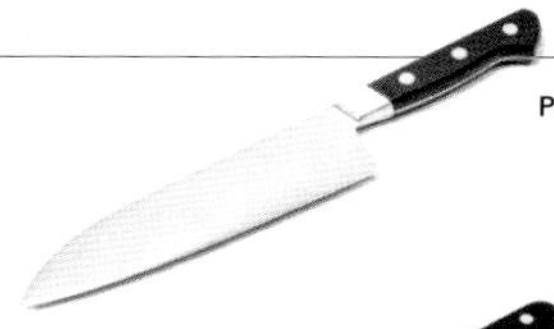

PERFORMANCE ★ ★ ★
EASE OF USE ★ ★ ★

Our favorite santoku wowed testers of all abilities, who raved that it felt "agile, sharp, and really good in hand." "Solid but light," it made "fine, level cuts" with "great precision and control." This knife features an asymmetrical blade with a 70/30 bevel that the company hand-sharpens specifically for either right- or left-handers.

ZWILLING Pro 7" Hollow Edge Rocking Santoku Knife
MODEL: 38418-183 PRICE: $129.99
BLADE ANGLE: 10° BLADE LENGTH: 7 in
THICKNESS OF SPINE 1 INCH FROM HANDLE: 2.04 mm

PERFORMANCE ★ ★ ★
EASE OF USE ★ ★ ½

With a deeply curved cutting edge, this "rocking" santoku permits the full Western rocking motion when chopping and slicing. Its tip is also much less curved than most, which helped it pass through food without resistance, as did its slim spine and very acute 10-degree cutting angle. Its handle was comfortable, if a bit too long for some testers.

MAC Superior Santoku 6½" *BEST BUY*
MODEL: SK-65 PRICE: $74.95
BLADE ANGLE: 15° BLADE LENGTH: 6.5 in
THICKNESS OF SPINE 1 INCH FROM HANDLE: 1.97 mm

PERFORMANCE ★ ★ ★
EASE OF USE ★ ★ ½

Thanks to its sharp cutting edge and skinny spine, this knife produced razor-thin slices and broke down a whole chicken and cut carrot matchsticks "like butter." The wooden handle felt a hair too thick and bulky to testers with smaller hands, and its blade was on the shorter end of what we prefer.

RECOMMENDED

KRAMER BY ZWILLING J.A. HENCKELS Euroline Essential Collection 7" Santoku Knife
MODEL: 34987-183 PRICE: $199.95
BLADE ANGLE: 15° BLADE LENGTH: 7 in
THICKNESS OF SPINE 1 INCH FROM HANDLE: 2.12 mm

PERFORMANCE ★ ★ ★
EASE OF USE ★ ★

Heavy, with a wide handle and a tall blade, this knife felt more like a modified chef's knife than a santoku. It was "sharp as get-out," easily breaking down a chicken, but several testers felt that they lacked control grasping such a large handle, especially during butchering when the grip became slippery.

VICTORINOX SWISS ARMY Fibrox Pro 7" Granton Blade Santoku Knife
MODEL: 47529.US2 PRICE: $54.00
BLADE ANGLE: 15° BLADE LENGTH: 7 in
THICKNESS OF SPINE 1 INCH FROM HANDLE: 1.81 mm

PERFORMANCE ★ ★ ½
EASE OF USE ★ ★ ½

A featherweight, this agile knife felt like the most petite santoku of the lineup, particularly where the textured handle tapered to a too-narrow neck near the blade. Mincing parsley was a pleasure, but the cutting edge felt a bit dull from the beginning, so the knife lost some performance points.

RECOMMENDED WITH RESERVATIONS

SHUN Classic 7-in. Hollow-Ground Santoku
MODEL: DM0718 PRICE: $182.00
BLADE ANGLE: 16° BLADE LENGTH: 7 in
THICKNESS OF SPINE 1 INCH FROM HANDLE: 2.36 mm

PERFORMANCE ★ ★
EASE OF USE ★ ★

Despite its sturdy, sharp blade, this "blingy" knife felt handle-heavy. Testers complained about the handle's D shape, too. It felt slippery as we cut carrots and onions, knocked into the undersides of our wrists, and was obviously oriented for right-handed cooks. Its spine felt sharp when we used a pinch grip.

MERCER Culinary Genesis 7" Forged Santoku
MODEL: M20707 PRICE: $39.99
BLADE ANGLE: 15° BLADE LENGTH: 7 in
THICKNESS OF SPINE 1 INCH FROM HANDLE: 2.60 mm

PERFORMANCE ★ ★
EASE OF USE ★ ★

While this bargain blade "rocketed" through butternut squash and slid through an onion, its balance felt awkward, and it didn't hold an edge as well as others. It struggled to slice through raw chicken skin, and by the end of testing it had dulled slightly. The grippy, cushioned handle felt secure, but its width made smaller testers' hands splay out uncomfortably, and its spine was too sharp in a pinch grip.

GLOBAL G-48 7" Santoku Hollow Ground Knife
MODEL: G-48 PRICE: $165.00
BLADE ANGLE: 15° BLADE LENGTH: 7 in
THICKNESS OF SPINE 1 INCH FROM HANDLE: 2.10 mm

PERFORMANCE ★ ★
EASE OF USE ★ ½

"It can cut, but it's not comfortable," noted one tester of this sharp blade with a hard metal handle. The spine was sharp, and its tapered neck meant that our hands slid forward toward the blade, taking away a sense of control. Butternut squash proved challenging, but the knife got through.

WÜSTHOF Classic 7" Santoku, Hollow Edge
MODEL: 4183-7 PRICE: $129.99
BLADE ANGLE: 10° BLADE LENGTH: 7 in
THICKNESS OF SPINE 1 INCH FROM HANDLE: 2.47 mm

PERFORMANCE ★ ★
EASE OF USE ★ ½

Despite the ultranarrow angle on each side of the cutting edge, this "light," "agile" knife didn't feel especially sharp. That might be because its spine was nearly 2.5 millimeters wide; it thus took "some force" to dice onion, which sprayed juice into our eyes.

NOT RECOMMENDED

OXO Good Grips Pro 6.5" Santoku Knife
MODEL: 11162200 PRICE: $24.99
BLADE ANGLE: 15° BLADE LENGTH: 6.5 in
THICKNESS OF SPINE 1 INCH FROM HANDLE: 2.17 mm

PERFORMANCE ★
EASE OF USE ★

This knife felt duller, heavier, and more wedge-like than the rest from the get-go, and testers complained that its handle was too long. It stuck in the center of two squashes, leaving us with the dodgy job of gently nudging the blade back out.

The Best Supermarket Turkey

The holidays are no time to gamble on a bird that cooks up dry and bland—or, worse, exhibits off-flavors.

⇛ BY KATE SHANNON ⇚

Is there any holiday food more fraught than the turkey? First it hogs the refrigerator, and then it hogs the oven. Never mind the logistics of thawing, seasoning, and roasting. After all that, it often turns out dry and bland. A well-tested recipe and the right equipment go a long way toward a better bird, but there's another variable: The turkey itself matters just as much. To find the best supermarket bird, we purchased eight best-selling turkeys from both national and regional brands. All birds were in the 12- to 14-pound range, which we like for its 10- to 12-serving yield and easy maneuverability. Four were processed without added flavorings or seasonings, and four were treated: one was kosher, which means it was completely covered in salt and rinsed in cold water during processing in accordance with Jewish dietary law, and the other three were injected with salty broths that could also contain other flavorings such as sugar and spices.

We cooked the turkeys according to our recipe for Easier Roast Turkey and Gravy (November/December 2016), which calls for salting the birds for at least 24 hours before roasting. This step seasons the meat and helps it retain moisture while also ensuring crispy skin and good browning. Because the kosher and injected turkeys in our lineup were already treated with salt, we didn't salt those birds. A

We tasted 120 pounds of turkey to find the best holiday bird.

panel of 21 tasters evaluated the flavor, texture, and overall appeal of each turkey's light and dark meat.

Surprisingly, half the turkeys disappointed. Tasters complained that the meat tasted "weak and washed out," or worse, had musty or funky off-flavors, like "canned tuna" or "dirty water." Turkey is naturally lean, so we expected some of the meat to be a little dry. We didn't expect samples to suffer from the opposite problem. Tasters described some of the slices as "wet" or "gummy," drawing comparisons to a "dampened washcloth" or a "waterlogged sponge." But there was good news, too. Four turkeys were "amazingly flavorful," juicy, and tender. What made these good birds good?

Breed, Feed, and Seasoning

First we looked at breed. Seven of the eight producers confirmed that they sell Broad-Breasted White turkeys or other similar breeds that mature quickly and have an abundance of white meat (the eighth, Butterball, declined to comment). Despite the similarities among the breeds, Professor Michael Lilburn of The Ohio State University's Turkey Center explained that producers work with outside companies to make genetic modifications that fit their specific requirements, so there are bound to be natural differences in flavor, even within the same breed. But other factors were surely also at play.

We next considered the birds' diets. Corn and soybean meal make up the bulk of turkeys' feed, but diets do vary. Michael Hulet, a professor of poultry science at Pennsylvania State University, pointed out that "Commercial diets may [also] contain antibiotics, animal products, and byproducts." And these components (which are sterilized), he said, "may affect

taste." Intrigued, we examined our lineup and saw that, according to their labels, only the untreated birds were antibiotic-free and were fed vegetarian diets. There's nothing wrong with an omnivorous bird (wild turkeys eat insects and worms in their natural habitat), but as we learned, bonemeal, feathers, or even blood (such byproducts are sterilized first) can go into the feed of commercially raised turkeys, contributing off-flavors. The producers of the three injected turkeys would not disclose whether their turkeys' diets contained animal products. Nevertheless, we found that birds labeled "vegetarian-fed" and "antibiotic-free" tended to taste better.

The salt-based solutions injected into the turkeys are meant to enhance flavor and moisture. But in fact, all the treated birds in our tasting were rife with texture issues. The kosher bird had a sometimes-dry, sometimes-spongy texture. And the injected birds were still dry or "borderline gummy" and "mushy," with an unpleasantly "sticky" quality. Although all the turkeys in our lineup were chilled in water (a routine part of processing that results in added moisture), the treated turkeys had 8 to 10 percent added moisture compared with a high of 6 percent for the untreated turkeys.

Fat played heavily into our rankings, too. The untreated turkeys all had far fattier dark meat, ranging from 2.61 to 4.11 percent fat, than the injected birds, which had between 1.50 and 2.71 percent fat. Analysis of the white meat produced similar results. As for the kosher turkey, its fat levels were similar to those of the untreated turkeys, but it had the most retained moisture (10 percent), resulting in a "strangely wet" texture and bland flavor that counteracted any advantages the fat should have provided.

A Better Bird

Any of the untreated, vegetarian-fed turkeys we tasted would be good candidates for your holiday table. All have clean turkey flavor, and we like that you can control the seasoning with these birds. That said, Mary's Free-Range Non-GMO Verified Turkey ($2.69 per pound) jumped to the head of the pack with "rich," "robust turkey flavor" and "very tender and juicy" meat. For a less expensive option, we recommend our second-place product, the Plainville Farms Young Turkey ($1.19 per pound), which features "concentrated" turkey flavor and "moist," "buttery" meat. Now that's something to be thankful for.

For a High-Quality Bird, Check the Ingredient List

Many supermarket turkeys are injected with salty flavored liquid that seasons the meat and changes its protein structure so it holds more water. When phosphates are included, they allow the meat to hold even more water. This type of processing may sound promising—after all, we commonly brine turkey and chicken in the test kitchen to improve flavor and moistness. But we've found that injected birds (these are often referred to as "self-basting") can contain funky-tasting spices and seasonings. Furthermore, their retained liquid (up to 9.5 percent) gave them a curiously "gummy" and "mushy" texture. We also had reservations about the Empire Kosher bird processed with salt: It was both wet and dry at the same time. For the best holiday bird, avoid those listing anything other than "turkey" on the ingredient list and follow our recipes' instructions for brining or salting.

TASTING SUPERMARKET TURKEY

We selected eight top-selling whole turkeys from both national and regional brands. All weighed between 12 and 14 pounds and all were widely available at our local supermarkets at holiday time. Our lineup included four untreated turkeys, one kosher turkey (salted and rinsed according to Jewish dietary law), and three birds that had been injected with flavored broths containing salt, sugar, or other seasonings. We roasted them (skipping the salting step on the kosher and injected birds) and then asked 21 America's Test Kitchen staff members to evaluate the white meat and the dark meat for flavor, texture, and overall appeal. An independent lab measured the fat levels in the white and dark meat; results are reported below as percentages. Age and diet information was obtained from product packaging and manufacturers. Most of the prices listed are what we paid in Boston-area supermarkets. Prices for the Mary's and Diestel turkeys are California retail prices; they're also available online for roughly double the cost. Products appear below in order of preference.

RECOMMENDED

MARY'S Free-Range Non-GMO Verified Turkey

PRICE: $2.69 per lb ($34.97 for a 13-lb turkey)

INGREDIENT: Turkey AGE: 10 to 12 weeks

PERCENT OF RETAINED LIQUID: Up to 6%

ANTIBIOTIC-FREE: Yes

VEGETARIAN-FED: Yes

FAT IN DARK MEAT: 2.61%

FAT IN WHITE MEAT: 0.48%

COMMENTS: "Tastes like what I think turkey should taste like," wrote one happy taster. Our new winner, which is from the same company that produces our winning chickens and heritage turkeys, has relatively high fat levels and is fed a vegetarian diet. As a result, it had "clean," "robust" turkey flavor and a slightly "nutty aftertaste." It had "great texture" and was "very tender and juicy."

PLAINVILLE FARMS Young Turkey

PRICE: $1.19 per lb ($15.47 for a 13-lb turkey)

INGREDIENT: Turkey AGE: 13 weeks

PERCENT OF RETAINED LIQUID: Less than 6%

ANTIBIOTIC-FREE: Yes

VEGETARIAN-FED: Yes

FAT IN DARK MEAT: 4.11%

FAT IN WHITE MEAT: 0.46%

COMMENTS: Our new Best Buy was "amazingly flavorful." Tasters especially liked the "rich, meaty" flavor of the dark meat, which was so good that there was "no need for gravy." Its dark meat had the highest fat level in our lineup and was deemed "firm, juicy, tender." Many noted that it was "just what I want in a turkey." Best of all, it's half the price of our winner.

DIESTEL Turkey Ranch Non-GMO Verified Turkey

PRICE: $3.49 per lb ($45.37 for a 13-lb turkey)

INGREDIENT: Turkey AGE: About 24 weeks

PERCENT OF RETAINED LIQUID: Up to 3%

ANTIBIOTIC-FREE: Yes

VEGETARIAN-FED: Yes

FAT IN DARK MEAT: 3.58%

FAT IN WHITE MEAT: 0.78%

COMMENTS: Raised for six months—the amount of time that heritage birds generally require to grow to full size—this turkey had dark meat with a purplish hue, "very savory" flavor, and "subtle minerality" that reminded us of duck and expensive heritage turkeys. In evaluations of texture, panelists commented that even the white meat was "perfect."

BELL & EVANS Turkey Raised Without Antibiotics

PRICE: $2.99 per lb ($38.87 for a 13-lb turkey)

INGREDIENT: Turkey AGE: 10 to 12 weeks

PERCENT OF RETAINED LIQUID: Less than 4%

ANTIBIOTIC-FREE: Yes

VEGETARIAN-FED: Yes

FAT IN DARK MEAT: 3.61%

FAT IN WHITE MEAT: 1.51%

COMMENTS: "Oh, this is good!" wrote one taster. Our panelists loved the "roasty," "surprisingly flavorful" meat and "nutty aftertaste." This bird also hit the mark with "tender and moist" meat. The white meat had by far the highest fat level of the bunch, and its dark meat was almost purple in color—a sign of older or relatively well-exercised birds.

RECOMMENDED WITH RESERVATIONS

NOT RECOMMENDED

JENNIE-O Frozen Whole Turkey

PRICE: $0.69 per lb ($8.97 for a 13-lb turkey)

INGREDIENTS: Young turkey containing approximately 9.5% of a solution of turkey broth, salt, sodium phosphate, sugar, flavoring

AGE: About 12 weeks

PERCENT OF RETAINED LIQUID: Approximately 9.5%

ANTIBIOTIC-FREE: No

VEGETARIAN-FED: No

FAT IN DARK MEAT: 1.50%

FAT IN WHITE MEAT: 0.16%

COMMENTS: The best of the injected birds was a far cry from the untreated turkeys. Given its lack of fat—the lowest in the lineup—tasters unsurprisingly found the white meat "very bland" and wished the dark meat were "a little richer." Some praised its texture, but others found it "almost mushy." A few detected "funky" off-notes.

HONEYSUCKLE WHITE Frozen Young Turkey

PRICE: $1.16 per lb ($15.08 for a 13-lb turkey)

INGREDIENTS: Turkey, broth, salt, sugar, natural flavoring

AGE: 10 to 13 weeks

PERCENT OF RETAINED LIQUID: 9.5%

ANTIBIOTIC-FREE: No

VEGETARIAN-FED: No

FAT IN DARK MEAT: 2.71%

FAT IN WHITE MEAT: 0.49%

COMMENTS: "Weak" and "generic" were apt descriptions of this bird's flavor. Some also found it "liver-y" and "musty." Its texture also took criticism: Like the Jennie-O bird, the Honeysuckle White turkey contains 9.5 percent absorbed moisture, prompting remarks such as "leaning toward mushy" and "a little waterlogged." The dark meat was a very similar color to the white meat, which may indicate that the birds get little exercise, and it tasted similarly mild as well.

EMPIRE Kosher Young Turkey

PRICE: $3.29 per lb ($42.77 for a 13-lb turkey)

INGREDIENTS: Turkey, water, salt

AGE: 13 weeks

PERCENT OF RETAINED LIQUID: Up to 10%

ANTIBIOTIC-FREE: Yes

VEGETARIAN-FED: Yes

FAT IN DARK MEAT: 4.01%

FAT IN WHITE MEAT: 0.57%

COMMENTS: The sole kosher bird in our lineup didn't exhibit any of the off-flavors that we detected in the injected birds (perhaps due to its vegetarian diet), but it was still "bland with a touch of generic turkey flavor." It had fairly high fat levels, but it also had the highest retained moisture level, 10 percent. The resulting texture was puzzling. Tasters described it as "too moist and too dry at the same time." As one taster summed up: "doesn't taste like much of anything."

BUTTERBALL Premium Young Turkey

PRICE: $1.19 per lb ($15.47 for a 13-lb turkey)

INGREDIENTS: Whole young turkey, contains up to 8% of a solution of water, salt, spices, and natural flavor

AGE: Manufacturer would not disclose

PERCENT OF RETAINED LIQUID: 8%

ANTIBIOTIC-FREE: Manufacturer would not disclose

VEGETARIAN-FED: Manufacturer would not disclose

FAT IN DARK MEAT: 2.61%

FAT IN WHITE MEAT: 0.47%

COMMENTS: Although ubiquitous in supermarkets during the holidays, this injected turkey met with strong dislike from our tasters. It had "no meaty flavor" and very noticeable off-notes. Tasters described it as "musty" and "greasy" and noted that it tasted "like fish" or "canned tuna." Although the dark meat was "relatively moist," the white meat was "too dry."

Tasting Dry Vermouth

Dry vermouth is a convenient alternative to white wine since it can be substituted in recipes in equal amounts. Like Marsala and sherry, vermouth is wine that's been fortified with a high-proof alcohol (often brandy) that raises its alcohol content and allows it to be stored in the refrigerator for weeks or even months after opening. Dry vermouth is also infused with botanicals, which can include leaves, roots, flowers, seeds, herbs, and spices. It is sometimes aged in barrels, a process that is intended to impart an oaky, vanilla-y quality and can allow harsh flavors or sharp tannins to mellow.

We bought eight nationally available dry vermouths, priced from $6.99 to $24.99 for 750-milliliter or 1-liter bottles. After sampling them plain and in place of white wine in Parmesan risotto, we found that they fell into two broad groups. Some were intensely flavored, with lots of warm spice and almost "medicinal" hints of pine and menthol that risked overpowering the milder flavors in the risotto. We preferred products that were "aromatic" and "more interesting" than a run-of-the-mill white wine and that provided background notes in risotto rather than dominating it.

Dolin Dry Vermouth de Chambéry, a French product that has recently become widely available in the United States, earned top marks for its "crisp" acidity and "green notes" of fruit, citrus, and mint. It's the best option for people who want to cook with vermouth and might occasionally drink it as an aperitif or mix it into cocktails. If you use dry vermouth primarily for cooking, our Best Buy, from Gallo in California, was slightly sweeter (but not cloying), with more subtle botanicals. It's also cheaper than the white wines we buy for cooking and will last far longer in the refrigerator. Cheers to that. For the complete tasting results, go to CooksIllustrated.com/dec17. –Kate Shannon

RECOMMENDED

DOLIN Dry Vermouth de Chambéry

PRICE: $14.99 for 750 ml

SOURCE: France

COMMENTS: Tasters loved this versatile French dry vermouth. When tasted plain, it was "crisp" and had notes of fresh fruit, citrus, and mint. It contributed a "distinctive" but measured herbal flavor to risotto. If you'd like to cook with dry vermouth and occasionally drink it plain or in cocktails, buy this bottle.

GALLO Extra Dry Vermouth

PRICE: $6.99 for 750 ml

SOURCE: California

COMMENTS: Our Best Buy was "sweeter" and had "less fragrant botanicals" than our winner but was still "crisp and fruity" enough for our panel. It earned top marks in risotto, where its "bright," "clean" flavor brought out the savoriness of the chicken broth and Parmesan cheese and didn't taste overly sweet. Best of all, it's less expensive than the dry white wines many of us usually buy for cooking.

MARTINI & ROSSI Extra Dry Vermouth

PRICE: $8.49 for 750 ml

SOURCE: Italy

COMMENTS: This ubiquitous dry vermouth, which ranked fifth in our tasting, contained a range of flavors when sampled plain. Our panels detected everything from "lemony," "almost tropical" flavors to "lavender" and "potpourri"-like notes. But when we used it to prepare risotto, those assertive flavors mellowed to something more "flat" and "mild."

What to Do with Escarole

A member of the chicory family, escarole can add crispness and personality to plain green salads. Its broad, white-spined, curly-topped leaves start out light at the bottom and darken to a rich green at the top. Unlike frisée, whose leaves should be trimmed of their bitter tips, a head of escarole yields very little waste.

Escarole is also a key player in many Italian soups, including our Tuscan White Bean and Escarole Soup (page 22). Though escarole is less assertive than its cousins Belgian endive and frisée, its bitterness brings complexity to the soup. Also, its resilient leaves turn supple when cooked but don't fall apart, and the base and spine of each leaf add a little texture. Look for heads bristling with sturdy, unblemished leaves. –L.L

SOUP AND SALAD GREEN

Yogurt Swap in Recipes

These days, grocery stores carry yogurt made not just from cow's milk but from goat's and sheep's milks, too. Since goat's and sheep's milks often have gamy, grassy flavors, we wondered how they would work in recipes calling for ordinary cow's-milk yogurt. We tried whole-milk versions of all three yogurts in Bundt cake, frozen yogurt, and a warm, savory yogurt sauce. In cake, the flavors of the goat's-milk and sheep's-milk yogurts were undetectable, but the sheep's-milk cake seemed slightly richer and more moist, likely due to this yogurt's high fat content (12 grams per cup versus cow's-milk's 9 grams and goat's milk's 6 grams). However, in the frozen yogurt and yogurt sauce, tasters found that those funky flavors came through quite clearly. **Bottom line?** If you enjoy the funk of goat's-milk and sheep's-milk yogurts, feel free to use them in recipes calling for ordinary yogurt. Their impact on texture will be minimal, and depending on the dish, their barnyard-y characteristics may come through. –A.P.

Freekeh: "New" Noteworthy Grain

WHOLE
Cooks in 45 minutes

CRACKED
Cooks in 20 minutes

Freekeh, a traditional Middle Eastern grain popular in Mediterranean and North African cuisines, has recently started appearing on restaurant menus and grocery store shelves in the United States.

Freekeh is made from roasted durum wheat that's been harvested while the grains are still young and green. The grains are polished (freekeh is a colloquialization of *farik*, which means "rubbed" in Arabic) and sold whole as well as cracked into smaller pieces. Simmered pasta-style in a large amount of water and then drained, whole freekeh took 45 minutes to cook, while cracked freekeh took about 20 minutes. Once cooked, both styles remained slightly firm and chewy and boasted smoky, nutty, earthy flavors. The freekeh also tasted surprisingly savory: Though it was cooked in only salted water, many tasters thought it had been simmered in chicken broth.

Freekeh can be substituted for other grains such as wheat berries or farro (try it in our recipes for Wheat Berry Salad with Orange and Scallions and Warm Farro with Cranberries, Pecans, and Herbs, which are available free for four months at CooksIllustrated.com/wheatberrysalad and CooksIllustrated.com/warmfarrosalad). It's also great in soups or hearty stews. –A.J.

Homemade Five-Spice Powder

Five-spice powder is a traditional Chinese seasoning blend with five components that imparts bitterness, sweetness, and pungency to food. We use it in spice rubs, glazes, sauces, and stews. Most Chinese blends include cinnamon, star anise, cloves, fennel, and Sichuan peppercorns, while American-made versions substitute white peppercorns for the Sichuan kind. This blend's impact is even greater when you grind your own from whole spices.

To make your own: Process 1 tablespoon whole cloves, 2½ teaspoons fennel seeds, and 2 teaspoons white peppercorns (or 4 teaspoons Sichuan peppercorns) in spice grinder until finely ground, 20 to 30 seconds. Transfer to small bowl. Process 4 to 6 star anise pods (depending on size) and one 5- to 6-inch cinnamon stick in spice grinder until finely ground, 20 to 30 seconds. Transfer to bowl with other spices and stir to combine. **Yield:** About ¼ cup. —S.D.

Microwave-Fried Shallots, Garlic, and Leeks

We love the bursts of crunch and savory flavor that crispy fried shallots, garlic, and leeks bring when sprinkled over soups, salads, stir-fries, and burgers. But they're easy to overcook. Microwaving them is more foolproof and doesn't require constant stirring. —A.J.

For Shallots: Place 3 shallots, peeled and sliced thin, in medium bowl with ½ cup vegetable oil and microwave at 100 percent power for 5 minutes. Stir and microwave at 100 percent power for 2 more minutes. Repeat stirring and microwaving in 2-minute increments until shallots begin to brown (4 to 6 minutes total), then repeat stirring and microwaving in 30-second increments until shallots are deep golden (30 seconds to 2 minutes total). Using slotted spoon, transfer shallots to paper towel–lined plate; season with salt. Let drain and turn crisp, about 5 minutes, before serving.

For Garlic: In place of shallots, use ½ cup garlic cloves, sliced or minced. After frying, dust garlic with 1 teaspoon confectioners' sugar (to offset any bitterness) before seasoning with salt.

For Leeks: In place of shallots, use 1 leek, white and light green parts only, halved lengthwise, sliced into very thin 2-inch-long strips, washed thoroughly, dried, and tossed with 2 tablespoons all-purpose flour (which accelerates browning).

Buttermilk Powder in Nonbaking Applications

We've long substituted powdered buttermilk for fresh buttermilk in baking recipes, but when we recently tried to use it in nonbaked goods, we ran into problems: It made for watery coleslaw, loose mashed potatoes, and fried chicken with a coating that didn't adhere properly. And curiously, when we added more powder to the same amount of water, the mixture didn't noticeably thicken.

That's because when fresh milk is inoculated with bacteria to create buttermilk, the proteins in the milk form a soft gel that thickens its consistency (some manufacturers also add thickeners). But when buttermilk is dried to make powdered buttermilk, the protein gel is disrupted, so reconstituted buttermilk ends up being thinner than its fresh counterpart.

DIY RECIPE **Chocolate-Toffee Bark**

For a sweet treat that's great for gifts, we make a buttery, nutty layer of toffee, let it harden, and then coat both sides with chocolate. A greased aluminum foil sling is essential for getting the sticky toffee out of the pan. —Julia Collin Davison

CHOCOLATE-TOFFEE BARK
MAKES ABOUT 1½ POUNDS

You will need a thermometer that registers high temperatures for this recipe.

8	tablespoons unsalted butter
½	cup water
1	cup (7 ounces) sugar
¼	teaspoon salt
1½	cups pecans or walnuts, toasted and chopped
8	ounces semisweet chocolate, chopped coarse

1. Make foil sling for 13 by 9-inch baking pan by folding 2 long sheets of aluminum foil; first sheet should be 13 inches wide and second sheet should be 9 inches wide. Lay sheets of foil in pan perpendicular to each other, with extra foil hanging over edges of pan. Push foil into corners and up sides of pan, smoothing foil flush to pan. Spray foil with vegetable oil spray.

2. Heat butter and water in medium saucepan over medium-high heat until butter is melted. Pour sugar and salt into center of saucepan, taking care not to let sugar touch sides of saucepan. Bring mixture to boil and cook, without stirring, until sugar is completely dissolved and syrup is faint golden color and registers 300 degrees, about 10 minutes.

3. Reduce heat to medium-low and continue to cook, gently swirling saucepan, until toffee is amber-colored and registers 325 degrees, 1 to 3 minutes longer. Off heat, stir in ½ cup pecans until incorporated and thoroughly coated.

4. Pour toffee into prepared pan and smooth into even layer with spatula. Refrigerate, uncovered, until toffee has hardened, about 15 minutes.

5. Microwave 4 ounces chocolate in bowl at 50 percent power, stirring occasionally, until melted, about 2 minutes. Pour chocolate over hardened toffee and smooth with spatula, making sure to cover toffee layer evenly and completely. Sprinkle with ½ cup pecans and press lightly to adhere. Refrigerate, uncovered, until chocolate has hardened, about 15 minutes.

6. Line rimmed baking sheet with parchment paper. Using foil sling, invert toffee onto prepared sheet. Discard foil.

7. Microwave remaining 4 ounces chocolate in bowl at 50 percent power, stirring occasionally, until melted, about 2 minutes. Pour chocolate over toffee and smooth with spatula, making sure to cover toffee layer evenly and completely. Sprinkle with remaining ½ cup pecans and press lightly to adhere. Refrigerate, uncovered, until chocolate has hardened, about 15 minutes.

8. Break bark into rough squares and serve. (Bark can be stored at room temperature for up to 2 weeks.)

There's no way to thicken reconstituted buttermilk, but you can still substitute it for the real thing in coleslaw and mashed potatoes: Decreasing the amount of water by 25 percent while using the full amount of powder recommended on the package will yield the same tangy flavor without introducing a lot of excess moisture. But because the more concentrated formulation isn't actually thicker, it won't help breading cling, so it is unsuitable for fried chicken.

In sum, except in recipes where buttermilk's viscosity is key, such as fried chicken, the powdered kind will work fine as long as you use 25 percent less water than recommended to reconstitute the powder. —A.G.

POWDERED BUTTERMILK
It's a sometime thing.

KITCHEN NOTES

⇒ BY MIYE BROMBERG, STEVE DUNN, ANDREA GEARY, ANDREW JANJIGIAN, LAN LAM & LISA McMANUS ⇐

WHAT IS IT?

CAST-IRON SAUSAGE STUFFER

This stout tool looks like an old fireplace bellows, but it's actually a sausage stuffer from the mid- to late 1800s. Made of cast iron, this 8-pound gadget was used to extrude ground sausage meat into casings to form link sausage. The handle would be raised to extract the plunger from the hopper so that meat could be placed inside. A casing would be placed over the extrusion nozzle and the handle pulled down to force the meat from the hopper into the casings.

To test the gadget, I whipped up a quick batch of sweet Italian sausage, loaded the hopper, readied a casing and . . . called for help. The long, unwieldy handle was tough to manage on my own, and I needed a fellow test cook to assist me. I needed both arms to generate enough force to pull the handle. Meanwhile, my helper held the unit steady and regulated the flow of meat into the casing. In the end, the press made fine sausages, but it was cumbersome to use. Later models evolved to include crank handles and gear mechanisms, which more easily and evenly forced the meat through the machine. –S.D.

Why It's Important to Let Cookie Sheets Cool

If you're baking a lot of cookies but have a limited number of cookie sheets, it can be tempting to load more batches onto the sheets before they've fully cooled. We ran a test to see the degree to which placing dough on a hot or merely warm cookie sheet would impact the cookies' spread. We made the dough for our Chewy Sugar Cookies (November/December 2010) and baked three batches. We arranged the first batch on a room-temperature cookie sheet (72 degrees), the second on a sheet that we let cool for 5 minutes (110 degrees), and the third on a hot sheet (172 degrees) that we did not allow to cool at all after removing the previous batch. What did we learn? Cookies baked on the warm sheet spread more than those started on the cool sheet; while not ideal, the cookies did not run into each other. But the cookies baked on the hot sheet spread so much that the cookies fused together.

The takeaway: For the best results, let your cookie sheet cool completely before reusing it. If time is tight, you can get away with letting it cool for as little as 5 minutes. Never reuse a sheet straight from the oven, as its high heat will cause the dough to spread and the cookies to fuse together. –S.D.

COOL SHEET
Best results

WARM SHEET
Not ideal

HOT SHEET
Too much spread

Cleave with Confidence

The tall, relatively heavy blade of a meat cleaver—such as the one on our favorite, the Shun Classic Meat Cleaver (see page 32)—is ideal for hacking up bone-in meat and poultry. But that's not all: The flat side of the blade can be used to smash aromatics, including garlic, ginger, and lemon grass. You can even use a cleaver to transfer chopped food from the cutting board to a cooking vessel. Many cooks are intimidated by cleavers. Here are a few tips for how to use this tool with confidence. –M.B.

TO HACK UP MEAT OR POULTRY:

➤ Stabilize ends of long cuts (such as rib or backbone) with your nonknife hand. For shorter pieces of food, keep your nonknife hand away from board.
➤ Grip handle of cleaver as if using hammer; for an alternate grip, place your thumb on blade spine.
➤ Let weight of blade do most of work, raising your arm only slightly from your elbow before bringing cleaver down on food.

➤ If cleaver gets stuck, press down firmly on spine with your nonknife hand to help push blade downward, or use slicing motion to finish cut.
➤ If cutting board is wooden with one-way grain, cut at angle to grain to avoid splitting board while chopping.
➤ Go to CooksIllustrated.com/cleaver for more information on how to use a cleaver.

Darning Turkey Skin

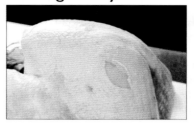

BEFORE AND AFTER: AN EASY FIX
A simple wooden toothpick is all you need to mend this tear.

As the showpiece of the holiday meal, a roast turkey should look as good as it tastes. We have many tricks for ensuring moist and tender meat and a crisp, golden-brown skin. But every so often, a turkey emerges from the packaging with torn skin. Besides marring the bird's appearance, the patch of exposed meat tends to overcook without the protection the skin provides.

Fortunately, there's an easy fix. Before placing the bird in the oven, arrange the skin so that the torn edges are lined up, and then use toothpicks to pin the skin to the flesh underneath. Toothpicks should be spaced ¾ to 1 inch apart. Roast per the recipe instructions, and when the bird comes out of the oven, remove the toothpicks. As heat sets the proteins, it helps glue the torn skin to the meat, and only the most discerning eyes will be able to pick out the patch. –L.L.

Guide to Chocolate Dipping

A glossy chocolate coating can enhance anything from simple fruit to fancy cookies, but not if it looks thick and clunky. Follow our foolproof technique for tempering chocolate (CooksIllustrated.com/temperchocolate), and then use these tips to create an elegantly thin coating. —A.G

1. Maintain a chocolate temperature of about 90 degrees to ensure that the chocolate stays fluid (and tempered).

2. Dip the item in the melted chocolate to the desired depth and pull up. To remove excess chocolate, tap the item against the surface of the chocolate 4 or 5 times, pulling up sharply each time.

3. To prevent a thick "foot" of hardened chocolate from forming beneath the item, gently scrape its bottom against the edge of the bowl as you transfer it to a parchment paper–lined baking sheet to set.

Why Do Some Blades Have Hollows?

Santoku and slicing knives often feature oval hollows carved into the sides of their blades. Many sources claim that this innovation, patented in 1928 by what's now the Granton Knives Co. in Sheffield, England, and often referred to as a "Granton edge," prevents food from clinging to the blade. However, the Granton edge has an additional purpose: The scallops make the blade thinner and lighter to help it slide through food while maintaining some rigidity at the spine for control. The hollows are especially effective on Granton-brand knives, whose deep scallops are carved down through the cutting edge on alternate sides, unlike those of most imitators, which are symmetrical, shallower, and set higher on the blade.

We've tested dozens of Granton-edge knives over the years and found the hollows valuable on slicing knives, including our favorite, the Victorinox 12" Fibrox Pro Granton Edge Slicing/Carving Knife ($54.65). The hollows reduce friction and make it easier to carve even slices, whether using it on a roast or a delicate side of salmon. But when testing santoku knives (page 23), we didn't find them necessary since these blades are short (6.5 to 7 inches) and are already razor-thin. Our winning santoku lacks a Granton edge, and we didn't miss it. —L.M.

Grate Advice for Ginger

Even with a sharp rasp-style grater, grating large amounts of fresh ginger can be a chore. Here are some tips to help improve your grating game. —A.G

➤ Start with a large piece of peeled ginger. Because some waste is inevitable, it takes a 1¼-ounce piece to produce 1 tablespoon of grated ginger.

➤ The fibers in a piece of ginger run from the top of the root to the bottom. Positioning the cut end of a piece of ginger perpendicular to the grater's surface so that the fibers meet the teeth of the grater straight on will result in clogged teeth. Instead, hold the ginger so that the fibers run perpendicularly across the teeth.

➤ If the teeth do clog, rinse the grater under warm running water and pass a moist sponge along the grating surface from the bottom toward the handle to avoid tearing the sponge.

Tip: There's a lot of flavor in the ginger's juice. Be sure to scrape it up with a bench scraper and include it in your measurement.

SCIENCE Why Brisket Is the Toughest Tough Cut

Brisket takes about twice as long to turn tender as do other braising cuts. We've always thought that's because brisket has more chewy collagen (the main component in meat's connective tissue) than other cuts, which needs more time to convert to soft gelatin for the meat to fully tenderize. But while developing our recipe for Braised Brisket with Pomegranate, Cumin, and Cilantro (page 8), we were puzzled to see that the braising liquid was thin and runny rather than silky and unctuous, the way you'd expect liquid full of gelatin to be. Could some other dynamic be at work? We decided to compare the gelatin produced by brisket with that of chuck roast, which often produces rich, thickened braising liquid.

EXPERIMENT

We sealed multiple 100-gram portions of brisket and chuck roast in bags and cooked them using a *sous vide* device at 195 degrees for 8 hours; at that point, we knew that both cuts would be tender and that they would have released as much gelatin as possible. We also included samples of veal breast—the same cut as brisket but from a calf—to see if age influences collagen (and thus gelatin) content. We drained the liquid from each bag, chilled it overnight, removed the fat, and then examined the gels for firmness.

RESULTS

To our surprise, the brisket and the chuck roast produced similar amounts of gel, and both gels were loose. Meanwhile, the gel from the veal breast was significantly more firm.

GEL TELLS ALL
Brisket and chuck have mainly insoluble collagen and produce watery gel (top two spoons), whereas veal breast gel is very firm (bottom spoon), indicating more soluble collagen.

EXPLANATION

Collagen is most abundant in muscles that get the most exercise. For this reason, brisket (from the breast, which supports 60 percent of the cow's weight) is naturally higher in collagen than chuck (from the shoulder). But over time, exercise creates cross-links in collagen that transform it from a soluble form to a stronger and more insoluble form. Insoluble collagen can only weaken and soften with prolonged exposure to heat; it won't break down into gelatin. Thus, while brisket has more collagen than chuck, the collagen in both these well-exercised cuts is mainly insoluble, so neither produces

COLLAGEN, UP CLOSE

Soluble collagen: few cross-links

Insoluble collagen: many cross-links

Collagen is a triple helix made of three protein chains that unwind during cooking to form supple gelatin. But age and exercise can create cross-links that allow collagen only to soften, not to fully unwind.

enough gelatin to create full-bodied juices. Because veal breast (young brisket) comes from a calf that hasn't experienced much exercise, its abundant collagen is mainly soluble and breaks down readily into gelatin.

TAKEAWAY

Brisket does indeed take more time to cook than other tough cuts because of its greater amount of collagen. However, much of that collagen is insoluble, so little of it will break down into gelatin. That's why we needed to bolster the viscosity of the thin braising liquid in our recipe with powdered gelatin. —A.J.

EQUIPMENT CORNER

⇛ BY MIYE BROMBERG AND EMILY PHARES ⇚

HIGHLY RECOMMENDED	RECOMMENDED	HIGHLY RECOMMENDED	HIGHLY RECOMMENDED	RECOMMENDED WITH RESERVATIONS
FINUM Brewing Basket L MODEL: 63/451.66.00 PRICE: $9.95	**MARCATO Biscuit Maker** MODEL: 8307 PRICE: $42.00	**SHUN Classic Meat Cleaver** MODEL: DM0767 PRICE: $149.00	**CALPHALON Tri-Ply Stainless Steel 14-inch Roaster with Nonstick Rack and Stainless Steel Lifters** MODEL: 1767986 PRICE: $75.69	**NORDIC WARE Microwave Omelet Pan** MODEL: 63600 PRICE: $5.12

Tea Infusers

Tea infusers are great for making a single cup of loose-leaf tea. They come in several styles: sticks, balls, and baskets made of perforated metal or wire mesh. With each, you simply insert the amount of tea you want to use into the infuser, stick the infuser into a cup, and pour hot water over it. We wanted to know which tea infuser was best, so we bought nine models, priced from $5.96 to $16.95, and used each to brew herbal, white, green, and black teas.

The size of the infuser proved critical. Smaller strainers couldn't hold a single serving of loose-leaf tea and were both fussy to fill and a challenge to clean. We strongly preferred larger, basket-style models, which allowed the tea to circulate and infuse the water more fully. All the basket-style infusers also had openings of 2 inches or more in diameter, making filling and cleaning them easy. Our winner, the Finum Brewing Basket L ($9.95), had the greatest capacity in our lineup, and its tightly woven mesh basket kept even the finest leaves out of the finished tea. Plus, its top can be used as a saucer to hold the basket and catch drips after or between infusions. –M.B.

Cookie Presses

Cookie presses are handheld gadgets that portion soft cookie doughs into a variety of shapes, from hearts and flowers to snowmen and turkeys. These cookies are typically called "spritz" cookies, from the German word *spritzen*, meaning "to squirt." The press has a tube that holds the dough, with a perforated shaping disk at one end and a handle at the other. After loading the dough, you place the cookie press base on a baking or cookie sheet, squeeze the handle, and out pops a perfect, oven-ready dough design—if the press works well.

To find the best cookie press, we purchased four, priced from $25.99 to $42.00, and put them through heavy use in the test kitchen. After pressing and baking more than 1,400 cookies, we found one with the qualities that matter most for a cookie press: consistency of shaping, durability, and, most important, the appearance of the cookies. The Marcato Biscuit Maker ($42.00) consistently produced attractive, well-formed cookies with few jams or misshapen designs. We experienced a couple of minor issues that required extra attention when loading the dough, inserting the disk, and operating the press, but the payoff—cookies in fun shapes—was worth it. –E.P.

Meat Cleavers

Designed to take abuse, meat cleavers are ideal for tough jobs that might wear down the blade of your chef's knife, such as cutting through whole chickens, whole lobsters, or butternut squash. With these functions in mind, we set out to determine the best meat cleaver for home use, buying 13 cleavers priced from $10.67 to $179.95. We put the cleavers to the test, chopping chicken parts and butternut squashes and breaking down whole ducks into serving-size pieces. In the end, the Shun Classic Meat Cleaver ($149.00) won us over with its even weight distribution; long, tall blade; and comfortable handle. This durable cleaver also came out of testing minimally scathed. For a more affordable option, we also recommend the Lamson Products 7.25" Walnut Handle Meat Cleaver ($59.95) as our Best Buy. A favorite of many testers, this old-school cleaver performed well and was easy to use, but it was not as durable or as well-made as our winner. –M.B.

Small Roasting Pans with Racks

We love our favorite roasting pan, the Calphalon Contemporary Stainless Roasting Pan with Rack ($99.99), for roasting turkeys and larger cuts of meat. But sometimes we want a more petite version for roasting chickens, vegetables and smaller cuts of meat. Curious to know which small roasting pan and rack were best, we purchased five sets priced from $17.99 to $159.95, each about 14 inches long. We used each set to roast potatoes and a whole chicken and to make gravy on the stovetop with the chicken drippings. Almost all the sets cooked the food well, but a few design factors made certain sets perform and handle better than others. Our favorite model, the Calphalon Tri-Ply Stainless Steel 14-inch Roaster with Nonstick Rack and Stainless Steel Lifters ($75.69), offers thick, tri-ply stainless-steel and aluminum construction and a flat cooking surface, which produced perfectly cooked, evenly browned food. Large handles made it easy to maneuver in and out of the oven, and its U-shaped rack nicely cradled the chicken. –M.B.

Microwave Egg Cookers

Microwave egg cookers promise cooked eggs in a flash with no pots, pans, or utensils to wash. To see how well they worked, we purchased seven products—five poachers and two omelet makers—and tested them in multiple microwave ovens at varying power levels. None of the microwave cookers could replicate the quality of eggs cooked on the stovetop; instead, this testing gave us eggs that were undercooked, rubbery, or even both at once. Why were the microwaved eggs inferior to stovetop eggs? Egg yolks contain less water and more fat than egg whites, so the two parts of the egg absorb energy at different rates, making it challenging to get nicely cooked eggs from a microwave oven. The best product, the Nordic Ware Microwave Omelet Pan ($5.12), is only recommended with reservations: It was easy to use and clean, and it produced the most evenly cooked eggs in the lineup, but they were nothing like a tender, well-cooked stovetop omelet. –E.P.

For the complete testing results, go to CooksIllustrated.com/dec17.

INDEX
November & December 2017

FOLLOW US ON SOCIAL MEDIA

facebook.com/CooksIllustrated
twitter.com/TestKitchen
pinterest.com/TestKitchen
instagram.com/CooksIllustrated
youtube.com/AmericasTestKitchen

BONUS ONLINE CONTENT

More recipes, reviews, and videos are available
at **CooksIllustrated.com/dec17**

RECIPES

Cilantro-Mint Chutney
Easy Holiday Cocoa Sugar Cookies
Mustard-Cream Sauce
Quick Roasted Red Pepper Sauce
Roast Beef Hash
Salsa Verde
Skillet-Roasted Brussels Sprouts with Chile,
 Peanuts, and Mint
Skillet-Roasted Brussels Sprouts with
 Gochujang and Sesame Seeds
Skillet-Roasted Brussels Sprouts with
 Mustard and Brown Sugar
Turkey Rice Soup with Mushrooms
 and Swiss Chard
Warm Farro with Cranberries, Pecans, and
 Herbs
Wheat Berry Salad with Orange and Scallions

▶ RECIPE VIDEOS

Want to see how to make any of the recipes
in this issue? There's a free video for that

EXPANDED REVIEWS

Tasting Dry Vermouth
Testing Cookie Presses
Testing Meat Cleavers
Testing Microwave Egg Cookers
Testing Santoku Knives
Testing Small Roasting Pans with Racks
Testing Tea Infusers

BONUS TECHNIQUES

How to Sharpen Santoku Knives
How to Use a Meat Cleaver
Tempering Chocolate

America's Test Kitchen
COOKING SCHOOL

Visit our online cooking school today, where we offer 180+ online lessons covering a range of recipes and cooking methods. Whether you're a novice just starting out or are already an advanced cook looking for new techniques, our cooking school is designed to give you confidence in the kitchen and make you a better cook.

➤ **Start a 14-Day Free Trial at**
 OnlineCookingSchool.com

Cook's Illustrated on iPad

Enjoy *Cook's* wherever you are,
whenever you want.

Did you know that *Cook's Illustrated* is available on iPad? Go to **CooksIllustrated.com/iPad** to download the app through iTunes. You'll be able to start a free trial of the digital edition, which includes bonus features such as recipe videos, full-color photos, and step-by-step slide shows of each recipe.

Go to CooksIllustrated.com/iPad to download our app through iTunes.

Roast Whole Turkey Breast with Gravy, 5

Skillet-Roasted Brussels Sprouts, 19

Gingerbread Layer Cake, 21

Chinese Pork Dumplings, 13

Chorizo and Potato Tacos, 18

Duchess Potato Casserole, 9

Tuscan White Bean and Escarole Soup, 22

Easy Holiday Sugar Cookies, 15

Braised Brisket with Pomegranate, 8

Turkey Barley Soup, 11

PHOTOGRAPHY: CARL TREMBLAY; STYLING: MARIE PIRAINO

Pişmaniye

Mamoul

Turkish Delight

Namoura

Baklava

Nazook

Barazek

Sweet Simit

Moushabek

Knafeh

Tahini Buns

TURKISH
AND MIDDLE EASTERN
SWEETS